# EVERYONE HAS A BEAUTIFUL HOME IN THEM.

# House Beautiful

# THE HOME BOOK

House Beautiful

# THE HOME BOOK

## CREATING A BEAUTIFUL HOME OF YOUR OWN

## Carol Spier

**HEARST BOOKS**
A Division of Sterling Publishing Co., Inc.
New York/London
www.Sterlingpub.com

# Introduction

There are as many ways to make a home beautiful as there are people who care about the design and ambience of their home environment. Or maybe more, since those who do care are often passionate about it, recognize many kinds of beauty, and tend to have lots of ideas and be eager and happy to change their décor every so often. In a world rich with options, how do you decide on a look that's right for you? And once you decide, how do you go about creating it?

*The Home Book* is a guide that will help you find, define, and articulate the interior design that will make you happy. In it you'll find ideas and inspiration and also pragmatic information to help you think through the development of an aesthetic that is meaningful and workable for you and your home. It will give you the language and insights with which to plan a look that you love and want to live with, and prepare you to work with design professionals who can refine your vision and bring it to life. Throughout the pages are questions that prompt you to think about your goals, the nature of your space, and the things that make you smile. There are hundreds of photos of room interiors of many different styles, in many different kinds of homes, with captions that share the thoughts (and end with the name) of the designers who created them.

The book is divided in three parts, each of which approaches interior design from a different perspective. The first considers the physical character of your dwelling: the site, the architecture, and the interior layout, and discusses the way these affect the interior design and urges you—whether you love them or want to change them—to acknowledge them in your planning. The second part considers the design components that are present in all interiors—the colors, fabric, wall coverings, flooring, lighting, and other elements that create the look. Each chapter in Part Two concludes with suggestions for the hunt, discovery, and organization of the elements you want to use: Interior design calls for lots of shopping. Part Three

approaches design room-by-room, discussing the purpose and requirements of each part of the home and showing myriad ways of meeting the
challenges and celebrating the possibilities found in each space. Every
chapter in Part Three ends with tips for pulling together the look you want
in your rooms.

Scattered through the book are options for colors, ideas for mixing fabric,
tips for shopping, insights from professionals in the design field, and inspirations for using different design elements or decorating specific spots.
There's a special feature on decorating green in this age of global warming,
and others on designing outdoor living spaces, open-plan interiors, and

studio apartments. At the end of the book is an appendix with more in-depth
information on planning and living through a design project—your role,
the designer's role, budgeting money and time, and the work process are
all discussed here.

There's a lot to look at in this book, and many things to think about. You
can browse at random or dive deeply as suits you. Interior design isn't linear; nearly every choice you make has an effect on all the others, and each
part of this book complements the others. Every one of us has different
taste and a unique situation: Enjoy the photos, consider the ideas, and find
the look you love.

# WHAT DO YOU WANT YOUR HOME TO BE?

- A sanctuary

- A gathering place

- A showcase

- An entertainment hub

- A place to hang my hat

- A legacy for my children

# PART ONE

# Understand Your Home

While each of us will answer the question "What do you want your home to be?" in a different way, basing our responses on personal goals, tastes, and needs, we all want a home that is beautiful and makes us happy. You are most likely to respond to this question by describing emotional qualities and physical characteristics that are important to you, using words that indicate the purpose, ambience, and style you may have in mind. If you haven't thought about your dream home this way, take a few minutes to do so. At the same time, ask yourself what your home is now, and see where it meets or differs from the ideal you have in mind.

Defining your dream home is a complex undertaking—where should you begin? The house or apartment you live in is a frame for the activities of your domestic life as well as the basic environment upon which to create your décor; the more you know about it, the better you'll be able to envision the way you really want it to be. So start with your house itself and consider three basic aspects of its design: The site—where is the house and how does it relate to its environment? The architecture—what are its physical characteristics and emotional qualities? And the layout—how does it work, does it answer your needs?

Together the site, architecture, and layout create the space you live in, inform the way it looks and feels, and provide the assets and challenges with which you'll begin to create your décor. Following are chapters considering home design from each of these perspectives; as you think about how each affects your home, ask yourself what you like and don't like, which things you wish to retain, which you'd prefer to change. Ask also, why? What is causing you to think the way you do?

# What's the setting for your home?

- ☐ A bluff near the beach
- ☐ A clearing in the woods
- ☐ A corner lot in a small town
- ☐ One floor in an urban row house
- ☐ A meadow
- ☐ A large yard in a gated community

# 1. THE SITE

OPPOSITE: **A distant view of a city skyline beyond a chain of lakes draws the eye from the interior living area through a loggia and then over this pool and terrace. The classical, vine-covered pergola and reflecting water make this area a lovely waypoint in its own right, framing the view from within, and complementing the breathtaking setting beyond.** (Fern Santini)

Where is your home? How does it relate to its environment? How do you describe the setting? Is it secluded? Is it exposed to the elements or sheltered by trees? Is there a fabulous view? Is the property landscaped as a park, with cottage gardens, or left au naturel? Are there neighbors nearby, do you see their houses, does sound or light carry from their yards to yours? Is your house close to a road? Is it an apartment in a setting over which you have absolutely no control?

As you describe the setting, separate the aspects that are givens—physical qualities such as the terrain or prospects that can't be changed—from those such as trees or garden structures that have been imposed upon it. Are you in a neighborhood where there is a common aesthetic? How aware of the landscape are you from within the house? Have you noticed where and when the sunlight enters? Ask yourself what you love or dislike about your environment. Then ask if these preferences are based on the way the property looks when you are outside, on the way you use the grounds, or on your perception of the setting from within. Are there conflicts among your answers?

If you love your landscape as it is, give thought to how your interior can take advantage of it. If it falls short of your dreams, try to articulate a vision for it that complements the exterior of your home and let that vision inform and be informed by the design you choose for your interior.

# LOCATION, LOCATION.
## Why Does It Matter?

The environment in which your home stands affects the views—an extension of your décor; your privacy or lack thereof; and the natural light you experience indoors. The setting is either an asset to be enjoyed or a challenge to be met, or very likely some of each. With terraces, porches, and garden rooms it can also be an extension of your living space. If it is an asset, you want to be sure you take advantage of it by providing the right access—doors convenient to the garden or porch, windows open to the view and light. And you want this access to enhance your living experience inside, so those doors should not interfere with traffic nor be blocked by furniture, and the windows should complement your arrangements for sitting, sleeping, bathing, cooking, and other activities. If you have a challenge somewhere on your grounds, you'll want to make changes to the landscape to overcome it, or arrange your interior in a way that minimizes its impact.

Take the time to fully understand the relationship of the site to the interior, because a change to one may affect the other. If you identify something you wish to alter, it's possible you'll have a choice between making the change inside or outdoors. For example, a room made dark by overhanging branches could be brightened by removing the tree shading it, adding or enlarging a window, repainting in a pale color, or adding lights. If the shade tree is a beautiful feature of your landscape, removing it might not be the best option, but if it's dying and the space it fills could be a pretty garden, losing it could be the ideal solution.

RIGHT: **Transparency is a key component of this Florida weekend house. Secluded on two and a half acres on a private dead-end street, the long, low building seems as one with the enormous sky surrounding it, while the furnishings introduce a manmade, graphic contrast that is readily apparent to anyone spending time in the backyard.** (Architect: Michael Damore)

ABOVE, LEFT: **Rustic design with multiple rooflines, overhanging eaves, and quirky twig embellishment typifies the vernacular architecture of the Adirondacks. This new home is a charming example, sitting with fairytale style in its deep forest locale, where the residents awaken to squirrels and woodpeckers investigating the bark exterior.**

ABOVE, RIGHT: **A screened sleeping porch offers a soothing summer connection to the woods. Decorated with whimsical detail and enhanced by a locally crafted birch bed, it's brightened by varnished walls that glow in the sunlight and cheerful patterned textiles. The twig web adorning the gable was fashioned in homage to spiders—described by the owner as "the ultimate designers."** (Mimi Maddock McMakin)

LEFT: **Elevated from the lawn and embraced by trees, this all-glass room provides a sitting hub and breakfast area at one end of a large kitchen. Composed with floor-to-ceiling steel windows and spanned by a low banquette, the space combines the enchantment of an outdoor room with shelter from the elements and the aromatic companionship of meals in the making.** (Sally Markham)

# INDOORS. OUTDOORS.
## How Will They Meet?

As you add elements of style to the plan, the relationship between inside and out moves beyond doors placed where you most need them and windows situated to give the nicest view. If your architecture is formal, chances are at least a portion of your landscape and your interior will be as well. If you live in a cottage, then your gardens and interior are more likely to be casual. If your landscape features various garden rooms, you'll want them designed to be understood and appreciated from the interior as well as when you stroll around the grounds.

Your interior design may take a style cue from the environment as well. If you live near the sea, you might choose a beach theme for your décor, a woodland setting might prompt rustic accessories, a home in a gated community with groomed grounds may suggest modernist or traditional furnishings. Or the ambience of your setting may evoke a decorating style with a similar emotional quality, with both suggesting romance, energy, tranquility, or even glamour.

Porches and terraces are natural transitions from outdoors to inside. Decorate them to suit their purpose and architectural style if it's apparent. If you wish to create continuity between home and garden, incorporate elements of your interior style with some from the garden. On the other hand, these spaces can be fun, surprising, or eccentric, and you might want to indulge some aesthetic whim here that you wouldn't choose elsewhere.

Keep your assessment of your site in mind as you think about the details of your architecture (Chapter 2) and interior layout (Chapter 3), continuing to consider the best way to link it with your décor. Here are questions to ask:

**Can you celebrate it?** Can you take better advantage of a view by pruning or moving shrubs? Will your décor look incomplete if you leave the windows bare to a spectacular prospect? Can you rearrange your kitchen in order to get the sink under the window, or borrow space from an adjacent room to create a pantry so you can replace the upper cabinets with a bank of windows?

**Can you change it?** The windows are great, but the house feels gloomy hemmed in by surrounding woods—can you thin the trees? The barren landscape is foreboding—can you plant a copse or a formal garden or put in a pond that will give your eye a place to rest? You like natural light in your bath, but the neighbors are very close—can you screen the window with shrubs? Should the driveway be moved to keep traffic away from a bedroom?

**Can you accommodate it?** Your home office gets too much sunlight but has a great view; should you add an awning or portico to cut the glare? You'd like to add skylights to your daughter's room, but you live in a historic district where they're not allowed on the front of a house; is there another room she could use or a way to break through to the adjacent room to bring in more light? You feel exposed to the city street, so a window treatment is a given; what style suits your décor? Your breakfast room is charming but the neighbor's yard is not; what about a wisteria-covered fence to mask it and create a private terrace at the same time?

ABOVE: **A parterre garden of boxwood and lavender is an unexpected, formal feature in front of this simple stone cottage, which was built in the 1920s. The garden is low—a contour that complements the house. Architectural in structure, it feels fresh and modern, and hints at the crisp, contemporary turn given to the décor inside.**
(Betsy Brown)

# EXPERT INSIGHT

## BRIDGING OUTSIDE AND INSIDE

Designer and architect Debbie Gualco, founder of Reynolds Gualco Architecture—Interior Design in Sacramento, California, believes interior and exterior elements are inextricably connected. She uses a process she calls "inside-out-outside-in" design to "integrate interior and exterior space in order to achieve optimal balance."

### What's the first thing I should consider in the relationship between inside and outside?

Every client says, "give me the light" but I think it's most essential to facilitate movement. Windows and doors must relate to "circulation"—the movement of users and air—through the space. Clients will request French doors to the patio, wanting them right in the middle of the back wall. But that placement obstructs the wall in terms of the interior design, interfering with ideal furniture placement—and ultimately, circulation. Rather than put double doors in the middle of a back wall, we might recommend putting one on either side.

RIGHT: **This picture of the back-yard greets visitors when they walk in the front door of this Sonoma county home. The glass wall in the back of the house disappears when pocket windows slide aside (note the tracks in the floor) and the polished concrete floor flows from the interior onto the back porch, where whimsical iron chairs invite one to admire the wisteria covered dining arbor and contemplate the pool beyond.** (Myra Hoefer)

OPPOSITE: **Open-air dining extends living space and brings the experience of any house closer to its setting. In Hawaii, where weather is warm and humidity low, a lanai—a covered terrace—is traditional and common. This one sits between the family room and pool, is outfitted with commodious teak furniture custom designed to mimic Hawaiian colonial style, and offers a generous view punctuated by indigenous palm trees.** (Douglas Durkin and Greg Elich)

## What about the outside spaces?

Exterior spaces also need to reflect circulation. Being an architect as well as a designer, I usually take a fairly unconventional approach. If, for example, your home has a traditional layout, you can redirect visitors by installing French doors in place of a picture window in the living room. The doors could open into a front-yard courtyard with terraced walls. This gives dinner-party guests the chance to sit outside and watch people walk by, but still have a sense of separation. You could start that dinner party with cocktails in the front and then serve a barbecue in the backyard, letting the interior provide a transition area between the two. There are a lot of unique and interesting ways like this to coordinate indoor and outdoor spaces.

## What are the other big considerations in linking outside and inside?

Interior design and exterior view should complement one another, whether you're looking out at Lake Tahoe or just a modest backyard. Look to create a terminal point of interest, such as a trellis or arbor, or a waterfall, giving the eye a destination so that it is not just wandering. Folding windows or doors (or pocket doors that take less space) are excellent ways to tie inside and outside together. These types of systems are especially powerful in corners, where they can seem to make the corner disappear. They're a great way to open the layout to the exterior, although they may not be practical where the weather is severe.

You can also tie the inside and outside together graphically. You can carry flooring out at least a little ways into the exterior area—such as slate flooring from a kitchen into a backyard area, where it meets the edge of a pool deck—to help connect interior space to the outside. Or you might take the burgundy from a maple tree and intensify that a few shades, making the color stronger for paint on a wall. It's like seasoning food. •

# DESIGNER'S TOP TEN

Architect and designer Mark Rios, of Los Angeles, California, reveals how to blur the lines (both real and imaginary) between your garden and your house.

**1.** Align windows and doors to create views that look right through the house, making it feel transparent.

**2.** Exterior lighting is essential. It leads the eye into the garden and captures the space at night. Add an outdoor fireplace or pit.

**3.** Get rid of traditional corners by adding corner windows or frameless corners with clear seals joining the edges of the glass. It's the corners that define interior spaces.

**4.** Open up your interior walls to the outside: think sliding doors, pocket doors, pivot doors, and double doors. Take away the lines of separation.

**5.** Consider reflective surfaces to make light and views bounce around a room. Make a floor reflective, a ceiling glassy, or a wall lacquered. Reflections make a room feel larger and more connected to its surroundings.

**6.** Add sounds in the garden—gravel crunch, water spills, your favorite CDs.

**7.** Invent ceremonies and occasions for the garden. Rituals create memories that last.

**8.** Furnish and accessorize the garden like you would a room. What are its colors, patterns, ideas, and emotions?

**9.** Take inside materials outdoors. Bring outside materials indoors.

**10.** Use glass and mirror elements in the landscape. They create a sense of mystery and make the garden feel larger.

LEFT: **Situated in open countryside in Missouri, this home is a series of small buildings linked by brick walls to enclose several garden rooms. With each building just one-room deep, the surroundings are ever available and wherever you are—indoors or out, you can see both the groomed and natural landscapes. The exterior palette of "misty lake and wet bark" is echoed inside with calm, grayed tones of natural wood, green, and blue.** (Susan Ferrier; Architect: Bobby McAlpine)

# GET ORIENTATED:
## Where Is the Sun?

Natural light makes your home pleasant during the day, filling it with an overall glow and creating pools of sunlight and casting shadows that give character. But the quality of natural light varies with the locale, the time of day, season of the year, the surrounding landscape, and the direction from which it comes. Why should you care? Light affects colors and your mood, and while it changes often, it has characteristics that are worth observing.

Because the sun moves to the south as it passes from east to west, light entering a window on the north side of your home is always indirect, soft, and colorless, which is why artists like studios that face north. Rooms that face east will be bright in the morning, and indirectly lit as the day progresses. Rooms that face south are bright for much of the day, filled with warm light. Western exposures are bright and warm later in the day. Some people love to awaken to the sunrise and insist their bedrooms face east, others curtain their bedroom to block the daylight and don't care which way it faces. If you like morning sun with your coffee, you might want your kitchen on the eastern side of your home, but if sunsets are glorious where you live, you may prefer a western exposure that will light your evening culinary feats.

Geographic location affects light too—some areas experience frequent cloud cover, which grays the light, and others are always sunny, which make it more yellow. Light at the seashore is often brilliant. Light in the woods may be filtered and muted by the time it reaches your home. You can control the character of light to some extent by planting or removing shade trees or choosing a home with an overhanging roof, awnings, or other shade device.

Colors look different under warm (yellow) and cool (blue) light, and so fabrics and paint may become more intense or shift their hue as the light changes. That's why designers and books like this urge you to check samples where you plan to use them and at different times of the day and suggest you refine your choices by considering the time at which the room is most often occupied.

LEFT: **Originally a garden shed and now renovated with a bay window, French doors, and a cupola to bring in maximum natural light, this freestanding home office appears one with its setting of mature trees and enjoys the sun filtering through them. A small walled terrace provides a charming sitting spot in fine weather; a series of informal paths link the building to the nearby main house and a marsh-side tree house that serves as summer sleeping quarters for four.** (Jill Morris)

OPPOSITE: **This porch offers a clear and sheltered view of the water, with windows that welcome or block the salty breeze as needed. The green-and-white décor is crisp and fresh; the wicker furnishings with striped and floral pillows are "summer porch" classics, informal, and comfortable.** (Markham Roberts)

# The house you call home is . . .

- ☐ A contemporary traditional
- ☐ A Greek revival farmhouse
- ☐ A stone castle
- ☐ A Nantucket cottage
- ☐ All glass

# 2. THE ARCHITECTURE

OPPOSITE: **A gabled side entry porch, turned columns, and fish-scale shingles are typical of Queen Anne cottages. This one, which is in New Orleans, is trimmed with fleur-de-lis cutouts and a quirky balustrade, probably handmade by Creole craftsmen. The entry leads to a gracious, long, side hall with a 14-foot ceiling and a charming bay window, which is just visible on the right in this photo.** (Karyl Pierce Paxton)

What does your house look like? Is it a particular style? One, two, or three stories? Square, rectangular, or maybe an octagon? With wings or a courtyard? Does it have gables, a mansard roof, or a turret? Is there anything distinctive about the building material—perhaps stone or logs—that affects the interior? Does it have a gracious front porch or a generous rear deck? Is the front entry centered or off-center? Are the windows tall? Are there elaborate moldings? Are the ceilings high or low? Are the rooms cozy or grand? How many fireplaces? Is it like its neighbors?

The architecture gives your home its inherent character and style. As you come to understand it, you'll appreciate the underlying structure it gives to your interior design, and see the ways it enhances or obscures the look you'd like to create. How do you respond to the exterior as you approach the house? Do you see ways in which it defines your experience of the interior? Try to see the interior bare, without furnishings. Does the space offer you the comfort you long for? Does this house make you happy? Does it feel like you? Do you think it reflects your personality? Think of all the things you like about it. Are there things you don't like at all? When you assess it, take note of both exterior and interior features and think about the ways they work together. What do you wish this house to look like?

# IT SHELTERS YOU.
## Why Does the Style Matter?

Every period of American history and every region of the country have produced domestic architecture with distinct characteristics; we recognize the way certain profiles, proportions, rooflines, arrangements of doors and windows, chimney placements, and trim details come together as specific styles. Even if you don't know a particular type of home by name, or if it is a contemporary suburban home that doesn't neatly fit into any named style, you'll probably see it as familiar in some way and have assumptions about the way it looks inside. Those assumptions are the key to why the architecture matters—it sets a style, provides the proportions for the interior space, dictates a basic floor plan, and very likely provides at least some of the interior finishing details. Of course houses are frequently remodeled, but unless they're totally rebuilt, it's likely their inherent style is evident to some degree. And if they are entirely redesigned, they become a new style.

Look around the inside of your home. Are the rooms large or small? Dark or light? Do they open into one another, or onto a hall? Are there architectural elements that impart style to the interior? Paneling, divided-light or stained-glass windows, fireplace mantels, balustrades, light fixtures, doors, floorboards, arches, built-ins, and moldings all add character, which varies with their style. Are there regional or vernacular details such as adobe walls or rustic beams, or opulent or modest elements that give your home personality? How does what you see feel to you? Elegant, stuffy, dull, warm, cold, charming?

While you're assessing your home, be pragmatic too; don't focus solely on aesthetics. Is there enough space for your family? Are you thinking of an addition? Or of adding dormers or raising the roof? What will this look like? How might it affect the style of your home? Will the change you have in mind alter the way you enjoy your property? Will it be appropriate for the neighborhood?

LEFT: **Glass walls convert this aged barn to a modernist home so transparent that it nearly disappears into its setting. Seen from without, the skeleton structure gives the interior an intriguing sculptural presence and the limited palette of the décor is sophisticated and noncompetitive with the surroundings.**

OPPOSITE: **The juxtaposed new and old post-and-beam frames dominate the interior; simple modern furnishings foster an appreciation of the architecture, natural light, woodland, and view.**
(Robert Berman)

ABOVE: A Mediterranean aesthetic is a comfortable fit for California, where the terrain and climate are similar to those in southern Europe. Designed to conjure the look of Provence, this Napa Valley house features native California stone, stucco walls with integral color, and reclaimed roof tiles from France. Each generous exterior doorway serves as both window and entry and keeps the indoor-outdoor connection constant whether open or closed. (Architect: Wayne Leong)

RIGHT: Indoors, massive stone walls are complemented by good-size furnishings, many of which came from France or Spain. The large blue-and-white toile used for the slipcovers is in scale with the room, reiterates the romance with all things French, and echoes the palette of the kitchen beyond. (Erin Martin)

# KEY CONCEPT:

## PROPORTION

In design, elements in different sizes or amounts are combined to create an overall effect; "proportion" is the relationship of these quantities to one another and the whole. It's a bit abstract, but this concept is important because successful proportions appear balanced and harmonious. Proportion is key to our perception of a design as aesthetically pleasing. And in architecture and interior design, the size of the occupants is part of the equation, so proportion also affects our comfort in a space.

When you look at your home or other homes you like, think about the height, width, and depth of the rooms—these dimensions establish the proportions. Adjectives we use to describe a room's proportions include, among others: ample, large, small, spacious, cramped, lofty, and squat. If we want to describe our emotional reaction, we might refer to proportions as beautiful, or conversely, unfortunately unattractive.

We also use the word "scale" to describe the size of one element as it relates to another. Notice how large or small the trim moldings are relative to the size of the room. Are they nicely balanced, so big they overwhelm the space, or so small they seem lost? What about the furniture? Does it make the room look crowded or increase a cavernous feeling? Good designers know how to use proportion to enhance their work with drama, wit, or intimacy, and you can learn from them—once you start to observe this aspect of design, you'll develop an eye for the scale or proportion of the elements.

ABOVE: **In this room, a large, decorative window placed diagonally in the gable wall, right below the roof peak, creates a dominant focal point that's reinforced by the four-poster bed tucked below the rustic beams. Acres of balloon-print toile cover the bed, walls, and ceiling, making the room cozy and charming.** (Diamond Baratta)

LEFT: **Open to the high roof peak, with floor, walls, and ceiling all composed of boards and all painted white, this simply furnished bedroom appears serene and spacious. The white bed, linens, and easy chair sit lightly, as does the delicate drop leaf table, which provides the only color aside from the views and the opened Dutch door.** (Ruthie Sommers)

# LOVE IT OR CHANGE IT?

As you develop your design plan, you'll be balancing dreams and reality, and ultimately, making those dreams real. Because you need some parameters and goals in order to move forward, this is a good time for a dream session in which to conjure your ideal interior. Even if you haven't a clue about the details, try to think of the overall ambiance — formal, casual, tranquil, opulent, or bright and colorful for example, and the basic look — traditional, modernist, Scandinavian, romantic, beach-house, or whatever you wish. And then do a reality check: Is this house the structure you dream of? Does your ideal interior fit here?

If the reality of your home and your initial vision for it mesh, you can develop the specific details of your design. If there are disparities, you should decide how to resolve them. You're just beginning to plan, so be open — you may decide to change your home or adjust your vision for it, and you may not know which way you'll go until you've learned more, considered a number of alternatives, and dealt with practical things like time and money. First be clear about the issues — is the problem one of size, proportion, or layout that stems from the way the house is configured? Or is it more cosmetic, due to surfaces or finishing details with the wrong character? The latter is fairly easy to change; the former requires more effort.

If you are thinking about structural changes, you'll need professional help: a designer, engineer, architect, or all three. Your role is to articulate your needs and dreams and understand that the design of the structure affects the ambience of the interior, and vice versa. It's easy to forget that window size, shape, and location are part of the façade, not just the interior, or that a room with a cathedral ceiling steals space from the second floor.

Interior finish details can be altered more easily, and in many cases, these changes are naturally part of the interior design process. But before you remove things like moldings and paneling, ask yourself how doing so will affect the integrity of the architectural design and whether this matters. If it is likely to have a negative impact on the home's value, you might learn to love the details.

LEFT: **In a room devoid of architectural details, thoughtful use of color and furnishings alone can be enough to create style. Beige, taupe, and wicker hues in several values give a calm overtone to this living room, supplemented with solid helpings of chocolate and touches of sky and royal blue. The coffee table, red-lacquer cubes, and large screen impart an Asiatic aesthetic that furthers the quiet mood.** (Garrow Kedigan)

OPPOSITE: **Impressive moldings, including ornate corbels around the ceiling, give stature to this small dining room. Full-length windows and bookcases emphasize the vertical proportions and take advantage of the height. The rustic wood slab table is a surprising and modern complement to the formal, albeit it simple, traditional décor.** (Kathryn Scott)

ABOVE: **Interior architectural details, such as the column-supported arches that frame this entry hall, lend unmistakable character to a home. Columns and moldings can be celebrated with elaborate paint treatments or honored simply as they are here, painted to match the walls and allowed to frame the stairwell with quiet intrigue.** (Myra Hoefer)

RIGHT: **When this small beach house was renovated, board and batten paneling was added to evoke the style typical at the turn of the twentieth century. Cream paint in a satin finish gives the paneling extra depth. The furnishings are almost all pale blue or cream to feel light—like the beach—while textured fabric and plump, down cushions lend richness to the relaxed, comfortable ambience.** (Mona Hajj)

## The room layout in your home . . .

- ☐ Features a central hallway
- ☐ Rambles through many wings
- ☐ The rooms open one to the next
- ☐ There's one large open living area
- ☐ All the bedrooms have private baths
- ☐ Adults and kids have separate quarters

# 3. THE LAYOUT

OPPOSITE: **A central entry hall divides the music and dining rooms in this home (the front door is to the left in the photo). Gracious archways frame the passage from each room to the hall and through to the opposite room; the chaise next to the piano was chosen for its low back, which keeps the view open. The other rooms in this home also flow one into the next, and the warm taupe palette is used throughout— inspired, serendipitously, by the particular granite chosen for the kitchen counters early in the design process.** (Kathy Smith)

Is it easy to walk about in your home? Can you gracefully move from the living room to the dining room or is the passage awkward? Can you see from one room into another? Do you feel isolated in some rooms? Do the exterior doors lead to warm, welcoming spaces, or do you almost trip over a bench when you enter? Is there privacy where there should be, or does the powder room open into the parlor or your guest room share a bath with the teens? Do you have to leave the closet door open because there's no way to swing it past your king-size bed? Is there a room that you simply can't figure out what to do with?

Every home has a kitchen, living area, dining area, bedroom, and bathroom. Most homes have several of some of these rooms, and other rooms as well. The overall floor plan—or layout of the rooms—can be configured in many different ways and its arrangement affects the way you move about in your home as well as the ambience and sense of openness or privacy. The layout is often linked to the architectural footprint (square, rectangular, or with one or more wings, for example) and style of the home, at least to some degree. However, if you have remodeling or an addition in mind, there are lots of options for the size and shape of each room, and for which room goes where.

# WHAT'S NEXT TO WHAT?
## Why Does It Matter?

In many ways, your enjoyment of your home begins with a layout that suits the way you live. If the rooms are not configured so that circulation, activities, communication, and privacy are each accommodated, making your home comfortable may be challenging—even the most gorgeous furnishings can go only so far to overcome an awkward or inconvenient layout.

To understand the implications of your layout, take a moment to identify the principal paths of circulation—the main traffic arteries, if you will—and the routes they provide from one area to another. Where are you when you first enter? In a central or side hall or a large foyer, or are you already in the living room? If you are in a hall or foyer, it provides a natural passage to other rooms. If you enter directly into a living room, your furniture must be arranged in a way that permits you to pass to the adjacent room or rooms, and this obviously limits the options for setting up

the living room. If there is a hall or foyer, do the rooms it leads to also lead to one another, or must you return to the hall in order to reach another room? If there is a second floor, where are the stairs? The answers to questions like these affect the way you move through the house and the way furniture can be arranged.

Think next about the location of the different rooms and their proximity to one another—does this work for the way you live? If you like company while you cook, is the kitchen convenient to the living and family rooms? Do guests have to walk by the master suite or a home office in order to reach the powder room, and does that mean doors must be kept closed, blocking daylight from the hallway? Is your youngest child's bedroom directly above the dining room, with the sound of running feet or late-night conversation passing from one to the other?

And now consider the qualities of the individual rooms. Are they large enough for their purpose? Can the furniture be arranged within each to facilitate conversation, activities, and enjoyment of any view while allowing space for you to move about?

OPPOSITE, ABOVE, AND ABOVE RIGHT: **A galley kitchen is by nature a hallway; the one on the facing page has a barrel-vault ceiling that gives a sense of ceremony to the narrow space, which leads to the charming octagonal breakfast room seen from the exterior and inside above. Work areas in this kitchen are divided between the two long walls. Five sides of the breakfast room form a bay that projects like a small temple into the garden. Inside, a table centered in the room ensures easy access to the French doors and the terrace beyond. The glass doors open to give the pleasant sense of eating outside but the interior is sheltered from the elements.** (Michael S. Smith)

# LOVE IT OR CHANGE IT?

LEFT: **The foyer in this home is really just the end of the narrow center hall into which the stairs project. The large opening to the living room makes the transition between the spaces gracious and to move about you can pass behind the love seat or between it and the sofa. A smaller, more private, opening leads to the dining room.** (Susan Tully)

How do you feel about the current layout of your home? Delighted and happy that everything flows nicely, there's appropriate room for furnishings, and public and private areas are discrete? Or do you wish the kitchen and living room were closer together, or want more storage upstairs? Do you wish you could rip it apart and start over? Before you answer, go back and revisit your thoughts about the architecture—were you thinking of making changes to the structure? How would they affect the layout?

If your assessment of the layout induces you to reconfigure the floor plan, make a list of the changes you envision. Are you thinking of moving doors in order to facilitate flow? Removing a wall in order to combine two small rooms, or moving one to change the relative size of adjacent rooms? Or of switching the kitchen and dining room locations? Of bumping out the back wall to enlarge a room? Or of a total gut and redesign?

Depending on the role the existing walls play in holding your house together, layout changes can be easy, or not so easy, to effect, and which case applies to you may not be immediately apparent. Given enough time and money,

## LOCAL CODE RULES

Why, you probably ask, should you care about the local building and zoning codes while you dream about your décor? Depending on where you live and how restrictive they are, these codes affect some things you might not think about—setbacks from a lot line, minimum and maximum size of a home, permitted uses for outbuildings, whether a third floor can be used as living space or stairs built without risers, the minimum size of new windows and doors, the ratio of baths to bedrooms, and even the placement of electrical outlets. If you live in a historic district there may be rules about the exterior design; if you're in an environmentally sensitive area, construction or clearing permits may be required or certain building materials prescribed. So educate yourself before you get too far in your plans—you can save a lot of headaches and disappointment if you work within the system from the outset.

nearly anything is possible to do, but stop now and ask a builder or architect for an informal opinion of the feasibility of your dream layout. This will give you an idea of the time, disruption, and expense involved, and you'll know whether to explore this dream further, with professional help if needed, or edit it to be more attainable for you.

ABOVE: **If one room can truly be the heart of the home, this may be it. The kitchen area is state of the art, there's a table where the whole family can sit down to eat just beyond it, and at the end, a big fireplace with a couple of comfy chairs looks delicious and is removed enough from the action to permit a quiet read. Old-fashioned beadboard on the walls and ceiling join the stone fireplace to give a homey tone to the open space, while large windows and a glass door provide natural light, air, and access to the garden.** (Architect: William F. Holland)

# TYPICAL FLOOR PLANS

There are many ways to get from here to there within a home.
Size, shape, and the use and position of a hall all play a role.
Does one of these floor plans look familiar to you?

**One story with central foyer**

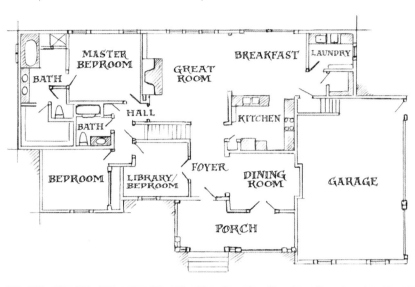

## Two story with center hall entry

### first floor

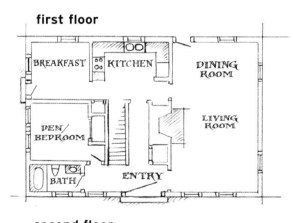

### second floor

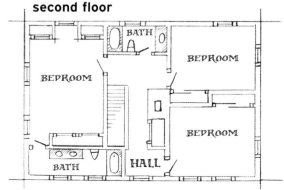

## Two story with entry into living room

### first floor

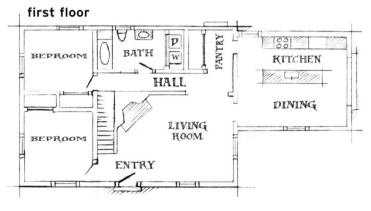

### second floor

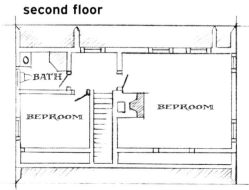

## Two story with side hall entry

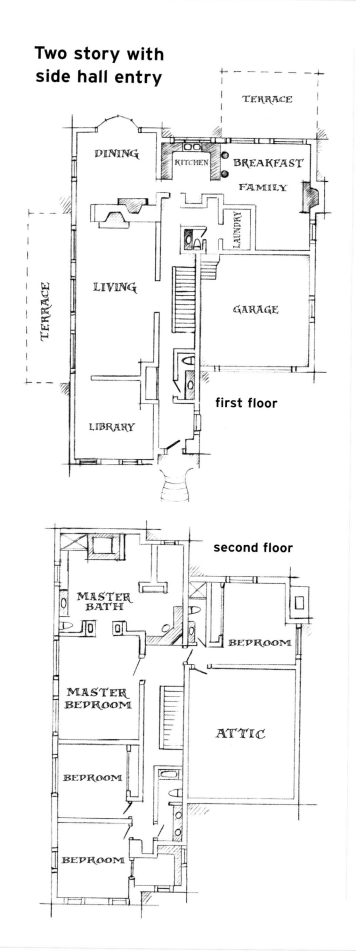

TERRACE

DINING

KITCHEN

BREAKFAST

FAMILY

LAUNDRY

TERRACE

LIVING

GARAGE

LIBRARY

first floor

MASTER BATH

second floor

BEDROOM

MASTER BEDROOM

ATTIC

BEDROOM

BEDROOM

## Two story with central foyer open to second floor

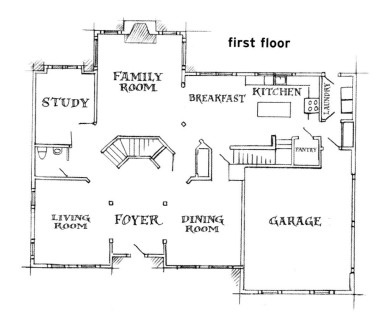

first floor

STUDY

FAMILY ROOM

BREAKFAST

KITCHEN

LAUNDRY

PANTRY

LIVING ROOM

FOYER

DINING ROOM

GARAGE

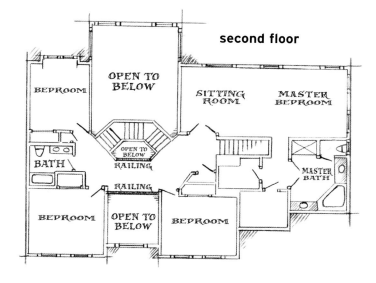

second floor

BEDROOM

OPEN TO BELOW

SITTING ROOM

MASTER BEDROOM

BATH

OPEN TO BELOW

RAILING

MASTER BATH

BEDROOM

RAILING

OPEN TO BELOW

BEDROOM

# WHERE'S THE DOOR TO THE GARDEN?

Moving or adding exterior doors may enhance the layout of your home in several ways. Relocating a door may improve efficiency—say to provide more wall space or improve the circulation. Adding one may provide convenient access to the pool, the trash, or the potting shed that is otherwise only reached from some formal or distant part of your home. (Sometimes removing a door is a smart idea, especially if there are several in one room, making it feel like Grand Central Terminal.) French and sliding doors enhance your aesthetic experience too, by deepening the connection between the inner décor and the landscape. When deciding where to place an exterior door, consider the impact it will have on the interior circulation and furniture arrangement as well as the way it will affect the façade of your home; if it's a glass door, site it so it reveals and shows off a specific portion of the your landscape (there's more discussion of this in Chapter 1).

RIGHT: **A long sofa and coffee table feel perfectly at home in this long narrow room, finding virtue in the given proportions instead of working to mask them. Armchairs and a bench angled around the sitting area relax the geometry. The door at the end of the sofa gives access to the garden from this room and others without interrupting the conversation area.** (Robert Stilin)

# EXPERT INSIGHT

## ACHIEVING A BALANCED LAYOUT

Shawn Henderson, of Shawn Henderson Interior Design in New York City, feels that for a layout to be effective there must be equilibrium between the space and the decorative elements within it.

**What makes a successful room layout?**

To me, a good layout has balance, and balance does not necessarily mean just the furniture. It can include what's on the windows, the color of the walls . . . there are so many different levels. The right balance is the common denominator.

**How do you achieve balance?**

I start with the balance between the furniture and the space. It's a matter of scale; people often buy furniture that is oversized for the space. They need to measure. I feel that a successful layout is not jam-packed; I like to really pare down the elements that I'm using. Also I look for continuity in finishes.

## What do you mean by "continuity"?

For instance, I like to have continuity in the trim color throughout a house, or window treatments. I'll use the same window treatments in a living room and dining room—I may change fabrics, but use the same type of window treatment.

## How important are focal points in your layouts?

Focal points play a really important role. They formalize and organize the space visually. When I see a really great fireplace in the center of a room, my layout revolves around it. I draw an axis through the fireplace and another axis line perpendicular to that and that's how my layout unfolds: The furniture is placed with consideration for whatever the focal point may be.

## What are some of the more challenging areas in terms of layout?

Small spaces are hard, but I actually like them because they are a little puzzle I like to solve. They force me to be more creative. The more troubling rooms are huge great rooms—wide open spaces with big vaulted ceilings. Rooms where you have to fill up different areas with unnecessary furniture start to outweigh other areas of the house.

## What solutions do you use for layout challenges?

I'm a huge fan of long sofas. A long sofa elongates a room and allows you to use, for instance, a pair of coffee tables instead of a single one, and you start to split the room up that way. I always use the biggest possible area rug, because it makes the room feel more unified and connected, even if there's more than one sitting area. You can put an Oriental rug over a seagrass rug, for instance, to divide the seating areas.

## How would you recommend people approach layout?

Start by analyzing how your family lives and how they use the room. It's really a matter of thinking about how people live, and trying to accommodate that in the space. •

LEFT: **Symmetry is inherently balanced. Here a bed centered on the wall is flanked by space in which traditional nightstands would look lost; a pair of chests provides better balance as well as a bit of storage, and striped rugs spread color that completes the ensemble.** (Katrin Cargill and Carol Glasser)

ABOVE: **An area rug defines the principal sitting area in this lofty multi-purpose room; balancing it is a very large dining table. The settee in front of the doors suggests a tête-à-tête; the wing chair can be pulled from the table to either sitting area or join them into a whole. Throughout, restrained forms and light and dark tones offset one another; the few large patterns add weight to the neutral palette.** (Paul Siskin)

# THE RULES OF . . .

## SMOOTH TRAFFIC FLOW

Just as lanes on a freeway are standard widths, there are general rules for the space to allow between furnishings to ensure ease of movement and visual appeal. You can consider these guidelines as minimums; depending on the size of your furniture and the room, you may decide that more space creates a more pleasing balance.

- Hallways must be 3 or 3½ feet wide to allow basic passage. If you intend to place a table or item such as a lamp or sculpture in a hallway, the hallway should be at least 3½ feet wide plus the width of the object.

- A primary pathway through any room should ideally be more than 4½ feet wide. In a room where social activities are conducted and people will pass each other, the pathway should be at least 5 feet wide.

- The standard allowance for space between a sofa and other furnishings, such as the coffee table, is 18 inches, which allows for unencumbered movement when sitting and rising. If the room is large and you are going for a more spacious layout, increase this distance to 2 feet.

- Don't be fooled by the position of your dining table with the chairs pushed in. You need at least 3½ feet behind the chairs to allow for unfettered access as well as pass-by space behind seated diners—an occupied chair will be moved out from the table 1½ to 2 feet. The more room around a dining room table, the better.

- Keep 3 to 3½ feet open in front of bookshelves and cabinets or other furniture with doors and drawers. This open space is especially important in the kitchen, where efficiency and comfort are so dependent on having room to maneuver; if possible, allow 4 feet or more so you can stand in front of fully extended drawers and lowered oven doors.

- Leave at least 2 feet open at the bedside to allow easy access and bedmaking.

# CLOSETS:
## Plan Now, Not Later.

It's hard to imagine a home with too much closet space, so chances are providing storage for clothes, linens, toys, tools, and other miscellaneous bits is part of your dream. You may feel closets aren't decorative, but they absolutely affect the layout and thus the way your interior is designed, so don't overlook them while you're dreaming.

Closets commandeer a surprising amount of space; if they're not planned from the beginning, they can jut awkwardly into a room, spoil its proportions, and block light and air. If you can't place them on interior walls, you may have to sacrifice a window to include them. This is why the wall between adjacent bedrooms is often formed of side-by-side closets, with one opening into each room—and why those bedrooms seem smaller than expected from the hallway. A standard clothes closet is 24 inches deep, plus you need room to stand in front of it, so bear that in mind as you explore and experiment with potential layouts. If you have room overall, a walk-in closet may be a better option because less wall space need be devoted to the doors.

OPPOSITE: **An alcove is at once private and public: As a space, it's removed from the room it fronts, yet open to it too. Size has a lot to do with the way you take advantage of one of these architectural delights; this one sits at one end of a master bedroom sitting area and is large enough to serve as an office. While this room serves two functions, it's the layout that defines them, not the aesthetics of the décor.** (Bunny Williams)

# UTILITY SPACES:
## Where Will You Put Them?

Washer and dryer. Linen closet. Mudroom. Workshop. Housecleaning gear. Where do they go? Well, it depends. Things to consider are the size of your home, the way you live, and the plumbing plan. For each of these rooms, ask "who uses it?" "how often?" "how large should it be?" and, for the laundry and workshop, "is outdoor access needed?" Contents for most of these rooms don't mix well, so be circumspect if you're dreaming of combining two or more in one space.

Do you do the laundry, or does a housekeeper do it? How do you feel about the noise of the machines? These are key points, because you can put the washer and dryer anywhere you can put plumbing: basement, first floor, upstairs with the bedrooms. With the bedrooms minimizes carrying of laundry baskets, in the basement obscures the noise. If you like to line-dry the wash for energy-saving and environmental reasons, locate the machines near an appropriate exterior door. Many machines will fit in a standard closet, but

having a larger space makes sorting, folding, and ironing easier. Some people like to dedicate a large room to laundry and devote some of the space to creative pursuits or even a playroom—be careful, though, if paint and glue are among the amusements.

Damp is not a good long-term companion for textiles, so try to find somewhere other than a bathroom for your linens storage. If you don't have built-in closet space, consider a good-looking cabinet that can be an enhancement in a bedroom or large hallway. If there's space in the laundry room, that's another option—the machines don't give off steam the way a shower does.

Find a dedicated place for cleaning supplies, the vacuum, broom, mop, and so on. The chemicals don't mix with other parts of your life; the broom and mop don't belong in the coat closet. Someplace with a utility sink is nice, so soiled water can be dumped. If your laundry room is large and has a closet, it may work, as long as you are good about putting cleaning gear and clean laundry away. You don't want the sheets to have an accident with the cleanser.

Mudrooms are underappreciated spaces. If it's large enough, a back or side entry can serve as flower arranging headquarters or store sports or garden gear.

The location of a workshop depends to some degree on what sort of equipment is in it, and what sort of work comes out of it. Generally a basement or heated garage makes sense, with plumbing if it is required. If the tools are noisy, a location some distance from your house may be preferable.

OPPOSITE, LEFT: **You don't need a lot of room for a laundry, but it's nice to include a utility sink for hand-washables if space permits. Make the space fun to be in—this one has been painted to look like a cabana.** (Alison Spear)

OPPOSITE, RIGHT: **The cushioned bench in this mudroom makes it easy to change footwear. Light-weight baskets in cubbies above encourage neatness—they're a lot easier to access than overhead drawers are.** (Kari Cusack)

RIGHT: **Fitted with a sink, cabinets, and shelves as well as pegs for caps, this charming mudroom multitasks for flower arranging.** (Paula Perlini)

# FURNITURE PLACEMENT:
## Plan Now, Not Later.

While you're assessing the layout of your home and thinking of ways you may wish to change it, give some thought to how you'll place the furniture. You may not know exactly which furniture you'll use, but you should be able to list the items you expect to incorporate—for instance, one sofa, three easy chairs (one with an ottoman), a coffee table, and two end tables in the living room. It's not too early to think about the way these items will fit in the space because the shape and proportions of the room and the location of the doors, windows, and other elements such as a fireplace all affect the way the furniture can be arranged to facilitate both conversation and circulation. Plus you'll want to think about the scale so you can anticipate how large or small, ornate or spare the furnishings should be in order to look balanced in the space.

If you're feeling a bit at sea in this area, begin by looking at photos in this book and elsewhere to find rooms that seem similar in shape and size to yours and take note of the way they are set up. Read Expert Insight: Achieving a Balanced Layout on page 44 and Expert Insight: Arranging a Conversation Group on page 52 for some good tips on this process. It's smart to be practical while you do this—use a scale drawing on graph paper, with scale cutouts of the furniture that you can move around, or a computer program to see how various options work.

ABOVE: **Tall cabinets flanking a large window could create an awkward space, but here they embrace a window seat and help define a breakfast area.** (Suzanne Kasler)

LEFT: **French doors opening to a garden or balcony may be the ultimate romantic touch for a bedroom—think of Juliet. Position the bed to take advantage of the fresh air as well as the view. Draperies can provide privacy as needed.** (Paul Wiseman)

OPPOSITE: **"Warm, inviting, and intimate" was the mantra guiding the design of this room, where the seating arrangement is focused on the fireplace, with the sofa offering the best view of the fire, easy chairs flanking it, and an ottoman tucked close enough to warm a sitter. The high ceiling has been brought down with the addition of old pine beams, waxed so they glow, and the honeyed tones of the palette cloak the room with mellow romance.** (Fern Santini)

# EXPERT INSIGHT

## ARRANGING A CONVERSATION GROUP

Glenn Gissler of Glenn Gissler Design in New York City combines the spatial awareness that is the product of his architectural training, and his finely honed interior design sensibilities to choose alluring furnishings and combine them in engaging arrangements.

**Are there basic rules or guidelines you use in creating furniture arrangements?**

As a professional, I always start with a measured floor plan and try to look at things objectively, more intellectually, just to consider traffic flow through a room. Even a layperson can sketch out a floor plan on grid paper. The other macro issue for me is that I like to have furniture in a room "greet you." What I mean by that is, if you see a friend on the street, you greet them with open arms. As a room accommodates the furniture, it should open its arms to you. When you see a friend or relative, you don't turn to the side, right? There is a certain logic that makes the space seem welcoming.

## What's the best way to compose a "seating group?"

There's a natural and normal way in which conversation ensues. If you want to have a room that encourages interaction with people, proximity becomes important. It's very difficult to have conversation leap over a circulation path, whether people are passing through or not. It's a psychological barrier. So chairs need to be near to each other. If your knees are an inch away from each other it's very intimate. If you're sitting at a right angle to somebody, it's a little more comfortable and still feels personal. And the further away you get, the less personal it becomes. Which is why in the increasingly big houses these days the rooms are actually problematic—they are too big for intimate interaction.

## What are the risks and rewards of making a piece of furniture a focal point?

For me, art is probably a more appropriate focal point for a room. My approach is that classic pieces anchor a room, which then allows for more free-spirited self-expression—in large upholstered pieces, large case goods, and area rugs. But overall, art should be the actual focal point.

## What techniques do you use for innovative furniture placement?

One of the most important has to do with views. Rarely do people just sit and stare blankly out into the garden or out at their view. For me, views are great backdrops for furniture, and I would position a sofa in front of the view. I actually think views within a home are more interesting—what you see when you look down a hall, what are you going to discover? When you're sitting on a sofa, the view through to the next room can be the interesting one.

## What about quality? How do you ensure quality in furnishings?

I suggest that people buy the best quality they can afford. That said, people have to honestly assess what the truth is, or they will be spending money for a living room set that they never use. A good piece of furniture is not good if it doesn't work with who you are, the size of your sitting room, and your home. •

# WHICH ELEMENTS OF DESIGN MAKE YOU HAPPIEST?

- ■ Serene hues
- ■ Ethnic textiles
- ■ Elegant wallpaper
- ■ Hand-painted Italian tiles
- ■ Funky, old wood floors
- ■ An unusual, ornate chandelier

# PART TWO

# Elements of Design

What are the things that will make your dream interior come to life? Every décor is composed of specific elements; recognize this and the task of creating a look you'll love becomes manageable, and enjoyable too. Defining the look is key, once you do that, you'll have a direction to follow as you choose the pieces that bring it to life.

You may know the look you want, or you may be exploring options. As you gather photo references of interiors you like, take a moment to analyze them and you'll see that the way color, lighting, fabric, walls and ceilings, floors, and window treatments are handled creates the ambience to which you are responding. These components are common to every room; an understanding of the way they work will help you select the specifics of your décor.

Following are chapters devoted to each of these components—first the ambience, or look, and then the concrete elements that create it. What about furniture? Of course, furniture is essential, but it's linked to the function of each room and in this book, you'll find it discussed in Part Three: Design, Room by Room, as well as in many of the photo captions. As you read the following chapters, be nimble—you'll see that color itself is a component of fabric and of wall, ceiling, and floor finishes; that fabric is part of window treatments; and that lighting affects everything. This is the magic of design—there is such a wealth of ingredients with which to work. Think about the ways these elements interact and you'll have a better understanding of and appreciation for all the materials you find when you shop, and be able to focus on what makes an option right for you.

# How do you want your home to look?

☐ Tailored and crisp
☐ Totally modern
☐ Relaxed and informal
☐ Serene
☐ Like a Mediterranean country house
☐ Traditional but not stuffy

# 4. AMBIENCE

OPPOSITE: **With a spectacular antique birdcage and misty white and gold furnishings set against dark, elegant, hand-painted walls, this living room appears very French, very romantic. The pure white silk taffeta curtains add contrast, like brides in billowy dresses lined up around the room.** (Anne Miller)

Design is more than an iteration of a particular, named style with furniture that has specific lines and proportions, and accessories to match; interiors that faithfully reproduce a period style are often museumlike and not so inviting. Successful interior design has character—it sets a mood and says something about the occupants of the home. The colors, textures, light, and yes, the kind of patterns and the shapes of the furniture, combine to create an ambience or look—an environment that expresses some sort of emotion as well as style. When you decide to decorate your home, one of the first things you want to do is find the ambience that will make you happy.

How do you know what's right for you? If you don't have an inherent preference, inspiration is everywhere—in the photos in this book, in other books and magazines, on television, in films, museums, home furnishings stores, and the homes of your friends. There are no rights and wrongs here, just myriad options that have worked for other people, who may or may not share your lifestyle, taste, or resources. If something pleases you, take note of it. See which looks you respond to, and ask yourself why. Start a clipping file so you can review the things you like and share your preferences with others. Choose some adjectives that name the ambience for you, but don't get hung up on specific style names if you're unsure of them; your clipping file will visually convey that information to salespeople or whichever professionals you engage to help you. Look through this chapter; you'll see that style and emotion are partners that help us name the looks we love.

# LOOKS WE LOVE

Most of us lead busy lives and want our homes to offer refuge from the world at large. We also want them to celebrate the riches of past and present design, so we fill them with things we enjoy seeing. When we describe the ambience of a room we love, we often use words that evoke emotion, that indicate the way we feel when we're in the room. What describes the emotions you'd like your home to express? Serene, relaxed, dreamy, formal, luxurious, glamorous, simple, warm, intimate, welcoming, and happy are words you might suggest. As you answer, think about the way you use your home, who lives there, and your lifestyle. What sort of ambience suits your family?

Think too about aesthetic style—are you drawn to the look of a particular period or region? What do you like about it, the lines, materials, or colors naturally associated with it? Is there a specific type of furniture or vernacular embellishment that tugs at your heart? Does the architecture of your house suggest a particular style, and if so, how do you wish to complement it?

Be imaginative as you assess the looks you see here and elsewhere in this book. Professional designers generally create a look that carries throughout a home; they don't shift gears between rooms unless there's a compelling reason for doing so. While you're looking for an overall aesthetic that pleases you, concentrate on your response to the ambience you see in each photo and don't get stuck on which room is shown and whether it has something in common with the same room in your house; simply ask yourself first what it is you're liking, and then how you see it working in your home.

OPPOSITE: **Wearing its elegance with restraint, this bath just may be the ultimate retreat—spacious and gracious, with quiet, sepia hues and hand-painted striée walls opening to a pastoral view; the simple draperies soften the look and add privacy when needed.** (Jeffrey Bilhuber)

BELOW: **The mandate for this master bedroom was comfort and peace. Hand-painted silk panels cover the walls in an Old World elegance; the striped bed skirt shares their palette and makes a nice foil for the pure white linens. A velvet-covered headboard and the carpet complete the soft background; lots of mirrors bring in light.** (Allesandra Branca)

OPPOSITE: **Casement windows wrap the dining area in this small lakeside cottage, giving a wide-open view above the banquette. With watery hues on the banquette, soft white on the board walls and ceiling, and an aqua-gray on the floor, color is key to the informal, lighthearted décor, where factory lamps mix with the rustic table and very contemporary chairs.** (David Reed)

ABOVE: **Brand new and finished with traditional formal details (beamed ceiling, fluted moldings, swagged valances over draperies), light and inviting with cream and honey colors and layered with pattern and texture, this living room has a timeless, unmistakably American style.** (Bunny Williams)

OPPOSITE: **A charcoal-colored cabinet framing the back wall sets off the whitewash color that unifies everything else in this tranquil dining room. The lyre-back chairs and fluted legs of the table put a dressy spin on the casual look.** (Ruby Beets)

ABOVE: **Mahogany paneling gives a timeless, traditional background to a library. Wanting to brighten the inherent darkness of this one, the designer chose paler fabrics, a honey-colored rug, and turquoise vases set as lamps—all things that pop yet keep the elegant room cozy.** (Markham Roberts)

# REGIONAL LOOKS WE FALL FOR

South of France? At the shore? High on a mountain? Is a sense of place part of your design dream? Perhaps you live where a particular aesthetic is common and feels comfortable, where the vernacular style has great character, or the local traditions and craftsmanship are unique and beautiful. Or maybe you wish you did.

The smaller the world gets, the more opportunity there is to enjoy the diversity of design found all around it. We're more exposed to different styles, and products are easier to find and acquire. Whether you're drawn to a particular regional look because you live there and it's a natural fit for your home or because it makes you happy even though it's got nothing to do with your address, give some thought to the degree to which you want to incorporate its hallmarks in your home. Are you looking for total immersion, with architectural elements involved—if so, what will be required to achieve it? Or do you want to use fabrics, furnishings, and accessories, perhaps collected on your travels, to flavor but not rule your décor? Both are good options, the choice is yours.

LEFT: **Pale, grayed blues and greens, distressed surfaces, whitewashed floors, and delicate carved and painted furniture are the hallmarks of Swedish period style, where the look is spare and contemplative, with accessories edited. Both French and Swedish eighteenth-century furnishings work, either old or reproduction, and stripes and checks are always appropriate for this look.** (Katrin Cargill and Carol Glasser)

RIGHT: **Old World ambience and modern convenience mingle in this kitchen, where the antique French tiles that line the walls cued the other features: the poured concrete countertops have the weight and texture needed to balance the tiles, the apron sink, cabinets, and hardware are classic, the Italian worktable and English pot rack old and authentic, and the appliances state of the art.** (Shannon Bowers)

# FORMAL OR INFORMAL?

What's your dress-up quotient? Do you lean toward prim or laid-back, glitz or jeans and a slinky tee? Which way do you want your décor to go? While you're choosing a look for your home, think about how formal or casual you want it to be, and whether different parts of your home might vary in this respect. Some decorating styles are inherently formal, some naturally casual, but most can be swayed one way or the other by your choice of materials, patterns, and surface finishes. Mixing metaphors can work too—say hanging a crystal chandelier in a rustic country dining room or having elaborate window swags made up in muslin—if the overall effect is balanced and pleasing. In fact, a touch of the unexpected may be what gives a room soul, history, or wit and keeps it interesting and personal. Keep an eye on the way designers use materials to create ambience.

ABOVE: **Sophisticated pastels and forms with clean lines and strong personality make a dressy ensemble in this bedroom corner, which is trimmed with oversize formal moldings and a graphic carpet on which Japanese-inspired flowers sit on a giant Glen plaid. The effect: grown-up and lighthearted.** (Diamond Baratta)

# DESIGNER'S TOP TEN

Designer Vicente Wolf knows that the secret to a great looking room is all in the mix of furnishings and accents.

**1.** If you layer a space with color, texture, and array of styles, your décor choices will have a much longer life.

**2.** Accessories can keep a space from getting locked into one time period or a thematic look.

**3.** I like to put something primitive next to something very refined. Each sets off the other and the best of both comes into view.

**4.** I'm always playing one period against another to bring out both similarities and contrasts. Look for elements that say the same thing, but from a different point of view.

**5.** An unexpected choice of paint or fabric can help you see a common piece of furniture in an entirely new way.

**6.** Opposites attract: A sleek white Saarinen table looks wonderful surrounded by dark, elaborately carved Anglo-Indian chairs.

**7.** I'll mix delicate French Limoges china with clear glass dishes, or Fiesta ware with Chinese blue-and-white. Nothing is more deadly than a dining table set with perfectly matched silverware and plates.

**8.** Irreverence is appealing. I might roll out an Aubusson rug on a concrete floor. The Aubusson cuts the edge of the concrete, and the concrete underscores the lyrical softness of the rug.

**9.** Sometimes I'll find an architectural fragment, like a building cornice, and mount it on the wall as if it were a console table. A little chunk of antiquity can give a contemporary room the dimensions of time and add more weight to a featureless space.

**10.** I'll group hefty Italian Baroque candlesticks on a slim glass-and-brass 1940s French table—usually at least three, rarely just one. There's safety in numbers.

## WHAT TO DO NEXT:
# Make a Clipping File.

Choosing the look you love is the first step in creating your décor, and your choice will inform the way you assemble everything you include. You'll need visual reference for this project, so assemble a file of clippings—pictures from magazines, including ads as well as editorial, printouts of things you find on the Internet, photocopies of book pages, and whatever you find in the way of postcards, brochures, catalogs, and the like.

Be greedy as you begin your file—include anything that appeals to you, even if you can't explain why or it seems inconsistent. In addition to pictures of interiors, include images of fabrics, graphic motifs, various surfaces, color combinations: whatever triggers a positive emotion and seems relevant. Later you may sort some of these into other files that are dedicated to specific things you'll need to choose. To trigger your imagination or focus your thoughts, include a list of words that describe the look you'd like, or even cut them out of magazines or type them on your computer and print them out. Use a box or file folder with bellows sides, or a big cork board if you like to have everything in view. You'll visit this file many times; as you do, your eye will become more refined, your sensibilities will narrow, and you'll be able to edit the visual materials you've collected so they represent a look you love and give you a direction to follow.

ABOVE: **Sand dune, sea oat, and pale, sea glass hues are a natural palette for beach house décor, making a subtle bridge between the interior and landscape—in this case a spectacular setting right on the ocean. A few striped fabrics add a crisp accent, and while the shell-pattern on the tufted chair is pretty and sophisticated enough to avoid cliché, no one will begrudge the local color topping the sofa table, where celery vases filled with collected shells flank a carved fish sculpture.** (Valerie Smith)

# What tone do you want your colors to set?

- ☐ Dreamy
- ☐ Earthy
- ☐ Upbeat and bright
- ☐ Fun
- ☐ Light and airy
- ☐ Luxurious

# 5. COLOR

OPPOSITE: **Color shyness was left at the door here, where deep, rich colors meet with aplomb. Dark, walnut floors and walls painted a complex green set off the bright orange upholstery and ivory accent pieces.** (Chad Eisner)

Whether composed of warm, cool, dark, light, gently varied or highly contrasting hues, the palette used in any room is immensely influential in setting the ambience. Color is subjective, personal, and to many people, intimidating. There are so many options, with limitless possible effects that may be dramatically different, or so subtle we barely notice them. We each recognize "the perfect" color combination when we see it, but many of us stumble when we try to describe or explain it. Add to the choice of colors the way they are used—how much of each, and where—and this part of interior design gets more complex. Color seems such an abstract entity, and unless you are mixing pigments or dyes, it is not something you can create. It is, however, something you'll need to work with, and there's no reason to be nervous about this; if you trust your emotional responses to color you will enjoy the process and find combinations you love.

Finding the colors you love isn't as complicated as you might think; three things will help you choose with confidence: Your eyes are a given, use them to discover color combinations that you like and to analyze how color is used in different rooms you admire. A basic understanding of the language of color will help you understand what you see and communicate your preferences; a discussion follows next in this chapter. And perhaps most comforting, the fact is you don't have to create the colors, but just choose them—stylists and manufacturers have already colored their wares.

# THE LANGUAGE OF COLOR

Artists and designers who are adept with color know it as both science and creative talent. While there's no need to become an expert on color theory in order to find the colors for your décor, it's comforting to know there is logic to the way it works. A grasp of the vocabulary experts use to discuss this subject will help you understand the colors you see, give you an appreciation for the way color has been used in the rooms you admire, and help you share your color preferences with your family, designers, and vendors.

The color wheel is a common and handy tool for understanding the relationship of colors. You can find a variety of portable color wheels at art supply stores, some feature revolving layers with windows that isolate various color schemes or show how colors change when mixed together. But the color wheel is just a beginning—the world of color is far too vast to capture in a single small illustration.

Different wheels are set up somewhat differently, but on all, twelve colors are arranged in wedges radiating from the center. Three of the wedges, at equidistant intervals, show the primary colors, red, blue, and yellow. Opposite each primary color is a wedge showing one of the three secondary colors, green opposite red, orange opposite blue, and violet opposite yellow; each secondary color is a blend of the primary colors it sits between. The six remaining wedges are the tertiary colors; each is a blend of the primary and secondary colors it sits between. Notice that black, white, and their blend, gray, do not appear as wedges on the wheel. Note also that while there are some tans and rusts in the red-orange, orange, and yellow-orange wedges, there is no chocolate brown on the wheel.

OPPOSITE: **The very pale, chalky chartreuse tint on the walls and draperies in this living room was chosen to meld with the greenery outside and keep the interior light. The sconce is both whimsical and perfectly proportioned; its antique-gold finish balances the olive-brown rug (reflected on the coffee table) and the lively, deep chartreuse, turquoise, and pink accents that complete the palette.** (John Oetgen)

## COLOR PRIMER

Here are terms to keep your color discussions clear rather than muddy.

**Hue:** A color.

**Tint:** A color mixed with white.

**Shade:** A color mixed with black.

**Tone:** A color mixed with gray.

**Intensity:** The brightness or dullness of a color.

**Value:** The lightness or darkness of a color.

**Pure color:** A color that is not mixed with white, gray, or black.

**Warm colors:** Reds, oranges, and yellows.

**Cool colors:** Greens, blues, and violets.

**Complementary colors:** Colors that appear opposite each other on the color wheel. When a color is mixed with its complement, an artist will say it is "neutralized." Adding a small amount of a color to its complement tones down the hue with the greater volume. A mix of more equal amounts creates a muddy or brown hue; chocolate brown is a mix of red and green.

**Analogous colors:** Colors that are adjacent on the color wheel.

**Color schemes:** An arrangement derived by selecting two or more colors based on their relationship on the color wheel. These schemes can provide a starting point for your palette, or help you identify the way a palette you like is composed, but remember the wheel shows only a few hues and may not correlate directly to the ones you are drawn to. Any of these schemes can include many values of the featured colors and the colors can be used in equal or unequal amounts.

- A complementary color scheme features any two colors that lie opposite one another on the wheel. If the colors are pure, this scheme is quite vibrant—think of Pop Art. Adding a small amount of a dominant color's complement to a palette will enliven the overall effect.

- An analogous color scheme, usually with three or more colors that are adjacent on the wheel, is always harmonious.

- A monochrome scheme features only one color.

- A diad scheme uses any two colors that lie two colors apart on the wheel.

- A split complement scheme features one color and the two colors that are adjacent to its complement.

- A triad scheme features three colors equally spaced on the color wheel, for instance red, blue, and yellow.

# BEAUTIFUL HUES.
## They Make Us Smile.

When you walk into a room, the colors greet you. How do you respond? Are you happy to be there? Do you feel relaxed? Cheerful? Close to nature? Serene? Pampered? Surprised? How do you want to feel when you enter the different rooms in your home? What is guiding your choice of a color palette? Color evokes an emotional response that is based on the colors themselves, for instance, sunny colors make us happy, smoky taupes and lavenders calm us, and on associations we have with them—perhaps blue, ocher, and terra-cotta remind you of the charms of the South of France or sandy hues bring the nearby beach to mind. Both perspectives are valuable when you are choosing a palette;

you want colors that create the mood you desire and support the style of the décor if it makes sense to do so.

We all have favorite colors. You might start with yours as a basis for your palette. But the colors you wear, or the colors of your most beloved possession or favorite flower may not be hues you want to dominate your décor; as you put together a color scheme decide which hues will be prominent and which used for accents. Be practical too, paint is fairly easy to change, but materials such as flooring, bathroom fixtures, and kitchen cabinets generally are not, and your palette applies to them as well. Give some thought to the future when you're choosing: Do you plan to be in this home a long time? Are you falling in love with a trend that will date?

It's not always easy to imagine how colors you see on paint chips or fabric swatches will look once they're on your walls and furnishings, so keep your eyes open for photos of rooms whose palettes greet you the way you want your home to welcome you. Once you put a palette together, look at it over a period of time; if your response to it isn't happy after all, shift direction slightly, or start afresh. Change is easy at this stage—so trust your instincts.

LEFT: **Earth tones are warm and soothing. Done here in natural fibers, the mix includes ocher, reed, and orange hues, all framed with woods indigenous to Hawaii and the South Pacific.** (Douglas Durkin and Greg Elich)

OPPOSITE: **Color is endlessly surprising—or at least the way you use it can be so. Here a plaster wall in a rustic, eighteenth-century stone house is playful in violet.** (Eldon Wong)

RIGHT, TOP: **If crisp, classic, and fresh is what you have in mind, you can't go wrong with blue and white. Here a Chinese-lattice wallpaper gives a fun 1950s resort look to a large dressing area where time can be idled away in correspondence or reading.** (Meg Braff)

RIGHT, BELOW: **Color is fun and uplifting when raspberry, fuchsia, orange, and golden yellow play in front of pale lilac walls. Blocks of mostly solid color keep the effect simple, warm, and comfortable—this combination has inherent energy and does not need much pattern.** (Angie Hranowsky)

OPPOSITE: **Color is pretty when deep purple, warm blues, and touches of green mix with soft white, straw, and gold.** (Robert Goodwin)

# Colorful Opinions: **FEEL-GOOD COLORS**

We can't think of anything more uplifting than clear yellow, real red, restful blue. Designers reveal the colors that make them smile.

ROBERT STILLIN:
**FARROW & BALL**
**COOKING APPLE GREEN 32**
Right now I'm in my office looking out at this field where horses graze, and the sun has turned the grass this rich, vibrant yellowy green, and it just looks so happy to me. Happy isn't about being ecstatic all the time. It's about feeling good, and when I see this color I feel alive and grounded.

JOHN YUNIS:
**FINE PAINTS OF EUROPE**
**SUNNYSIDE LANE 7014T**
It's hard to get yellow right—usually it's too green or too red or too muddy. But this is nice and clear, without being shrill. If it's too vivid, it's like living in an omelet.

LIBBY CAMERON:
**BENJAMIN MOORE**
**MILANO RED 1313**
It's a funny combination of pink and red and coral. Colors in that range are very stimulating—good for conversation, they keep people's minds going. It looks luscious in a satin finish. You can make most colors happy if you put enough sheen into the paint.

MARY DOUGLAS DRYSDALE:
**BENJAMIN MOORE**
**JAMAICAN AQUA 2048-60**
This is a pale teal, a really lovely neoclassical color that goes with high heels and beautiful earrings and sixteen sets of china. It's also sassy and romantic. It reminds me of sitting on a beach where a wonderful waiter asks, "Now, what would you like?"

JAMIE DRAKE:
**BENJAMIN MOORE**
**WHITE SATIN 2067-70**
It's an ahhhhhhhhh color, a pale, ethereal blue with a touch of periwinkle. Completely uplifting—like floating on a cloud surrounded by fluffy down pillows. As soon as you walk in, you feel the weight of the world lifted from your shoulders.

ALEX JORDAN:
**BENJAMIN MOORE
RIVIERA AZURE 822**
My bedroom is delphinium blue. What I like about the color is that it's restful, cool—there's a sense of depressurizing. If you are in a bad mood, it's not a color that intensifies the condition.

SARA BENGUR:
**DONALD KAUFMAN COLOR COLLECTION DKC-30**
It's the color of afternoon light—that end-of-day moment when it feels warm and mellow and everything has a glow. I'm thinking Sardinia, in some beautiful house right on the Mediterranean, and we're sitting outside and eating figs off the tree with a bottle of white wine.

SUSAN ZISES GREEN:
**DURON MT. VERNON ESTATE OF COLOURS
LEAMON SIRRUP DMV070**
This is the color of a pistachio nut—a clear, sharp yellow-green with no sadness in it at all. I used it in a showhouse for Kips Bay and there wasn't a person who came in who didn't break into a smile.

PETER VAUGHAN:
**BENJAMIN MOORE
SPRING IRIS 1402**
I started out as a painter, and I'd always add purple to other colors to give them depth and richness. Lavender reflects light well, which is why you see it all over Scandinavia. In the depth of winter, it's a very cheerful color to walk into.

DAVID MITCHELL:
**BENJAMIN MOORE
SWEET DREAMS 847**
Sweet Dreams is like a hug. I know that sounds sappy, but this is the perfect nice, comfortable blue, with just enough gray, and just enough robin's egg blue, and just enough teal. Paint any room with this and it becomes the happiest room in your house—but not in a clownish, perky way. My kind of happy means serenity and atmosphere.

MATTHEW PATRICK SMYTH:
**PRATT & LAMBERT
VINTAGE CLARET 1013**
This is a real red, a true red that's not trying to be anything else but red. I used it in my living room and it never fails to get a reaction. I once had someone look at the color and say, "I wish I could go through life with these walls behind me."

THOMAS GUNKELMAN:
**BENJAMIN MOORE
BLEEKER BEIGE HC-80**
This isn't beige as we think of it beige—so boring. This has warmth and depth. It's a very sophisticated color that makes me feel good, and I know I look good against it.

# THE MOTIF.
## Adding Pattern to the Mix.

Pattern plays a number of roles in décor. It can add visual excitement, establish a period or regional style, and alter the perception of proportions, plus it offers a readymade way to disperse multiple colors within a room. Obvious sources of pattern are fabrics, wallpaper, and rugs; tile and decorative painting are two others and both can be easily customized. Pattern can also serve as a source for your palette: a multi-colored wallpaper, fabric, or rug with a mix of hues that you love is all you need to get started—and you needn't like the pattern itself to adopt the color scheme.

Most patterns are inextricably linked to a specific style, locale, or era; fortunately there are copious options and you'll have little trouble finding a motif that suits your chosen ambience. Fabric and wallpaper patterns are often developed in families of companion designs, with coordinating florals, geometrics, or abstracts in several scales, which makes it easy to mix them. There are designers who don't use pattern because they feel it obscures the lines of the furnishings and others who've built their careers on it; those who like to mix several patterns in a single space and others who'll choose a single pattern and fill a room with it, and still others who limit pattern to a few accessories; you can follow whichever path appeals to you. If you decide to incorporate pattern, consider the scale of the motifs when you make your choices: very small patterns will blend into a solid color when viewed from a distance, larger patterns can overwhelm whatever they cover or show it off to great advantage; and multiple patterns can complement or compete with one another—a distinction that's sometimes in the eye of the beholder. When mixing, a classic rule of thumb is to choose three scales.

LEFT: **A mix of cheery, sophisticated patterns in different scales fills this pretty Florida room. The striped fabric at the windows billows in the breeze, nearly tenting the room—like a Mediterranean beach cabana; the club chairs are covered in a block print of big bouquets on a ribbon stripe, the fauteuils are covered in a more delicate, tone-on-tone tendril pattern, and the pile rug repeats the aqua, pink, and fuchsia palette.** (Michael Whaley)

OPPOSITE: **Lots of pattern, lots of color: While textiles are an obvious source of both, accessories such as decorative ceramics can be equally effective. Here plates in a variety of styles add individual and collective pattern to the wall, as do the vessels peeking through the screened doors of the pink cupboard, creating a lively background for the vibrant Guatemalan and Pakistani pillows on the sofa.** (John Oetgen)

# SOFT OR SLEEK?
## Incorporating Texture.

Smooth, rough, multidimensional, slippery, hard, soft: Every material you use in your décor has a tactile quality. The nature of a surface is important because matte finishes absorb light and shiny ones reflect it, affecting our perception of color. A single hue used in a variety of textures will appear subtly different from one to the other as shadows and sheen add nuance to its intensity. Monochrome textures can add recognizable pattern to your décor; tile laid with matching grout or in a checkerboard of honed and polished pieces, glossy stripes painted adjacent to eggshell, and cut velvet, damask, and basket weave fabrics are a few examples. You can add interest to a limited palette by incorporating a variety of textures; this is a good way to make something simple appear more complex.

Surface also affects the ambience of your home. Slick surfaces tend to be restrained or austere, soft ones relaxed or inviting. Of course this varies with the situation and both can be elegant or informal, but texture can be used to sway a look one way or another or add an element of contrast. Depending on the application, metallic, glass, and polished stone surfaces can convey luxury (think of a foyer, bath, or dining room) or a professional quality (think of a kitchen). Draperies made in velvet appear seductive, in taffeta, crisp and assertive, in gauze, airy and informal. Texture affects the experience of using your home too—plush fabrics are nicer to sit on than scratchy ones, shiny floors can be slippery.

Texture may not be the first thing you consider when you're selecting colors, but it's an important component in the execution of your décor, so give it some thought early on. You can add textured accessories as a finishing touch, but materials chosen for floors, walls, and built-in components make a fixed contribution that goes beyond their hue.

LEFT: **Texture can be hard, and if so it's often appreciated more by the eye than the hand. Wood paneling and hand-troweled plaster are two examples, stone and tile two more. Terra-cotta tiles face the chimney of this wood-fired pizza oven, creating a diamond grid on the front, a small square one on the sides; embossed tiles frame the top and bottom.** (Sandra Bird)

ABOVE: **Fabrics with subtle dimension add a caressing finish to the furnishings in this living room. The sofa is covered in soft, indestructible mohair, which makes the embrace of the high arms and back especially sumptuous, the ottoman is topped with an embroidery-like cut velvet, the throne chair to the left of the cabinet is covered in tapestry, the striped chair in a luxurious cut chenille. Beneath them, a woven, soft jute mat is topped by a small Oushak carpet.** (Kathy Smith)

RIGHT: **Cut velvet always adds a touch of elegance; the tone-on-tone vine pattern on this pillow is graceful and prettily framed with a silk flange that echoes the sheen of the velvet pile. In contrast, rough stones add varied hues to the chimney breast.** (Christopher Maya)

# ENVELOPE OR ACCENT?
## Proportioning Color.

Chances are one color on your palette will play a dominant role in your décor. Which color stars is up to you, but it's helpful to think about the impact of light and volume (the amount of color used) on the overall effect.

Colors change under different kinds of light. That's one reason why it's always smart to look at samples of materials in your room at different times of day and under artificial light. But you should also bear in mind that indirect bright sunlight will intensify colors, while direct rays will lighten them and even wash out very pale hues. Yellow hues in particular become more yellow in sunlight. Evening light, candlelight, and dimmed artificial light subdue color, blurring subtle distinctions between hues and making light colors quieter and deep colors darker.

Easier to visualize is the influence of volume. The more there is of a color, the more impact it has. A pale color you barely perceive on a paint chip may not have sufficient contrast to use on moldings against white walls, but it will appear darker if it covers the walls themselves. A dark or bright hue that adds a wonderful highlight to a patterned fabric or

ABOVE: **Soft white walls and lots of natural daylight keep this breakfast/family room open to the cityscape beyond the window wall; blocks of red and purple bring the chairs and velvet-covered sofa into focus.** (Faye Cone)

LEFT: **Stripes in two tones of periwinkle surround this sitting room with mysterious depth; the sconce shades, flowers, and throw pop against them and bring up the bright red that travels through the carpet and upholstery. The whites are softened by the richer blues and reds.** (Meg Braff)

# DESIGNER'S TOP TEN

Designers William Diamond and Anthony Baratta share their considerable expertise on how to rev up your rooms.

**1.** A painted ceiling will influence a room without interrupting the eye. Paint the ceiling pink to add warmth and surprise, or sky blue for a feeling of the outdoors; for a more dramatic effect, try gold or silver leaf.

**2.** Buy a colorful quilt, old or new. Stretch it over a frame like a painter's canvas and hang it on a wall for an instant shot of pattern and color.

**3.** We love to paint floors. Use French blue, dark green, Chinese red or even black. If you're feeling adventurous, stencil a border or an overall pattern in a darker shade or complementary color.

**4.** Accessorize a neutral room with one strong color, for example, pick one big color—like hot orange— and find throw pillows in a geometric orange print, a stack of fabric-covered orange boxes, or orange ceramic bowls and vases.

**5.** Be creative with colorful paint. In an all-white modern room we might paint just one wall in a strong color. The colored wall will recede and give added dimension to the room.

**6.** Add colored lampshades, which can be custom made with almost any fabric or paper in every imaginable color.

**7.** We love to use antique Swedish, Austrian, or German painted furniture to add an elegant touch of color. For a more playful look, we'll paint or pinstripe a piece of thrift shop furniture.

**8.** Rugs are one of the easiest ways to introduce color into a drab setting without overwhelming a room. A strong rug will ground a room and add depth and drama to a neutral space.

**9.** Reframe a painting or print with a color mat that matches one of the artwork's dominant colors.

**10.** Slipcover a sofa and chair in a clean, bold color canvas with a contrasting welt. Slipcovers are a less permanent investment, so you can have fun experimenting. Try bold checks or stripes in crisp, clean colors, or a favorite large-scale print.

wallpaper may be overwhelming as a background color that surrounds you, or it may make the space feel intimate and cozy. If you wish, you can compensate for this effect by using the color in a different value, choosing a darker shade where you plan to use less of an especially dark or bright color, and a lighter tint where you plan to use more. When you look at the photos of rooms you like, notice how the colors are balanced: Are the hues in the palette of similar value or is there contrast of dark and light as well as color? This too influences the impact of an individual hue.

# EXPERT INSIGHT

## Choosing Appropriate Colors

As the principal of the New York City design firm that bears his name, designer Scott Sanders provides fine-tuned color strategies to his clients, tailoring his palettes to be the most appropriate and effective for any given interior.

**What's the most important role color plays in a room?**

It sets the mood for a room. The color you choose is really about what you want the room to feel like.

**Do you tend to use one color scheme throughout the entire interior, or mix it up room to room?**

In general, I feel it's important to have continuity throughout the entire house. I'll use one or two colors throughout the house, and then mix in other accent colors. That gives continuity, but at the same time allows the various rooms to have different personalities.

ABOVE: **Balance is everything when you choose a stimulating color for the walls; overdo it and you could find yourself in an amusement park. Traditional, serious furnishings keep this vestibule real.** (Mary McDonald)

LEFT: **Watercolor-aqua walls expand under the beautiful seaside light that alternately glimmers and bleaches in this tiny sitting room, which is gently grounded by the taupe rug and floorboards; the plump sofas look simple and not too big in clean white.** (Ruthie Sommers)

OPPOSITE: **The warm, earthy brown granite countertops inspired the autumn palette in this eat-in kitchen, where brown, beige, and gold neutrals are splashed with touches of coral.** (Kathy Smith)

### What kind of classic color combinations do you think work best?

Blue and white, yellow and green for a kitchen, red and black for a very formal dining room. For a library, I would suggest chocolate brown and camel or dark green and navy blue. I like burgundy and khaki, navy and khaki, or dark green and khaki. And grays and blues look really great together.

### What kind of guidelines would you suggest if someone wants to use bold colors?

You need to be aware that you will likely get tired of bold colors very quickly. If you really want to incorporate a strong, bold color, use it as an accent. Bold colors are often attractive because they are the color of the moment; this can quickly date a room.

### How should the homeowner account for different lighting in choosing colors?

Select three shades of the color you want: where you think you want to be, and one shade lighter and one shade darker. Do this with paint, wallpaper, or fabric swatches. Put the samples in two places: next to the window and in a darker corner. Look at them at different times during the day and at night. Then make your decision.

### Is a neutral color scheme always appropriate?

No. It totally depends on the house, the location, the architecture, and the personality of the homeowner. It's about trying to keep a balance. An entire neutral house can be boring.

### How do you use color to affect spatial relationship and the relationship with other decorative elements?

Color is key to how the décor is perceived. If it's a big room, paint it a brighter, warmer color to bring the walls in. Paint a smaller room a cooler color to push the walls out. Color also establishes visual weight and balance. If you put a bold primary-based piece of art in a pastel room, it's probably not going to seem right. The colors of the art should balance the colors of the space.

### What are the challenges homeowners face in choosing colors and color schemes?

Sometimes people are scared of color, especially dark colors. Ultimately, people should really follow their heart: If they love a color, test it, and like it in place, they should not be afraid to choose it. •

# OPEN YOUR EYES FOR INSPIRATION

Color is everywhere you look. When you are choosing the hues that make you happy, there's no reason to reinvent the wheel, you can take advantage of palettes already created by nature, artists, and designers. Inspiration can be found in the environment, in a flower garden or at the florist, on textiles and tiles, in a painting, in the produce section of your market, and of course, in photos of rooms you like. There are also lots of books about color, many with page upon page of different color combinations—the most useful are directed at the advertising community, interior designers, and craftspeople such as quilters who work extensively with color.

Are you a collector? Your collection could inspire a palette, either to complement the display of the objects or to evoke their flavor elsewhere. Do you wish to link your indoor and outdoor environments? Bring colors from your landscape into your home. Perhaps you wish to acknowledge your locale in your décor, for instance by using a nautical theme with blue, white, and hemp colors. Or is there a particular carpet, piece of pottery, painting, or multicolor rose that says it all to you; if so, replicate its hues.

LEFT: **Collections of yellow Quimper and assorted blue-and-white pottery suggested the soft French gray-blue that finishes this display shelf as well as all the other cabinets in the same kitchen.**
(Hilary Musser)

OPPOSITE, TOP: **What is chocolate and everything sweet? A French patisserie. Thus the theme for this kitchen, where the walls are chocolate-colored, the accessories brown, pink, and white, the decorative painting done** *à la Française.*
(Jamie Gottschall)

OPPOSITE, BOTTOM LEFT: **This country kitchen features a backsplash made from antique French floor tiles—a readymade source of bold pattern—that were found begging to be recycled. Brilliant green country pottery is equally graphic on the open shelves above, and rustic wood cutting boards add a warm touch.**
(Shannon Bowers)

OPPOSITE, BOTTOM RIGHT: **The natural landscape inspired a palette of "misty lake and wet bark" for the exterior of this country home; those colors moved indoors as washes of gray, green, and blue over wood.**
(Architect: Bobby McAlpine)

LEFT: **Subtle, nuanced grays, graduating from darkest on the floor to paler upholstery and mixed with white and flashes of silver, provide a shortcut to the modern, minimalist atmosphere of this apartment living room, where "real" color is added by the owner's collection of contemporary photographs.** (Franklin Salasky)

# WHAT TO DO NEXT:
## Create a Palette You Love.

Set up a file folder or box to hold your color inspirations. Put into it any clippings, photos, swatches, and other samples you collect. Most of these will represent some place or object that has its own design, and you'll find it easier to envision a palette for your home if you can isolate the colors so that you can work with them without seeing their source. One easy way to do this is to take a portion of your file to a paint store and collect sample cards that match the hues in the photos or samples. While you're at the paint store, collect brochures. Most paint manufacturers arrange at least some of their colors in palettes and provide suggestions for mixing and matching; you may see something similar to your collection or something else that you like.

Lay out the sample cards on a white background (a colored background will intrude on your perception of different combinations) and sort the samples in different ways. Cut the paint chips apart if you need to. Arrange them so they overlap, showing more of one color than of the others so you can get an idea of the effect when one hue dominates the group. Arrange them differently. Add or subtract colors. See what happens. Look at your files too; can you create the palette that inspired you with the paint chips? Are you beginning to find colors that make you happy? When you've edited the chips to your satisfaction, tape them onto a card that you can refer to often and carry along when you shop.

It's admittedly challenging to imagine how a group of small colored pieces of paper will translate to the decorated interior of your home. Some paint manufacturers publish magazines that show their colors in place. There is also a variety of interior design software that can show you the effect of different palettes. The House Beautiful Web site, www.housebeautiful.com, features many photos of rooms that you can recolor online—it's fun and fast to use and easy to relate the results to your home.

LEFT: **Soft blue-gray and ivory create a gentle, calm, and dreamy welcome in this small guest room, where cotton panels trimmed with matching velvet hang on a simple iron bed frame, a chinoiserie toile stripe meanders over the bed, and grass cloth textures the walls.**
(Alessandra Branca)

OPPOSITE: **Crisp and fresh, delicate yet strong, like springtime, this yellow-green and white palette gains complexity from the blue-green accent woven into the pillow and bench fabric and repeated for the lamp base. The bamboo window shade adds a neutral contrast with an undertone of yellow.** (Phoebe Howard)

# What effect should your lighting give?

☐ A romantic glow
☐ Daylight even when it's dark outside
☐ Soft, but bright enough for conversation
☐ Make my art collection shine
☐ Energize my kitchen and office
☐ Flatter me at the mirror

# 6. LIGHTING

OPPOSITE: **Fireside dining has an enduring appeal, but it can be toasty. Here a Gustavian crystal chandelier and a few candles against the wall supply all the romance that's needed, casting an intimate glow over the symmetrical décor. Tiny electric bulbs hidden in the frame of the chandelier shine upward and supplement its candles.** (Markham Roberts)

Sparkling. Flooded with light. Nuanced with intriguing shadow. Dramatically accented. It's a given that every home should be well lighted so that the occupants can see to move around and accomplish whatever tasks they turn to, yet the lighting should create an atmosphere that's not purely utilitarian but instead filled with the poetry, drama, or romance that eludes many of us. Natural light is all around us and we can flip a switch to supplement it with electric light. What should happen when you do this?

The kind of illumination you choose and its placement varies with the purpose of each room—there's no one answer to the question. Light can make you feel happy or sad and make a space seem inviting or cold, so controlling its effect is critical to your enjoyment of your home. Yet it has neither volume nor mass and you can't hold it in your hand; it seems mystifying. If you assess your lighting needs pragmatically, by asking what you want to do and see in each space, and how you want the space to feel at different times of the day and night, you'll see that accommodating these needs is not so daunting; indeed, there are fixtures and bulb types to create every desired effect.

Once you have an idea of your lighting requirements, creativity takes over. Fixtures are like jewelry; they add a finishing touch to your décor—one that changes whether they are lighted or dark. Think of what will suit your chosen look—something that sparkles opulently or has a restrained beauty? Something witty or tailored? Ultra-modern or very traditional? Something discreet that you don't especially notice, or something brimming with personality?

# BROAD OR FOCUSED?
## Two Types of Light.

Every room, no matter what its purpose, should have two kinds of light: general, ambient light that provides overall illumination, and specific, task and accent light that is focused on particular areas or objects. How much of which type depends on the way the room is used, whether there are multiple seating or work areas in it, and the ambience desired. Unless a room is windowless, as baths and hallways sometimes are, natural light can usually supply some of both types during the day (moonlight is great for romance, but not for reading). Artificial lighting should take into account the variable character of natural light and supplement it as the day passes or weather changes as well as at night.

Not all rooms require bright ambient light—kitchens do, dining and living rooms may not. If you do want bright overall light, plan it to be even in intensity and distribution, without contrasting areas of light and shadow. Artificial ambient light usually comes from overhead fixtures, which you might not find suitable for your décor. For a nuanced or more atmospheric effect, a combination of indirect sources such as uplights, sconces, hanging lights, and table lamps may be more appealing. You can install dimmers to modify the intensity of the light (you might want a room brightly lit for cleaning but not for sitting), and if there are multiple fixtures, have them controlled individually or in groups so that specific areas of the room can be lit as the natural light changes or to suit the occasion.

Artificial task light ensures that you'll be able to see what you are doing in specific locations—at kitchen work areas, at the mirror, wherever you read. You may use task light to supplement ambient light, for instance at your desk, or by itself, perhaps when you read in bed, so think about this when you are choosing fixtures to make sure they give enough illumination and will direct it where you wish. Accent light, usually from small fixtures, illuminates artwork and library shelves. You can also create drama with large or small accent fixtures, using them to wash or flood sections of a wall, floor, or ceiling with light.

RIGHT: **A glazed entry door spills daylight into this tiny house in New Orleans' French Quarter. Ambient light comes from table lamps—a pair of** *bois doré* **(gilded wood) lamps with silk shades sits on the consoles, there's a larger lamp on the chest; brass apothecary lamps with articulated arms provide reading light at the sofa while a picture light illuminates the painting above. A marbled glass pendant light can be seen in the room beyond, hanging over the bed.** (Tim Landy)

# HANGING OR STANDING?
## Mixing Function and Form.

Light fixtures come in many styles and materials, your first task is to decide on a basic type for each place you need light: table or floor, pendant (hanging from the ceiling), wall-mounted, or ceiling-mounted. Light fixtures should neither overwhelm a space nor be swallowed by it; their perceived scale is linked to their shape and style as well as their actual dimension and it's difficult to judge, so look at photos of similar fixtures in place to get an idea of what works. Part of the challenge is deciding how many fixtures to hang; your choice depends on their scale, the size of the room, the amount of light each fixture gives, and your design concept.

Table and floor lamps are versatile; they're not fixed in place and it's easy to try them out and move them around. Table lamp styles are vast; floor lamp designs are more limited. Many contemporary styles mix well with a variety of looks. They do need to be plugged in and their cords can be unattractive or a hazard; if you are placing them at a distance from a wall, consider floor outlets.

Pendant light fixtures include lanterns, chandeliers, and types with a single paper, cloth, metal, or glass shade. They're typically hung over dining tables and kitchen islands, in foyers, stairwells, and hallways, and sometimes in living rooms, bedrooms, and bathrooms. If you're in doubt about scale, larger is usually better; small can look lost unless the room is very small. Shaded styles may have globes or dishes that focus the light up, shades on others focus light down, and some are completely closed but clear or translucent. If there's no table or counter under a pendant lamp, make sure there is clearance for tall people to walk under it safely. There are also ceiling fans that incorporate lights—something to consider for warm climates.

Wall-mounted fixtures include shaded types with flat backs that sit flush to the wall, single and multiple arm sconces that project from it, and articulated, swing-arm styles ideal for bedside use, as well as library and picture lights, which have horizontal shades that focus light up or down. Track lights may be mounted on the wall and focused in any direction. Multiple-light wall fixtures designed for bathrooms come in a variety of styles. There are also small, discreet fixtures to affix under kitchen cabinets to illuminate the workspace below—their style isn't much of an issue, but you mustn't forget to wire for them.

Ceiling-mounted fixtures may be recessed or sit on or just below the surface. Recessed types include open cans and those with eyeball shades that can be focused in a particular direction. Track lights are versatile and adjustable, as are the more delicate types with individual lamps that ride on wires. Individual fixtures are available in various styles; some are adjustable. While you're planning, don't forget fixtures for closets and combination exhaust fan–lights that are ideal for baths and utility spaces.

LEFT: **Every desk needs a table lamp to light the work area without glare. On the wall behind this one, dramatic swing-arm lamps illuminate a frequently rearranged photograph collection.** (David Netto)

OPPOSITE: **Nothing is more ambient than candlelight. This candle lantern is one of four used to give a romantic glow to the corners of a large, feminine bedroom.** (Charlotte Moss)

ABOVE: **Simple sconces wearing shades that match the white bed linens and high wainscoting look sweet here and allow the marvelous twining-vine metal headboard to shine.** (Nancy Bozhardt)

RIGHT, TOP: **Swing-arm lights are the ideal for reading in bed; this vintage model has a pierced, red metal shade that adds a dab of welcome color too.** (Form Architecture and Interiors)

RIGHT: **The pleated silk shade on this bedside table lamp diffuses the light and adds nuanced texture in keeping with the tufted headboard, pleated bed skirt, and fitted table cover.** (Anne Miller)

OPPOSITE: **A pair of etched glass overhead fixtures bounces light onto the ceiling in this living room; they're interesting and large enough to balance the contrasting beams they hang below. Two floor lamps flank the sofa at the back.** (Andrew Flesher)

# The Choice Is Yours: **LANTERNS**

Talk about an entrance! These leading lights
steal the show in any hallway.

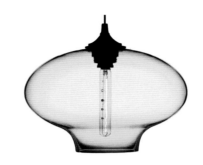

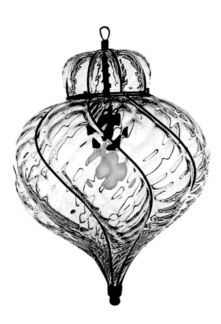

# LIGHT BULB PRIMER

You have a choice of three types of light bulbs; each is available in a variety of sizes and shapes.

- **Incandescent** light bulbs are the most familiar. They light instantly, can be dimmed, come in many shapes, sizes, tints, and finishes, and are inexpensive to buy. However, they are relatively inefficient and are usually the most expensive to operate. Incandescent light generally has a warm, yellowish cast. Reflector lamps are a type of incandescent bulb used for floodlighting, spotlighting, and downlighting. For indoor recessed fixtures, choose ellipsoidal reflectors, which focus the light beam about two inches in front of the enclosure and are twice as energy efficient as parabolic reflector lamps.

- **Halogen** light bulbs, more accurately tungsten-halogen bulbs, are a form of incandescent lighting. They are somewhat costly but extremely energy efficient, and are less expensive to operate than standard incandescent bulbs. Halogen bulbs get very hot and can cause burns, or even fires on direct contact. They do not work in standard light fixtures, need protective housing, and should be placed where nothing can touch them. Skin oils dissipate the life of these bulbs, so avoid touching the glass when you install them. Halogen light is bright and white, close to the color of natural sunlight.

- **Fluorescent** light bulbs have been held in distain for residential use for decades, but recent improvements have eliminated the slow start-up, flickering, noise, and harsh light commonly associated with them. Fluorescent light is very efficient, using only 25 to 35 percent of the energy required for comparable incandescent light, and the bulbs are long lasting. Compact fluorescent bulbs are approximately the size of standard incandescent bulbs, have screw-in bases and can be used in most fixtures; however most cannot be dimmed and they are temperature sensitive, so check the package for ideal operating conditions. They cost considerably more than comparable incandescent bulbs, but they last a very long time. They're heavily pushed as the energy efficient choice in this era of global warming. Two caveats: They're most efficient where the fixture is left on for a period of time; you won't see much payback installing them in closets. And because they contain mercury, there are some questions about disposing of them safely, so check with your local recycling program.

ABOVE: **Zinc lamps made from reclaimed architectural elements share the tones of gray and green washed throughout this living room and provide ample reading light when the drapes are closed.** (Susan Ferrier)

OPPOSITE: **A big Dutch cupboard and a large table with scaled-up, contemporary Chippendale-style chairs make this dining room spare and still. It's a beach house, and instead of a serious, formal chandelier over the table, there's a reproduction of a late eighteenth-century Gothic chinoiserie lantern that has a great, crazy scale and dark color that are just right for the room.** (Michael Smith)

# SHOWING IT OFF AND KEEPING IT SAFE

These often neglected aspects of lighting are unique but equally important: Making the most of artwork and shedding light on dark places to make them accessible and safe.

The entire surface of a painting or other framed artwork should be evenly lit, without glare, with the colors showing accurately, and with a minimum of heat and ultraviolet and infrared rays. To light art effectively without damaging it, mount a picture light with a long arm that directs light evenly onto the painting onto the back of the frame, and use a color-correct, ultraviolet-free, low wattage bulb. Fiber-optic lights are free of damaging ultraviolet and infrared rays, but they're expensive and best left to specialists to install. Sculptures, often less sensitive than framed art, should be lit to enhance their form and sometimes to cast shadows on the wall or floor. There are uplights and downlights of various sizes and configurations; select one that suits each particular piece.

Bookshelves and display cabinets often benefit from special lighting. Lights designed to clip onto shelves or mount beneath them are available.

Dark closets are irritating and, if someone reaches for precariously stacked items, can be unsafe. Install a fixture on the ceiling or wall—even a simple, frosted bulb will help. If there is no wiring to the closet, look for an inexpensive, easy-to-install battery-powered fixture at a home or hardware store.

LEFT: **Hung in the foyer of a beach house where the décor follows the romantic notion that the ocean is large and mysterious, lending only pieces of itself to us, this spider sconce has slender, curvy arms that reach out to support tiny shades. However you see the arms—as tentacles, seaweed, or the flower-tipped branches of a lovely tree—the sconce is delicate and graceful.** (Susan Ferrier)

OPPOSITE: **Projecting, articulated wall-mounted brass lamps illuminate the titles on the shelves of this formal library.** (Bunny Williams)

# EXPERT INSIGHT

## CREATING HARMONY WITH LIGHT

Stephanie Stokes, the owner of Stephanie Stokes, Inc. in New York City, brings the eye of a photojournalist to interior lighting. In her world, getting the artificial lighting right is key to creating a harmonious mood.

### Where does lighting fit into your design process?
I think lighting is probably, after space design, the singular most important subject in interior design. You have to concentrate on visualizing what you're planning. I think that the electrical plan should always allow for a lot of flexibility and change.

### How can the electrical plan allow for flexibility?
You just basically overwire. It's cheaper in the long run.

### What are your biggest lighting challenges?
My biggest challenges are probably creating mood, creating the poetry that you can walk into and feel. Achieving a mood and an ambience is partially technical. But it's mostly taste.

RIGHT: **Honey-colored plaster, amber and gold hues, and the patina of waxed wood set a mellow mood in this dining room, which glows with romance when softly lit by a chandelier, candles on the table, and delicate multi-light sconces in the corners.** (Fern Santini)

OPPOSITE: **Designer Stephanie Stokes suggests using picture lights to enlarge the scale of a room (and make the paintings sparkle like jewelry) and says to balance small accent lights with bigger fixtures. She prefers silk shades, like the fringed one in front of the painting here, because they diffuse the light "for poetry," an effect not possible with paper shades.** (Craig Schumaker and Philip Kirk)

## How do you approach lighting for theme and mood?

You have to focus on how you want to live and what face you want to present to the world. For example, if you're living in Seattle and you're going with halogen lighting, you're presenting a very cutting-edge, current face to the world. If you're living in an eighteenth-century French interior, your approach is more about traditional fixtures and the soft yellow light of incandescent lighting. Mood and theme are also intertwined with practicality. When I take on a client, I want to know how she uses a room. You also have to consider context. A lot of the furniture and fabrics we use today were originally seen in candlelight. Damask and crushed silk velvet, for instance. The lighting you use should replicate that softness.

## How will color be affected by artificial light?

First and foremost, by the color of your bulb. Halogen makes sense in a white room because the bright white light makes everything sparkle. But my living room at home is supposed to glow with sunlight whether it's day or night. So I use tung-sten light and try to correct whatever inadequacies I have by changing bulbs. If I painted a wall a little too green, I can correct it by putting a pink bulb in the fixture lighting that wall.

## What about fixtures?

Well, one size does not fit all. For me, I like to bounce light, so that it rains and falls, that's wonderful. That means using fixtures to direct the light at the ceiling. Another issue is the shade. With a paper shade, light is forced up and down in harsh ways, so you're not getting a general luminosity. It's a great way to modernize the room: You just put paper shades everywhere and you take ten years off the room. But on the other hand, you've given up the poetry, the glow. Fixtures also have to take into account purpose. My bedroom has two fixtures—on the bedside table and mounted next to the bed. The two lights work to cancel shadows, which is actually what you try to do in lighting a work desk. Have a light coming from overhead and one on the desk to cancel the shadow. •

# WHAT TO DO NEXT:
## Make a Lighting Plan.

Planning ahead is key to successful lighting. It's easy to understand that increasing the natural light by adding a window or skylight is not a last-minute option, and just as easy to assume you can enhance your ambience by simply plugging in a lamp when you're putting the finishing touches on your décor. The latter is a risky assumption: Adequate and appropriate artificial light depends on the correct fixtures being selected, wiring and outlets being properly sized and sited, and installation dovetailed with other parts of the design—there's no point in painting if the walls and ceiling need to be opened up to install power or support for the lights. Budgeting realistically is important too: fixtures can be costly and if you are looking for something unique, may take time to locate or manufacture. You won't be happy if you have to settle for something you don't really love because you've run out of money or the schedule doesn't permit a delay.

If all this technical information seems dry, just remember that form and function go together where lighting is concerned: decide what the lighting requirements are and you'll be able to choose fixtures you love to look at that do the right job. Don't fault yourself if the job seems complex and you feel a bit at sea; you don't need to figure it all out yourself. Gather ideas, stashing photos of fixtures and lighted rooms that have the aura you're after in a folder. Form whatever plans you can; then get some professional advice. A good lighting vendor will explain the reach of various fixtures and can do a plan for you. Or you can hire an interior designer to create a plan, and source the fixtures too, even if you don't wish to use his or her services for any other part of your job.

OPPOSITE: **Two stories high, with skylights, windows at two levels, and no upper cabinets to block the sun, this kitchen enjoys such an embarrassment of natural light that the electric fixtures are rarely used except in the evening. When they're needed, pendant lights with a vintage industrial look provide ample general light over the huge, marble-topped island and counters; sconces supplement them with task light by the sink and the range hood houses lights as well.** (Judith Barrett)

RIGHT, TOP: **Curtains at the bed head are no reason to skip good reading light—they can be made with separate panels that abut where sconces attach to the wall. Pleated lamp shades are a nice complement to the curtain folds.** (Mary McDonald)

RIGHT: **Golden metal-frame pendant lamps with shirred gingham shades add a final dressy touch to this kitchen, which is so pretty and well-appointed the owner often entertains in it.** (Anne Miller)

# Which fabric gives the ambience you love?

☐ Luxurious silk velvet

☐ Natural linen, simple as the sandy beach

☐ Iridescent taffeta that shimmers

☐ A charming toile with a tale to tell

☐ Muslin, it's so unassuming

☐ An avant-garde textured sheer

# 7. FABRIC & TRIMMINGS

OPPOSITE: **Versatile fabric, celebrated here in vivid hues and lavish application, offers instant style, color, and pattern. In this dining room it's stretched flat to cover the walls, gathered on rods to curtain the windows and doorway, and shaped into smart little dresses for the chairs. Trim is a great tool too; here woven multi-color ribbon edges the blue-striped portieres and the slipcovers are finished with a plain ribbon—check out the hemline, where the ribbon has been pleated into a teeny skirt.** (Diamond Baratta)

Color, pattern, texture, sheen, dimension, structure, and fluidity combine in nearly infinite ways to give fabric character that transfers to the room it adorns. It's among the most versatile of all the materials available for interior design. Even straight off the bolt, fabric offers instant style; once manipulated, it supports, and can easily transform, the ambience of your home. Unlike light, you can hold it in your hands, and it can be layered, flexed, stuffed, gathered, draped, stiffened, and stretched with an ease that is unmatched by paint, tile, metal, or wood.

There are luxurious fabrics, rustic fabrics, opaque goods, and sheers. You'll find crisp, soft, thick, thin, tight, open, smooth, and nubby weaves, and each behaves differently. There are printed fabrics, woven patterns, and cut pile surfaces, with each available in a range of scales to complement or alter the scale of an entire room or a single piece of furniture. If your dream is a room that envelops you in warmth, you can drape it in dense velvet or lofty mohair; if you want the cool touch of filtered light, gauze or lace will provide it. Ethnic prints and weaves can transport you to distant lands. Motifs with historical, regional, and wonderfully contemporary flavor will give specific identity to a décor. You can accent fabric with fringe, braid, ribbon, cord, or studs—all come in many styles. The possible combinations are exciting and endlessly beautiful.

# IT'S GORGEOUS.
## Where Will You Put It?

Your first thought for incorporating fabric in your décor is probably for window dressing or upholstery and, of course, these are logical and important uses that influence and support the overall ambience. Window treatments are so important and offer such a wealth of creative opportunity that there is a chapter devoted to them beginning on page 176. Fabric can be a fine wall covering too—applied flat like wallpaper, or over padding, like upholstery, or gathered to give softness, like draperies. If your walls are in bad shape, one of these options may mask the problems, but you needn't have something to hide to be drawn to this use.

Smaller and more particular uses of fabric can be as effective as artwork for adding character and style to a room. Use luxurious or ethnic textiles for throw pillows to toss like jewels on sofas, window seats, or beds. Curtain the inside of glass cabinet doors in a romantic or country kitchen or bath. Skirt a dressing table with something fancy, or a console sink with something tailored—or the reverse if it gives you the look you want. Make a soulless round side table elegant with a fringe-trimmed silk moiré cover.

Two important, and sometimes overlooked, homes for fabric are the bed and the dining table. Readymade options for covering both abound, but something custom-made, especially for a bed, enables you to indulge your dream aesthetic and may be more creatively integrated with the other furnishings in the room.

LEFT: **The red-on-cream floral stripe fabric covering the walls makes a pretty background for this breakfast room. It's repeated—just once—on the armchair; checks and solids in the same palette cover the banquette and loose pillows. Dressy embroidered monograms carry the red onto the natural linen window shades.** (Katrin Gargill and Carol Glasser)

OPPOSITE: **Use a bold pattern to make a bold gesture. This large, stylized floral stripe is fun in juxtaposition to the sweeping curves of the Victorian settee—it lightens the mass of the settee, emphasizes the verticality of the form, and puts the formal parlor piece happily in a country sitting room.** (Tom Scheerer)

# FABRIC JARGON

## GOOD TERMS TO KNOW

Fabric has its own lingo. Here are some terms that will keep communication clear when you shop for fabric or discuss it with a designer or workroom.

**Dye lot:** A single production run of a specific fabric, usually identified with a number. Color can vary slightly from one run to another; it's best to purchase the entire amount you need from one dye lot. There's no guarantee the same dye lot will be available should you run short, that's why good yardage estimates are important. Sometimes called color run.

**Embroidery:** Decorative thread embellishment applied by hand or machine to the surface of a fabric.

**Fiber:** The substance from which the yarns or threads that form fabric are created. Silk, cotton, linen, wool, and rayon are frequently used for home décor fabrics. Polyester, nylon and some other synthetic fibers are sometimes found, especially in sheer or novelty fabrics. Real and synthetic metals are also used. There is current interest in textile yarns made from bamboo and other renewable plant sources. Fibers are frequently combined in a single fabric.

**Finish:** A process through which fabric passes when it comes off the loom. Some finishes, such as moiréing (a watermark pattern), glazing, brushing, and embossing give the fabric a characteristic decorative surface. Others such as starching and sizing give it body. Still others make it stain- or water-resistant.

**Hand:** The body-language of a fabric when it is handled. Stiff, crisp, drapey, fluid, slippery, stable, flyaway, and sculptural are terms that can describe the hand of fabrics.

**Memo:** A sample cut that can be borrowed (taken on memorandum) from a store or showroom. Most memos include one piece that shows an entire pattern repeat and smaller pieces showing each color variation available, all stapled to a card. Some retail shops have memos that can be borrowed with a credit card number left for security.

**Pile:** Erect yarns forming a soft surface on the fabric, as with velvet, plush, and corduroy.

**Railroad:** To turn fabric sideways on a wall, window, upholstery, or any other application. Railroading eliminates seams in wide spans. Fabrics with directional patterns (motifs with an obvious top and bottom) or plush surfaces cannot be railroaded.

**Repeat:** The distance from the center of a motif to the center of the next identical motif. Motifs on patterned fabric should be matched and aligned when the fabric is cut and sewn, and an allowance for this must be included in the yardage requirement for any given use. You don't really have to worry about this unless you're in the DIY mode, however, the larger the motif, the more fabric is needed and this affects the overall cost of whatever you're using the fabric for. When you're budgeting, multiply the cost per yard by the number of yards needed for each fabric you're considering.

**Swatch:** A small sample cut of a fabric. Many vendors supply swatches at no cost. Swatches are useful for assembling a palette and matching colors, but they show only a portion of most patterns and may be too small for you to judge the impact of the fabric in your room.

**Weave:** The structure of a fabric; the pattern in which the yarns are woven. Plain, twill, and satin are the three basic weaves; there are many variations of each. The look of a woven pattern can be altered if different combinations of thick and thin, tightly or loosely twisted yarns are used.

ABOVE: **A plain fabric, even one as ordinary as muslin, can be an effective choice for slipcovers because all the dressmaker details will stand out. These dining chairs look fresh and light dressed in sleek tops and smartly pleated little skirts.** (Karen Cohen and Ani Antreasyan)

OPPOSITE: **A gentle mix of azure and white fabrics, some with quilted detailing, covers this bed with dreamy comfort. Fine, dark blue accents give definition to the design and bring the color from the curtains to the headboard and linens.** (T. Keller Donovan)

# TAFFETA OR CHINTZ?
## Fabric for Every Effect.

Fabric is tactile. The way it feels when you touch it has almost as much to do with the effect it creates as its color or pattern. And each type reflects or absorbs light in a different way. It's almost impossible to judge its effect from a photo. Good retail home décor fabric stores are scarce, but you can learn a lot about fabric by window shopping in a variety of places: Visit hotel lobbies, showhouses and museums (no touching), furniture stores, and home stores. Go to manufacturers' showrooms if you can. You can't fail to become excited by the possibilities.

There are hundreds of kinds of fabric and you needn't try to learn the names of all—indeed, it would be virtually impossible. Fabrics are often categorized by weight, which gives some indication of what they're best used for, but there are so many exceptions and so many ways to be creative that this is only so helpful. They are also sorted by pattern type: florals, stripes, checks, plaids, abstracts, and novelty prints, among others, as well as by type of woven pattern or texture and as solid colors. Bear in mind that manufacturers often give their fabrics individual names that evoke a motif, look, or theme, or are simply easier for people to remember than a product number. Names like these won't be meaningful to anyone other than that manufacturer and designers who are familiar with the fabric. When you're looking at fabric, if you don't know the technical name for it, try to describe it by weight, finish, hand, and pattern, for instance "medium-weight, shiny, crisp, and solid color," or "medium-weight, matte but slightly textured, soft, with a twining vine and rosebud print."

Lightweight fabrics: Gauze, voile, handkerchief-weight linen, cotton lawn, organza and organdy, some types of taffeta and fine silk, netting, and some lace are all examples of lightweight fabric. The type of fabric generically referred to as "sheers" falls into this category. There are many unusual textured lightweight fabrics, some with mixed opaque and sheer sections, some embroidered, some with ethereal prints, some shot with metallic or dimensional novelty threads. Some lightweight fabrics are very stiff and some very soft, and this affects their application at least as much as their weight does.

Lightweight fabrics are usually delicate so they're not good choices for anything where stress will be a factor; otherwise they offer tremendous design opportunities. They're perfect for reiterating a light and airy ambience, they add delicacy and femininity, and they can be used in interesting ways to blur and soften hard lines and juxtaposed with unlike materials to add sophistication. They can be gathered, draped, and swagged to create clouds of color or used sparingly, with elegant restraint. They're fun to layer too.

Medium-weight fabrics: Chintz, many cottons and linens, muslin, silk shantung, some types of taffeta, faille, cotton ticking, and silk, linen, and cotton damask are all medium weight. You'll find glazed fabrics like chintz, printed and plain, that have a gentle sheen, and dressy ones like taffeta that are lustrous and also stiff enough to show you a bit of attitude; simple and complex textures; all manner of prints and woven patterns.

Strong enough to withstand tension and yet light enough to gather or drape, medium-weight fabrics are versatile; most may be used for upholstery, slipcovers, bed and table linens, window treatments, pillows—really, anything you can make from fabric.

Heavyweight fabrics: Velvet, tapestry, many woolens, ottoman, canvas, duck, and chenille are examples of heavyweight fabrics. These fabrics are bulky and some are stiff. Heavy fabrics usually appear weighty and substantial, which can be a plus if you're creating a rich, lush ambience. They're effective as window treatments and upholstery and may work well elsewhere if their actual or visual weight is not an issue.

Use your hands as well as your eyes when you are selecting fabric; there are exceptions to all these generalizations and you'll very possibly find lightweight woolens, medium-weight velvet, and damask of all weights. Your goal is to find something with the right appearance that will give the effect you want, not to worry about what it's called.

OPPOSITE: **A beautiful textile is a work of art, so why not hang it on the wall? An eighteenth-century English tapestry sets the mood in this bedroom; its intricate, organic pattern of flowers and birds is complemented by the simple broad stripes of the vintage Tibetan cloth that covers the bed.**
(Waldo Fernandez)

RIGHT: **Velvet, always sensual, gives a luxe finish to the gathered cushion covers topping this banquette; gathered shades on the windows echo the soft effect. Alternating blue and floral print throw pillows and the striped ticking casually covering the ottoman exude relaxed charm.** (Alessandra Branca)

# WHISPER

Designer Brooke Gomez isn't afraid to admit she loves pink, especially in sophisticated, whisper shades paired with oatmeal and taupe. Here she uses fabric in these hues to create a romantic yet formal living room. Follow her cues to assemble your own group from the swatches in this palette or from the equally lovely aqua and chocolate array she suggests for another look.

## Start Here: Blush

The soft gradations of pattern and color make this large print ideal for a big sofa, says Brooke Gomez, who likes to match a fabric with the scale of the furniture while still thinking of the big picture. "If everything is loud, it's not going to work."

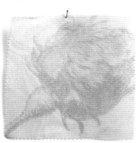

## ✚ Printed Linens Add one from this category

Balance this gutsy pattern with a sweet, petite chair frame.

A tile-like pattern makes great throw pillows—take them to the next level with fantastic metallic fringe.

Cover a pair of chairs with this; finish the seams with pink or gray welting.

## ✚ Stripes & Checks

Then add two from this category

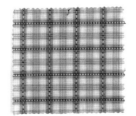

This stripe makes lovely curtains: leave it unlined for the beautiful translucency only linen can give, or line it with solid pink for a pretty effect.

This check is a chameleon—use it in a formal way or on seats in your kitchen.

This little plaid looks great on an ottoman—and really sings if there's a crisp pleated skirt.

The vertical nature of this stripe is perfect for curtains on a tall window.

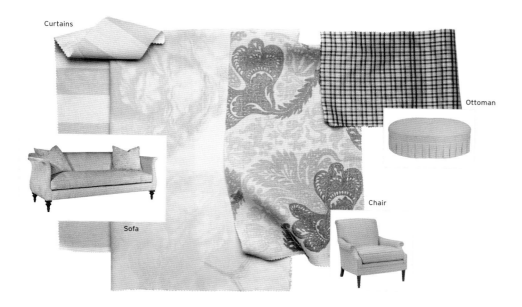

Curtains

Ottoman

Chair

Sofa

## Start Here: Aqua

With a fabric like this that's printed with layers of color, the paler motifs play second fiddle to the darker ones. This fabric really comes to life in natural light—it's a romantic with a lot of character.

## + Velvets Add one from this category

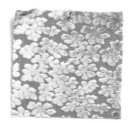  

You can't go wrong this light blue, delicately cut velvet. Brooke Gomez used it to cover a pair of settees.

This cut velvet has a chunkier motif; it's cozy and doesn't feel precious—good on a banquette.

A velvet like this adds a dose of texture to any room. The scale of this multicolor stripe is perfect for a bench.

## + Linens

Then add two from this category

This plain, vanilla-color linen is a blank canvas that screams out for jewelry. Accessorize it with fringe, welting, or buttons.

Gomez likes the way the rich tones of this print complement stained wood pieces.

A small print like this can look busy on a large piece of furniture, so use it on a chair seat or an ottoman.

Play with this pale, dreamy, medium-size stripe by using it for loose, cascading curtains.

# INSTANT ROOM

## HAPPY

If you love color and want a really happy room, designer Annie Selke shares your passion. Here's her vision of fabrics for the ultimate carefree bedroom: "It's a restful, serene combination," she says, "not as disparate as it might seem, because the colors are matched." Use her suggestions to assemble your own mix from one of the upbeat swatch groups she's put together here.

### Start Here: Golden

Annie Selke thinks of this bold pattern as a solid. Even though the scale is powerful, the "positive/negative makes it feel like one color." With only two colors, a pattern like this is easy to use, unlike when you have seven or eight colors to contend with. It's great for a bed, but you can put this anywhere.

### + Textures  Add one from this category

Mixing in a natural-color fabric that gets interest from a geometric weave is a great way to add texture to a casual room.

The handmade quality of this crewel adds depth to the room, and the scale of the pattern is good—it doesn't overpower.

A color-saturated plain weave cotton is totally versatile—use as an accent or to cover a small bench.

### + Complements

Then add two from this category

An irregular stripe like this acts as a big pattern, but if all the colors are the same intensity, as these are, it will sit back a little.

Choose a sweet fabric for a sweet shape. This two-color allover bitsy design breathes and is light, but it has some oomph.

Selke says there's usually a place for both irregular and regular stripes: a small-scale regular ticking stripe is a good mixer here.

Sometimes you need a little breathing room—use a solid parchment color when you need a break from pattern and color.

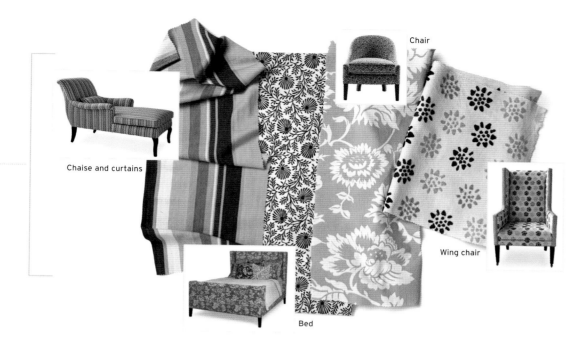

Chaise and curtains

Chair

Wing chair

Bed

## Start Here: Peony

Another bold positive/negative, this bright pink and white print works on everything. Annie Selke designs with the bed in mind, with a focus on comfort: "It's all about starting with a base cloth that you want to get into bed with."

## + Textures Add one from this category

Insert a little hand-crafted fabric—like this nontraditional crewel—into the room so it doesn't look like it's all bought off the rack.

You can't go wrong with a stripe like this; it goes with everything. It's great for furniture or curtains—or a bed skirt and top linens.

Cotton eyelet is very feminine, but when it's in a color like this it has some attitude. Use it for slipcovers, with a hit of color peeking through.

## + Complements

Then add two from this category

Classic matte leather in a fashion-forward color is just the thing when you need an accent. Try it on a bench or chair seat, or for a pillow.

For a bold statement, introduce a graphic pattern. One like this has a manageable scale that works in a variety of places.

When you're looking for a "go-with" print, choose one that can stand on its own too, like this small but bold allover pattern.

A plain fabric will give you some breathing space. This pale lilac is more interesting than white for this group of fabrics.

# FRINGE OR GROSGRAIN?
## Adding Trim to the Mix.

Ribbon, braid, fringe, and cord supply decorative accents to anything made from fabric; they're beautiful and diverse, and deserve to be part of the design from the outset—don't let them be afterthoughts. Narrow trims can discreetly add a band of color at an edge or highlight the contours of a chair or sofa. Deep fringe or elaborate tassels will add an extravagant gesture. Multicolor tassel fringe adds delicate contrast. Glass bead fringe adds sparkle; wooden beads an ethnic twist. Braid and ribbon can be appliquéd in simple or elaborate configurations that create a stylized motif, medallion, or border, and transform the supporting fabric.

Whether to incorporate a trim depends on your taste. But each trim will contribute its character to whatever it adorns, so it makes sense to choose fabric and trim together and design their application so the finished effect is as ornate or low-key as you like. You can achieve a look of luxury by adding elegant fringe and braid to a plain fabric, or quiet a shimmering fabric with a matte ribbon edge. Trim offers a subtle way to carry color from one part of a room to another: you can pick up a hue from the carpet and repeat it on a

drapery fringe or pillow edging. Or to add interest without adding color, select trimmings with different textures or sheens in the same color as your fabric.

If your eye is seduced by trimmings, note their price. They're often costly, and even if one yard of braid or a single tassel is not especially pricy, you may need miles of braid to edge all your draperies or a basket of tassels to trim all the pillow corners. There's nothing to keep you from weighting your budget toward fabulous trim and choosing less expensive fabric, as long as the mix is the one that makes you happy.

ABOVE: **A stencil-like border cut from wool felt outlines this dark, wool satin window treatment; it's decorative and also serves to separate the valance from the panels when seen from across the room.** (David Kleinberg)

LEFT: **Very long bullion fringe makes a luxurious skirt for a sofa covered in a solid color fabric. Soft, floppy tassel fringe gives a fancy edge to the large silk throw pillow. The color mix here is subtle and gives just the right importance to the details.** (Christopher Maya)

ABOVE: **Ivory, taupe, and chocolate bedding strengthens the lines of the Charleston rice bed in this master bedroom. Fine, graphic lines of chocolate ribbon break up the expanse of the lighter-color linens and tie the pillow shams, top sheet, and duvet cover to the quilted spread.** (Kathy Smith)

## SUBTLE

If a quiet, nuanced look is on your list, follow the approach of designers Wayne Nathan and Carol Egan to combine super-subtle fabrics in a way that keeps the room interesting. As an example, they propose a soft, sophisticated take on the study—no stuffiness here. Use their tips to select your own mix from one of the swatch collections they favor.

### Start Here: Oatmeal

To introduce a graphic element, put a stripe like this on a bench. On the other hand, if used for curtains, this pattern will go quiet because the stripes get pushed together. Wayne Nathan likes it for wall upholstery too.

### + Solids Add one from this category

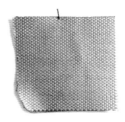

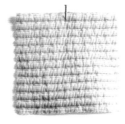

On a large piece of furniture such as a sofa, you want something light; this ecru linen makes a versatile background for colorful pillows.

A small, two-color woven pattern like this is so subtle you can use it like a solid and mix it with more pronounced patterns.

Something soft but dimensional, with the look of closely spaced quilting, is great for upholstery and nice for Roman shades too.

### + Textures

Then add two from this category

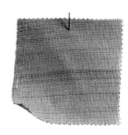

Add a dose of color with a velvet that has a high cotton content; it's luxurious but not precious, so it's even good for dining chairs.

An elegant wool in a color like this citron is good for upholstery and it drapes beautifully too—try it for a bed skirt.

Glossy leather pairs well with both wood and white furniture; choose a color that picks up one hue from the "start here" stripe fabric.

A little bit of a light-weight "horsehair" canvas with a bit of sheen and subtle stripes goes a long way; use on tailored cabinet doors.

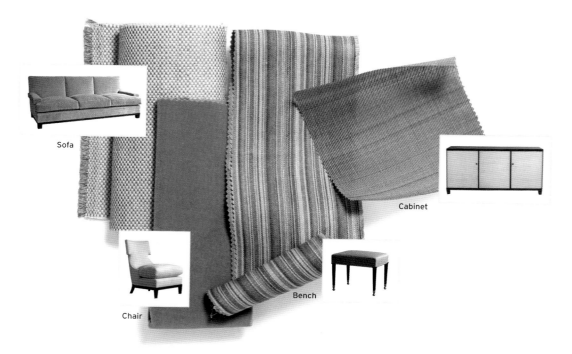

Sofa

Chair

Bench

Cabinet

## Start Here: Rust

Traditional plaids can be very dark. In rust and silver colors, this one tweaks a classic design and is light and modern with a nice scale. Wayne Nathan suggests using in on large ottoman, decorated with nailheads.

### + Solids Add one from this category

Wool flannel works well for wall upholstery, and looks chic and crisp as armchair skirting.

Bring in a very dark wool but use it in small doses—try it as a seat cushion, adding a contrast welt to the seams.

This tone-on-tone weave works as a solid and helps other colors stand out. It "really has a grounding effect," says Nathan.

### + Textures

Then add two from this category

A small, three-color stripe like this works for pillows or accent furniture like a stool. Egan would experiment with patchwork effects.

A dark napped fabric will really pop in a room; it's fun to wrap around an umbrella-stand bucket.

A touchably soft fabric like this wool begs for a home on a comfy sofa.

A durable fabric like this "horsehair" canvas is good for desk and dining chairs. There's a subtle stripe that gives it impact.

# INSTANT ROOM

## COMFORT

Relaxed elegance is designer Suzanne Rheinstein's signature style. To create the easygoing comfort of an English country house and keep it young and modern, she likes to use a mix of traditional and modern fabrics. Here she imagines a cozy living room. Follow her cues to select your own mix from one of the two lovely swatch groups she's put together here.

### Start Here: Chinoiserie

Suzanne Rheinstein suggests beginning with an oversize print with lots of character, like this chinoiserie multicolor cotton. "Use it for curtains, one beautiful chair, and nothing else." Then pull out the individual colors elsewhere with subtler but beautiful fabrics that have sheen and texture. Rheinstein would add a sisal rug to take the room down a notch. "Marvelous."

### ✦ Silks Add one from this category

The best thing about a double-sided silk and wool like this is you can show off the front and back: perfect for unlined curtains.

A glazed silk is like chintz, finished to have a subtle sheen. It's great for upholstery because it's not flimsy, but also not too stiff.

A pale stripe like this doesn't shout, it shimmers. Wrap it around bolsters or use it to cover accent pillows.

### ✦ Heavy Textures

Then add two from this category

Rheinstein likes a heavy, plain weave fabric for a tailored seat on a walnut bench, to make the room feel more relaxed.

A cut velvet with a medium-scale design works well with an oversize "start here" print. This one would add a vintage look.

A mix of silk, wool, and cotton gives velvet an especially sumptuous texture. Try it on a bergère with piping detail.

Use a subtle velvet stripe like this on an ottoman. Look for a durable viscose and cotton blend, then put your feet up.

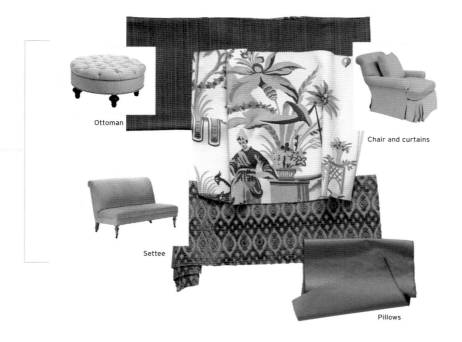

Ottoman

Chair and curtains

Settee

Pillows

## Start Here: Paisley

A motif like this is a fresh take on an intricate Italian paisley. Suzanne Rheinstein says "Back it with paper and put it on the walls, and keep everything else pale." Thanks to the water-color hues, "this print can create a very serene setting."

## + Stripes Add one from this category

  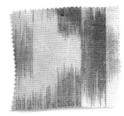

This delicate stripe calls for a big, squishy sofa. Rheinstein says she'd "run the stripe around the bottom to make its own trim."

To personalize stan-dard dining chairs, use a soft, twill stripe like this for slipcovers.

A large ikat with a vertical pattern makes beautiful curtains because it has more interest than a regular stripe.

## + Textures

Then add two from this category

  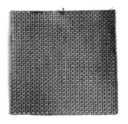 

Use a soft, subtle, two-color plain weave like this somewhere you can really enjoy it, like on a big club chair.

An Indian silk with a fine rib makes stylish curtains or a sweet accent. Or try it for throw pillows, adding a crisp pleated edge.

A heavier weave with nuanced color looks terrific on a pair of headboards in a room where the "start here" paisley makes the curtains.

A plain fabric woven from two colors reads as a solid. One like this is a true basic that's perfect for any type of upholstery.

# WHAT TO DO NEXT:
## Make a Swatch File.

There are so many choices in the world of fabric, how do you know which is the right one? Your perfect fabric is patterned in a way that suits your décor, is the right color, the correct scale, has the right character to drape or mold as needed, works with everything else in the room, and is within your budget. That's quite a list of requirements. But the perfect fabric is out there; you just need to be smart about choosing it.

If you are working with a designer, he or she will acquire and organize swatches for your approval. If you are not, organize your search. Find a large bellows envelope for your swatches. Put a copy of your palette into it. Make a room-by-room list of all the items for which you need fabric and trimming. Annotate the list to indicate the type of fabric you want for each item; be as specific as you can, including the color. Then go shopping; if there are no retail home décor fabric stores nearby, search online for "home decorating fabric"; you can order swatches. Many drapery and upholstery workrooms can also source fabric for you. Make sure the vendor attaches each swatch to a card that identifies the price per yard, the width of the fabric, and the size of the

repeat. If the fabric has a pattern name or number, it should be on the card. Make sure the card is marked with the store name too. You'll need all this information before you actually purchase your fabric and there's nothing more frustrating than being unable to remember where you picked up the swatch you love most—or how much that fabric costs.

When you have all your samples, spread out the swatches for each room and edit them. Group all the possibilities for each item together and lay all the groups out on a table. Mix and match swatches from each group until you have a selection you like. Label each one you've chosen with its intended use and pin the selection together. Pin the swatches remaining in each group together too; you may want to revisit them. Hold onto all the swatches while you assemble samples of other materials you plan to use.

You might wish to purchase a larger sample of each fabric (or borrow one from the vendor) so that you can see its full effect, but resist the urge to order the total yardage until after you've looked at the fabrics in conjunction with the other sample materials and in the room where you plan to use them. Before you purchase, ask the workroom you're using how many yards of each fabric they'll need. If you are working with a designer, he or she will know when it is appropriate to order your fabric.

LEFT: **A little bit of wonderful fabric can be magic—you don't have to use yards and yards. Silk throw pillows with panels of hand embroidery in vivid colors and exuberant patterns add an exotic finish to this bed and look fabulous against the ivory damask linens and rose suede-covered headboard.** (Angie Hranowsky)

OPPOSITE: **Pillows covered in bold blue-and-white prints strike up a spirited conversation on this spool bench, which is in the foyer of a Florida home. The block-print and batik designs are typical of India and Indonesia; calling to mind far-away shores, they evoke the feeling of the beach without direct reference. The frame of the Dutch cushion mirror echoes the swirly foliate patterns of the fabrics.** (Phoebe Howard)

# You'd like the walls in your home . . .

☐ To add color, color, color
☐ To create a cocoon
☐ I want an unobtrusive backdrop
☐ To masquerade as an arbor
☐ They must be handsomely detailed
☐ To shimmer by candlelight

# 8. WALLS & CEILINGS

OPPOSITE: **Why stop with only one wall covering when several are more fun? Tall wainscoting, made of vertical boards and painted white, adds a bit of texture to the walls of this breakfast room. Above it is wallpaper with a gold chinoiserie toile pattern on a black background. Pear-green paint adds zing to the interior of the niche and brings the gold from the toile down to eye-level; the dark table balances the wallpaper's black background.** (Mary McDonald)

Color, pattern, texture: which would you like as the background to your interior? Color for sure, but what about the others? Do you see a scenic mural in your home, an elegant backdrop of meandering branches filled with imaginary birds, a gentle wash of variegated hues, a stylized flower exuberantly splashed all over, the subtle nuance of tone-on-tone matte and glossy stripes, or a field of pure white that sets your furnishings into sharp relief? Do you favor hand-troweled plaster, catching shadows in its subtle furrows? Are you drawn to traditional wainscoting, or a formal backdrop of raised-panel woodwork, with pilasters and capitals, or simple boards installed horizontally for an unpretentious or even rustic effect? Would you like clouds on the ceiling, or antique beams?

If pattern is your dream, you can introduce it easily with wallpaper or fabric, or have it painted by hand. If you're looking for subtle texture, there are wallpaper-like materials with dimensional surfaces to consider, or textured woven fabric can be pasted or upholstered to the walls. For more dimension, you can curtain your walls with gathered fabric. Or turn to wood moldings and paneling for something more architectural and geometric—you can add them if your walls and ceilings are plain. Any of these approaches can be interpreted formally or informally, with the detail needed to create the look you want, and colored in any way you wish. Plus they can be mixed, with wallpaper or painted plaster above wainscoting, moldings added to break up a wall, or one wall or the ceiling handled differently to add drama or focus.

# PLAIN OR FANCY?
## Using Paint for Effect.

It's easy, fast, fairly inexpensive, not a problem to change. Simple—find the color you want and roll it on. If you've planned your palette, you should have a good starting point and need only to test the color to make sure it's the right value, neither too dark nor too light. Reality is you'll probably explore a number of related hues until you find the one that looks best with the other materials you're using. How will you use paint?

Deciding where and how to use paint is part of the initial design process, and the decision is really about color. How does the color of the walls and ceiling contribute to the ambience you've chosen? Will they be the same color, or contrast? Are there trim moldings, and if so, how will you color them? To match the walls but in a different finish, or in another hue so that the trim becomes a graphic accent? Will the window treatments be the same color as the walls, creating a uniform background, or be a contrasting color

that brings them into prominence? Do you want to treat one wall differently from the others, and if so, will you do it with paint, wallpaper, or paneling? Will you use paint to create a pattern on the walls or ceiling; if so, what are the colors? Is the surface you're painting flat or dimensional, will there be shadows that darken the color? Is there another architectural material, stone or brick for instance, that plays a prominent role in the room? How large are the windows and how will the wall color relate to the vista?

Painted color becomes more interesting when subtle variations in the hue or sheen are introduced. If your walls are being plastered, a skilled artisan can mix pigment into the wet plaster. This technique, known as Venetian plaster, produces nuanced color with intriguing depth. The plaster can be applied with visible trowel strokes or smoothed; it can be waxed and polished. (There is special wallboard designed to accept a skim coat of plaster; you need not begin with traditional lath walls.) Decorative effects in which painted color is applied in layers, such as ragging, rubbing, stippling, and striée, also produce allover nuanced results; these effects can be quite sophisticated or charmingly casual.

OPPOSITE, TOP RIGHT: **The color? Burnt marigold. The finish? Glazed to look as if caramel had been drizzled over it. The effect? Reminds one of a wonderful old French restaurant, where you just know you're going to have a good time. What could be better for a dining room? This one includes a mantel with a faux tortoiseshell finish.** (Myra Hoefer)

OPPOSITE, BOTTOM LEFT: **This daring peony pink covers only one wall in a small dining ell, making the space cozy. When you pick a strong color, look for the undertones—the shades mixed into the color you first perceive—they're what give it depth and balance. This pink contains a lot of gray and brown, which are colors the designer brought out elsewhere in the décor.** (Suzanne Kasler)

ABOVE: **Venetian plaster, a wall surfacing technique in which pigment is mixed into the plaster rather than painted on top, produces nuanced color variations with wonderful depth. Here, the plaster is rough and the color transitions are intentionally apparent to complement the assorted collections on display; you can have this done so the variation is extremely subtle.** (Jill Morris)

# PAINT FINISHES PRIMER

Interior paints are either latex (water-based) or alkyd (oil-based). Both are available in a variety of finishes, or sheens, which range in degree from flat or matte through eggshell, satin, and semigloss to high gloss. Some manufacturers offer some interim degrees of sheen to these.

- The glossier the paint is, the harder and more durable its surface. Glossy surfaces are reflective and can be used to add drama to a space. However, a glossy finish will highlight any imperfections in the surface it covers, so it's a poor choice for walls that are in bad shape; flat paint will visually smooth out bumps and small dings, though of course it doesn't repair them. As a rule, flat paint is used for walls and ceilings in spaces where hand contact is infrequent. Because they can be wiped clean, eggshell or satin paint are good choices for kitchens, bathrooms, stairwells, and spaces used by young children. Semigloss and high gloss paints repel water and can be washed; they are generally used for trim moldings.

- Washes and glazes used for decorative effects are paint that has been diluted with a specific medium; the terms mean different things to different people, but usually a wash is understood to be transparent. Artist's paints are used for some types of decorative painting, particularly stenciling, murals, and faux stone or wood.

- Painted surfaces can be sealed with varnish or wax, which add sheen and protect the painting. Varnishing and waxing are not easy to do, so leave them to a professional.

LEFT: **Stencil a frieze to carry the eye around a room. This one features arches in the Moorish-Venetian style and has been applied over glazed, combed walls. To balance the graphic effect, the windows, doors, and baseboards have been outlined with a contrasting painted band.** (Robin Bell)

# INSPIRATIONS

## Paint + Pattern = **Individuality**

Why stop with plain color when pattern adds so much character? Decorative paint effects can transport you to a whole new world.

Choose a representational effect that's real enough to fool the eye or intentionally stylized and mannered. Introduce a graphic motif, repeating it as a border, at regular intervals, or as an accent or focal point. Use layers of subtly patterned paint to add mystery and magic. Think of something fun, something quirky, something astonishingly gorgeous. Ask your designer or a local art association to recommend a painter who is skilled in the technique you favor. •

LEFT: **A hand-painted lattice suggests a gazebo or pergola and makes a charming background for this dining room.** (Albert Hadley)

ABOVE: **Allover decorative painting techniques can introduce subtle repeating pattern. A sepia glaze has been combed over the walls and ceiling in this dining room; the darker ceiling promotes a sense of intimacy.** (Jeffrey Bilauber)

RIGHT, TOP: **Indulge your love of a distant or imaginary land by painting a mural. Delicate chinoiserie foliage meanders above a Chippendale border that tops the (real) paneled dado in this foyer.** (Markham Roberts)

RIGHT: **Unabashedly pretty, this hand-painted arabesque-and-trellis motif gives a fanciful finish to a bedroom cabinet.** (Michael Whaley)

# INSTANT PATTERN:
## Using Wallpaper.

Wallpaper and related covering materials offer an easy way to bring pattern or texture as well as color to your walls and ceiling. You may be drawn to wallpaper because it's appropriate for the style of your home or typical of a specific regional or period look, or you may simply love the idea of having a patterned background in your décor. Either way, there are myriad choices ranging from discreet to dramatic, with options that replicate historical patterns, mimic other materials such as stone or metal leaf, give a trompe l'oeille effect of draped fabric or even orderly bookshelves, take the place of decorative painting, and feature patterns of every imaginable style.

Color, motif, and scale are all important to consider when you choose a wall covering. When you planned the overall look of your décor, which color did you select for the walls? That hue should be the dominant color in your wallpaper—probably the background, but it depends on the pattern. Where else in the room is pattern used, for upholstery, a carpet, window treatments? How important do you want the wallpaper pattern to be, what role should it play? Do you want it to tell a scenic story, establish the room style, provide subtle interest, or be eye-catching? If texture is the goal, do you want a subtle overall effect or one with a noticeable motif? Are you thinking of real or synthetic metal leaf for a touch of luxury, or of gluing up a collection of paper ephemera? How will you integrate your preference with the other furnishings? Is the wallpaper destined for the ceiling too? Is there paneling in the room?

Many wall coverings are available in coordinated sets that include companion patterns and borders in several sizes. Additionally, some are coordinated with fabric lines, making it easy to carry a design from walls to soft furnishings. If you are considering papering a flat ceiling, look for patterns that look good viewed from all directions.

ABOVE: **Grass cloth adds a subtle texture to walls; this one puts a pale, tailored, aqua grid on the walls of a study.** (Marshall Watson)

LEFT: **It's a big world, have fun with it—or with any other giant graphic that appeals to you. This den makes the most of the knee-wall/sloped ceiling dilemma by acknowledging it with a huge map and then painting the rest of the room in bold contrast.** (Chantal Dussouchard)

OPPOSITE: **Lovely, self-assured, and pink, the wallpaper in this hallway takes your breath away. Why not?** (Michael Whaley)

# WALLPAPER PRIMER

Various wall coverings are commonly referred to as "wallpaper." These include paper or vinyl, or vinyl- or acrylic-coated paper or fabric, and they may be laminated to a paper or fabric substrate.

- Coated and solid vinyl wall coverings are more durable than those that are not coated, making them good choices for any area where the walls could become soiled or traffic is heavy. If you are not working with a designer, you'll find wallpaper sample books at home design stores, some paint stores, and some retail home décor fabric stores; there are online sources too. Swatches, or sample cuttings, can be ordered; sometimes there may be a small charge.

- Wall coverings can be printed by a variety of hand and mechanical techniques and also hand-painted.

- Wallpaper is sold by the roll. Rolls come in several standard widths and lengths; each size covers a specific area (number of square feet). The amount of wallpaper needed for any job is figured in square feet and depends on the area to be covered, the number of door and window openings, and size of the pattern repeat. Your designer or paper hanger should calculate the amount you need, but if you want to get a rough idea, there are quick-reference tables that show the number needed of each type of roll to cover a given area.

## Some Terms to Know

**Color run:** A single production run of a specific wall covering, usually identified with a number. Color can vary slightly from one run to another; it's best to purchase the entire amount you need from one run.

**Embossing:** A raised pattern created by impressing a design into a wall-covering material by means of pressure or heat.

**Flocking:** A velvet-like surface created when chopped fibers are shaken onto a sticky pattern printed on a wall covering.

**Grass cloth:** A paper onto which woven grasses have been glued.

**Lining:** Plain paper applied horizontally to the wall before the decorative wall covering goes on. Lining improves the wall surface to ensure better adhesion of the decorative covering.

**Peelable:** A wall covering that can be dry-peeled from the wall but leaves its substrate on the wall.

**Repeat:** The vertical measurement from the center of a motif to the center of the next identical motif. Motifs on patterned wall coverings should be matched at seams and an allowance for this must be included in the square-foot requirement. The larger the motif, the greater the total number of square feet of wall covering needed for any given room. The pattern on a mural or scenic wall covering is designed to continue horizontally on adjacent panels and the amount needed is calculated differently from an allover pattern.

**Scrubbable:** A wall covering that can be washed with a sponge and detergent.

**Size:** A sealer used to prepare the wall before the covering is applied. There are also special primer paints that do this.

**Strippable:** A wall covering that can be dry-peeled from the wall leaving minimal adhesive residue and without damaging the wall.

**Prepasted:** A wall covering to which adhesive has been applied by the manufacturer; dipping a strip of this material in water will activate the adhesive.

**Top colors:** The colors that form the design on the background color.

**Washable:** A wall covering that can be cleaned with a sponge, mild soap, and water.

OPPOSITE: **Wallpaper sectioned with applied moldings creates a paneled effect that breaks up the space in this large bedroom. The small scale of the pattern and the light colors keep the room airy.** (John Oetgen)

# SOFT SURFACE:
## Fabric as a Wall Covering.

With the options for wallpaper so vast and appealing, why consider fabric for your wall or ceiling covering? You may simply prefer a specific fabric to any wall covering you find ready-made, especially if you want to repeat a window treatment or upholstery fabric. Or you may wish to curtain or upholster your walls to introduce a softer dimension than is possible with a flat covering: Perhaps you want to create a cocoon or tent effect, blur the distinction between your window treatment and your walls, or create a tufted or quilted surface—or maybe you need to mask walls that are in bad shape.

Fabric can be laminated to a paper backing and then applied like any other wall covering. There are services that do the laminating; if you are not working with a designer, ask your fabric retailer, paperhanger, or drapery workroom how to have this done. Some fabrics are sturdy enough to be glued directly to the wall using wallpaper paste. Fabric can also be stapled to the wall; for a slightly dimensional effect, install a layer of upholsterers' polyester batting first. To conceal seams and finish top and bottom edges, glue on gimp, braid, or ribbon in a matching or contrasting color.

LEFT: **Fabric gently gathered on rods mounted at the ceiling all the way around a room creates an intimate, tented effect, especially when paired with matching draperies. These panels, which were copied from a seventeenth-century Moghul fabric, make a dramatic backdrop.** (Michael S. Smith)

OPPOSITE: **The effect of fabric pasted flat against the wall is similar to wallpaper, but seen in the flesh the subtleties of the weave and surface finish are apparent and soften the effect. This red-and-white varied stripe makes a lively background for furnishings with solid fields of red and cream; note how it's finished with red braid above the white baseboard.** (Alessandra Branca)

# HARD EDGE:
## Using Paneling and Molding.

Walls covered in woodwork are naturally impressive. Even plain flat boards butted together add substance, simple beadboard gives an informal, tidy background, while elaborate, raised-panel walls suggest prosperity and emphasize grand proportions. Paneling adds a geometric texture to walls; depending on the style of paneling, this can be linear, include curves, feature X or rectangular motifs, and catch or create shadows in exciting ways.

Paneling is not the only use for interior woodwork. Exposed and boxed beams add character to a ceiling. Pilasters and fireplace surrounds provide interest on walls, breaking up the color or pattern on the surrounding surface. Built-in cupboards, kitchen cabinets, and bookcases are not merely functional; they contribute form, texture, and color to the ambience.

Paneling is integral to the construction of some homes, especially antique ones where it actually is the wall, not applied to another surface. But woodwork can be added where none exists, so don't eliminate it as a possibility if your house doesn't come with it. If paneling or wainscoting is on your list, give some thought to the style of the moldings and the doors too; there should be some aesthetic consistency.

What role would you like woodwork to play? Will it establish an architectural style? Will its texture provide rhythm, bring relief or a pattern to a plain surface? How will it be finished and what affect will that have? Do you want the rustic texture of rough-sawn boards? Will you stain it so that the grain shows but it takes on a color that works with your palette? Will you leave it natural, and wax it so it glows? Will it be painted a marvelous color?

LEFT: **The paneling in this dining room is exactly the kind you see in houses throughout Sweden. The lower portion is real; the upper section created with paint.** (Katrin Cargill and Carol Glasser)

OPPOSITE: **One entire wall in this kitchen eating area is a built-in display case. It's fashioned from reclaimed antique white pine, with paneled doors on the bottom, a fluted frieze across the top, and tall glass doors that show off a collection of blue-and-white pottery in between. Handsome pine paneling in the adjacent sitting room can be seen through the deep doorway.** (Joan Schindler)

ABOVE: **Substantial moldings cover the walls in this dining room in a strong but monochrome grid, making a geometric backdrop to the softer patterns and textures of the rug, tufted chairs, and distinctive painting. Hanging over the table is a Russian brass chandelier with applied organic ornament.** (Marjorie Slovack and Martha Davis)

# INSPIRATIONS

## Walls + Tile = **Stylish Protection**

Water and wallboard don't mix. Who cares?
Tile looks great and shrugs off the wet.

Tile conquers the water, steam, and splashes of sauce or shampoo that pose a challenge to paint and wallpaper in kitchens and baths. It adds color, pattern, and texture too — with low-key nonchalance or extravagance, whichever suits. Tile an entire bathroom from floor to ceiling, line the shower walls, add a backsplash or wainscoting; you'll find alluring ceramic and stone options for any spot you have in mind. •

LEFT: **Go for the impact of pattern. With five colors used, no color ever lands adjacent to itself in this harlequin design.** (Sandra Bird)

ABOVE: **Mirror is as fine as tile for protecting a bathroom wall and increases the light as well. Here moldings add sophistication and make the reflections endlessly intriguing.** (Alessandra Branca)

RIGHT, TOP: **Challenge: How to squeeze luxury into a tiny bathroom. Solution: Blitz it floor-to-ceiling with polished white marble bricks laid with straight, rather than staggered, joints. Lesson: Use massive quantities of a single material to create a feeling of indulgence.** (Franklin Salasky)

RIGHT: **Bold alternating bands of limestone and marble line this gentleman's bath, making it luxurious without being glitzy and masculine without being dark. They're graphic too, which suits the modern aesthetic of the accoutrements.** (Paul Siskin)

# WHAT TO DO NEXT:
## Make a Sample File.

Lots of options, lots of decisions to make. To keep the planning process under control, set up a system for organizing your materials search. If you are working with a designer, he or she will organize and do the materials search for you, but you can help by collecting visual reference of things you like. If you're working on your own, begin with a room-by-room list, deciding the kind of wall treatment you want in each room. Make another list, this time organized by material: paint, wallpaper, fabric, woodwork, and tile. Set up a file folder for each material so that you can collect brochures and samples (refer to page 130 to organize a fabric search). Keep your palette handy; if you go bricks-and-mortar shopping, take it along.

For paint, wallpaper, fabric, and tile you can acquire samples but woodwork calls for a different approach. If paneling or moldings are being added, your designer or architect will design and specify them. You can create a clipping file with photos of paneled rooms you like; include pictures of wood finishes that appeal even if the woodwork style differs from what you have in mind. If you are planning to paint or stain the woodwork, put brochures or sample chips in your paint folder. Cabinet vendors will provide small, finished, wood samples on request but for architectural woodwork, you'll probably review samples of finish options at a later stage.

You'll be able to acquire samples of fabric, wallpaper, and tile that are large enough to show their effect, but the paint chips provided by manufacturers are too small to guide a final choice. Some paint manufacturers will provide larger samples to professional designers and some package small sample jars of paint to make testing easy; if these are not offered, buy the smallest can available. You can paint samples on heavy paper or cardstock—a good idea because you'll be able to move them around to check their effect in different parts of the room. If you have trouble finding a color that matches another material you've chosen, for instance a fabric, the retail paint vendor may be able to scan a swatch and have his computer determine the equivalent paint recipe.

While you are planning, assemble as many samples as you wish. Keep them sorted by room within each of your folders, in envelopes or labeled in some way. If you acquire a lot of options for one use—which you easily may, edit them to select those you like most. Try to get at least a rough estimate of the amount you'll need of each material so you can include cost in your decision-making. Hold onto everything until you have samples of fabric for soft furnishings and window treatments, and have flooring and carpet samples too. You'll want to look at everything together in order to choose the mix you love.

LEFT: **There's very little going on colorwise in this hall; to add depth and interest, simple paneling climbs 7 feet up the wall to stop 18 inches below the ceiling—a pleasing proportion. Newel posts that resemble lighthouses are one of many marine motifs used in this home to express the owner's passion for boating.** (Jodi Macklin)

OPPOSITE: **Take this in, it's a simple, graphic, and very individual use of paint. Red enamel the color of old Chinese lacquer puts a shine on this stair wall, the banister and steps are black, the wall in front is white. Striking.** (Amanda Kyser)

# Where do you fancy your footsteps falling?

- ☐ In an ancient stone hallway
- ☐ On a loopy pile rug
- ☐ Wide boards that show their age
- ☐ Ebonized wood, very shiny
- ☐ On something truly easy-care
- ☐ Colorful tile, in a custom pattern

# 9. FLOORS

OPPOSITE: **Very dark, highly polished wood floors ground this cloud-level room with a sense of security, their reflective sheen a reassuring anchor for the velvet and chenille furnishings—and occupants—at the window wall.** (Marshall Watson)

Gleaming, soft, hard, warm, cool, a field of color or intricately patterned: what will go under your furniture and greet your bare toes? Are wood floors the answer, or natural stone? Do the beautiful colors and patterns of ceramic tile call to you, or would something more industrial, like rubber or vinyl be better? Is the retro appeal of linoleum a must for your mid-century kitchen? Or is softness critical, pointing you toward a cushy rug that looks elegant and absorbs footsteps and sound? Are new floors a part of your design plan, or will you refinish or cover what's there?

Floors play a double role in your décor; they support the ambience and they carry a lot of traffic too. The use of each room suggests its flooring as much as the aesthetic does, so when you consider options, think about durability, maintenance, comfort, and sound as well as appearance. Flooring materials can be loosely divided into two categories: hard, including wood, stone, and ceramic tile, and soft, including carpets and rugs and resilient materials such as linoleum, vinyl, and rubber. Of course, there are degrees in both groups, with wood being softer than stone, and rugs softer than vinyl, but these groupings are useful also because hard materials are as a rule more difficult or expensive to install and replace, while the softer ones are easier to change (though not necessarily less costly). An enticing array of colors, patterns, textures, and sheens exists for each type of flooring, and rugs can top any of the others (and be layered). Finding the right option for each room should be fun.

# NARROW OR WIDE?
## Choosing Wood Floors.

Timeless, sophisticated, rustic, stylized, quirky, dark, light, shiny, or matte; there's a wood floor to give you nearly any look you like. First there's the tree of origin: ash, beech, birch, cherry, fir, hickory, maple, mesquite, oak, pine, and walnut are the native options, each with distinctive color, grain, and character. Imports including mahogany, bamboo, cork, teak, and many exotics offer even more possibilities. Then there's the board width—narrow, medium, wide— and the pattern in which these are laid—straight, herringbone, random widths, parquet, or marquetry. Top these with a matte or glossy finish that brings out the natural color, tints it, or obscures it.

Wood floors can be enjoyed for their inherent beauty or stained, bleached, or painted to support a particular look. Cerused floors, which are rubbed with white color, are typical of Swedish-style interiors, ebonized floors are black and modern, multi-toned parquet suggests the Art Deco era, and opaque paint spattered with flecks of contrasting color gives a fun country accent. Very old wood floors often have a warm patina and obvious patterns of wear, which may or may not strike you as charming. If you have wood floors that don't appeal to you, investigate options for refinishing—to refresh their look or create new character—before you rip them out. Borders and medallions in contrasting wood may be incorporated in new floors; any style is possible. Additionally, wood strips can be interspersed with stone or ceramic tiles for interesting patterned effects.

Solid-wood flooring is graded; all grades are good quality and equally serviceable, the difference lies in the amount of color variation and degree to which character marks typical of each species are present. The different grades are chosen for the overall effect each produces when installed; a clear or light-color finish will bring out the character of the wood. Engineered flooring consists of layers of wood pressed together with the grains running in different directions; it is very stable. There is also acrylic-impregnated flooring, which is extremely hard and durable and most often used in commercial buildings.

LEFT: **Ebonized floors enhance the modern, sensual look of furniture with simple lines and forms covered with a variety of textures in beige and minky brown hues.**
(Vicente Wolf)

ABOVE: **Typical of antique American country houses, very wide boards, 10, 12, and even 20 inches across, can still be purchased today. Here they give warmth to the dining room in a new Vermont farmhouse.** (Susan Tulley)

RIGHT, TOP: **The medium-width oak floorboards in this bedroom are more casual than their narrower cousins in the sitting room beyond and reveal more of the swirling wood grain; here they complement geometric hooked rugs and stylish country furniture.** (Barbara Westbrook)

RIGHT: **Hand-scraped for character, medium-width walnut boards laid in a chevron pattern add quiet interest to this breakfast room, which is adjacent to a classic kitchen in a Colonial Revival home.** (Mick De Giulio)

# EXOTIC WOODS

Unusual wood flooring from South America, Africa, and Asia offers exciting possibilities for floor design. The various types are intriguingly colored and figured. Some exotic woods are more difficult to work and seal than the more familiar native species, so check with your contractor to see if he has any experience with or concerns about them before setting your heart on one. Additionally, some of these woods produce allergic reactions in some people. For ideas of what's available, visit www.woodfloors.org, the Web site of the National Wood Flooring Association.

- Cork and bamboo flooring are readily available and environmentally friendly. The material we know as cork is actually the bark of the cork oak tree; it can be harvested every six years without damaging the trees, which may live for centuries. Cork is long wearing, flexible, and resilient, plus it has terrific insulating qualities; it feels soft and warm to bare feet. It is resistant to liquid penetration, though seams between pieces of some flooring types must be sealed. Additionally, it is both hypoallergenic and antistatic, so it does not host mold, mildew, dust, or pollen—something to consider if someone in your family has allergies.

- Bamboo is a grass, not wood, but with similar qualities. Very fast growing, like cork it can be harvested frequently without damaging the plant, which replenishes itself by sending out new canes. It can be grown successfully in damaged soil and may help to regenerate the soil over time. Bamboo is both hard and durable, and is less affected by moisture than other hardwoods—making it a good choice for homes in humid climates.

ABOVE: **Glossy gray-green paint puts a watery sheen on the floors in this lakeside cottage; paired with the white ceiling, walls, and cabinets, they make the small space light, airy, and connected to its surroundings.** (David Reed)

OPPOSITE: **Old pine floorboards give a fresh-scrubbed finish to the recently updated kitchen in this mid-twentieth century beach cottage, helping to maintain its original charm.** (Thomas Jayne)

# INSPIRATIONS

## Floor + Paint = **A New Look**

What's more wonderful than a fine wood floor? One enhanced with a painted finish that gives new character to the room.

Go ahead, paint or stain your floor to make a statement with color or pattern or both—you can be as eccentric or sophisticated as you like. Create a trompe l'oeil effect with faux stone or marble, or opt for a classic graphic pattern like bold checks, stripes, or a border. If you're doing this yourself, consider a stencil to guide an organic motif, or set up a geometric pattern with masking tape. Be sure to seal the finished floor well to protect the paint. •

LEFT: **Fun is definitely an option for a painted floor. Here stylized citrus sections are scattered over brilliant turquoise.** (Diamond Baratta)

ABOVE: **Diagonal geometric patterns tend to open up a room. This one, a red grid on a soft white ground, picks up the pace in a big country kitchen and suggests an extension of the terrace outside.** (Shannon Bowers)

RIGHT, TOP: **If you love color, pick one that will surprise you every time—like the intense chrome yellow that floods this breakfast area—and run with it.** (Kim Freeman)

RIGHT: **Mimicking a carpet, the chevron pattern stained in this hallway adds a quiet accent that complements the stair runner and lightens the space. What's more, there's no way too-speedy feet can trip over it.** (Nancy Boszhardt)

# ROUGH OR POLISHED?
## Stone and Ceramic Tile.

Marble, limestone, granite, onyx, slate, terra-cotta, encaustic, glazed ceramic, riven, smooth, polished, honed, figured, flecked, embossed, painted, printed: The material and finish options for stone and ceramic tile floors are so diverse it's difficult to consider these tiles as one category. They have in common hardness, durability, and the fact that they are neither warm nor soft underfoot. Beyond that the variety is immense; there are numerous materials, colors, shapes, sizes, and surface finishes (not to mention ceramics that imitate stone); add to those choices the options for layout and creativity beckon.

Stone and tile floors are often chosen for entries, conservatories, bathrooms, and kitchens. In homes with architectural style in the tradition of European chateaus and Mediterranean villas they seem appropriate throughout. Which type to use depends entirely on the effect you wish to achieve. Highly polished stone is reflective and elegant, glazed ceramics are reflective and upbeat if not opulent. Coarsely hewn stone looks rustic, as does tile that mimics it. Honed surfaces and unglazed ceramics appear softer and warmer. There are tiles patterned with nearly every imaginable motif, including traditional folk and regional styles that may even inspire the look of a room. Tiles are often available

in sets of companion shapes or patterns or coordinated colors that facilitate layout options such as basket weave, inserted dots, and borders. Mixing and matching is a natural for some materials—wonderful patterns can be created by mixing different types of stone or interspersing matte with shiny pieces or tumbled with smooth. Some manufacturers will prepare custom arrangements of small tiles for you, gluing them to a mesh background so the installer doesn't have to create the design on-site. One caveat when you shop: Wall tiles are not strong enough for flooring, so be sure to inquire if you are unsure of the quality.

When you are looking for tile, consider how the color will work with the walls, furniture, and rugs, and also with the fixtures, appliances, and cabinetry in a bath or kitchen. Think about the role of pattern, including the effect of grout in the layout, and also the scale. With natural stone you have the option of using substantial pieces, and you can take advantage of this to emphasize the stature of a large foyer or grand room; a smaller space might be better served by smaller pieces. While some stone tiles may be arranged with edges touching to appear seamless, the grout lines of most applications will add some texture to the layout, so even if the floor is monochromatic, the size of the tiles has an impact on the scale of the pattern that emerges.

OPPOSITE, BOTTOM LEFT: **Large, rustic rectangular stone tiles in assorted sizes add an interesting counterpoint to traditional, semiformal white cabinets in this kitchen. The sand and ocean-green hues in the room give a clue to the seaside locale.** (Jonathan Rosen)

OPPOSITE, TOP RIGHT: **These stone pavers look ancient, but they're new, chosen to replicate the floor typical of an old Swedish country kitchen (the diamond cabinets were inspired by an antique Swedish sideboard); the herringbone layout distracts the eye from the narrowness of the space.** (Marshall Watson)

ABOVE: **The juxtaposition of a dark bluestone floor with the pale table and walls has quiet power in this foyer. The tiles are huge, about 18 inches square, like something you might use outside; bringing them inside feels very European.** (Kay Douglass)

# INSPIRATIONS

## Tile + Layout = **Pattern**

All those individual pieces beg for order. Take up the challenge—enliven your floor in a way that makes the most of their shape, color, and finish.

An astonishing diversity of stylistic design is possible when tiles in two or more colors are arranged together. Effects range from simple checkerboard patterns to scenic representations, words and phrases, and complex faux carpets. With the wealth of colored tile available nearly any palette is possible, and there are so many shapes and sizes that geometric designs are easy to compose. Look down when you visit a retail tile shop—examples are often underfoot. •

LEFT: **Looking for an ingredient with charm? Try little black hexes composed as flowers and set at regular intervals on a field of white. Inspiration came from a floor spotted at Harrods department store, in London, and the design adds a soft finish to this state-of-the-art kitchen.** (John Schindler)

ABOVE: **A big checkerboard of soft tan and cream tiles laid diagonally opens up the space in this long kitchen; it's bold but not busy between the cream and hunter-green cabinets.** (T. Keller Donovan)

RIGHT, TOP: **French in inspiration, the checkerboard floor in this tiny vestibule features two colors of marble and reflects to the max in the mirrored walls.** (David Kleinberg)

RIGHT: **Simple, imaginative, effective: a lattice of small beige tiles frames quartets of large white squares, adding a gentle rhythm to the large open area of this master bath.** (Jacqueline Derrey Segura)

# FUSS-FREE STYLE:
## Using Resilient Flooring.

If easy-care, easy-on-your-legs good looks are on your list, consider resilient flooring, which is relatively inexpensive to boot. Several types are on the market: linoleum, solid vinyl, vinyl composition, laminate, and rubber. Here are some things to know:

Linoleum was invented in the middle of the nineteenth century and has been around ever since. It's an all-natural product made from renewable materials and is biodegradable, something that can't be said for many building products. Currently popular for its retro look, it is very longwearing, and comes in a rainbow of glorious colors, all with a characteristic subtly marbled pattern. Linoleum is made from linseed oil, wood flour, tree resins, ground limestone, and pigment, which are combined and then pressed onto a jute backing. It is available in sheets, planks, and tiles; inlaid patterns can be created in the sheets by the installer, and patterned border strips are available in some

brands. Linoleum is naturally bacterial-resistant and anti-static. If you order samples, allow them to air for several hours so that the yellowish film that forms during the manufacturing process can dissipate and you can see the true color of the linoleum.

Vinyl is made from petrochemicals and sold in tile and sheet formats. Tile is available in solid vinyl (with the color or an inlaid pattern consistent from top to bottom) and in a composite form, with the color or a printed pattern in a thin layer laminated between a stabilized backing (sometimes cushioned) and two protective top layers. Sheet vinyl is available in composite format only. Solid vinyl tile can be as costly as ceramic, but the composite forms are less. Vinyl colors and patterns are myriad, with many wood, stone, and ceramic look-alike options available. Vinyl comes in various surface finishes that have different maintenance requirements involved.

Laminate flooring, like composition vinyl, has a layered construction, with an easy-to-clean surface layer topping a photographically reproduced pattern that is laid over an inner core of sturdy fiberboard and finally a backing layer of resin-saturated paper that provides a moisture barrier. Because the pattern is a photo, laminate flooring can represent virtually any material and is ultra-realistic; it's also easy to install and made with recycled materials.

Rubber flooring tiles are designed for industrial and commercial use, but they are a fine choice for a home if their look supports your style or the purpose of the room. Embossed and flat surfaces in a variety of colors and limited patterns are available. The tiles are durable, flexible, resilient, absorb sound, and have a nonslip surface. The manufacturing process for rubber flooring is environmentally friendly and disposal is nontoxic should you decide to remove it later.

LEFT: **A classic checkerboard of pomegranate-and-white vinyl tiles adds a cheerful finish and echoes the cabinets and walls in this newly updated kitchen in a Victorian home.** (Emily O'Keefe)

OPPOSITE: **Garden-fresh and charming, this breakfast room takes an air of whimsy from the cutout base of the old French picnic table, the curly iron park benches that flank it, and the iron-and-glass chandelier above. The checkerboard floor is pretty and indestructible in blue-and-white resilient tiles—perfect for kids who run in and out at will.** (Ken Fulk)

# FLAT OR PILE?
## Adding Style with Rugs.

Soft, warm, vibrant or soothing, large or small, solid, tweed, textured, boldly or intricately patterned, rugs ground your décor with color, character, and comfort. Traditional styles from around the globe introduce formal and informal patterns of every sensibility and graphic composition—there are stripes, plain and figured borders, central medallions, meandering or tossed florals, garden-like compositions, animal skins, complex and simple geometrics, realistic, whimsical, and stylized motifs. There are period and regional designs to complement specific interior styles, and tribal and oriental patterns with timeless appeal that easily adapt to many settings. The woven construction may be flat, have a low or deep pile that is looped or cut, be uniformly textured or feature a raised design. Natural fiber options include wool, silk, cotton, and linen, which all accept dye beautifully and have a naturally attractive surface, as well as sisal and related rustic plant fibers. Acrylic, nylon, polyester, polyolefin, and other synthetics wear well and can look terrific, though they may lack the luster of natural fibers. What role do you wish your rug to play?

A rug can be the focal point of a room or part of the background; it can set the tone of the overall design or support the other furnishings. How important do you wish yours to be? How should it influence the ambience, do you want an elegant, opulent, crisply modern, casual, or cozy feeling? Will your rug cover most or all of floor, define an area within a room, or direct traffic from one area to another? Will you use several rugs in one room? Will you use a single rug style throughout your home, or in adjacent rooms? Is there an element of pragmatism in your choice, are you trying to muffle footsteps or protect wood or tile from scratches or spills? Is maintenance an issue?

While you consider the options, think about where the rug will be used as well as what you'd like it to look like; the answer may influence the way you budget and search for it. Are you furnishing a weekend house, a cabin, a child's room? A stylish home store or catalog may have the perfect thing. If you're decorating a principal residence, a more upscale source could be indicated, perhaps an antique rug, something by a contemporary artist or small studio, or something custom made. You may find that working with a designer is the best way to find what you really want. Will you want to take the rug with you should you move, or could carpet that's cut to fit and attached to the floor be appropriate and provide the look you like?

LEFT: **Country stripes signal easy living. This style incorporates several weaves and three colors for the look of a traditional American handcraft; in this example the palette is muted, but more vibrant options and stripes of different proportions can be found too.** (Valerie Smith)

OPPOSITE: **Soft, deep, wool-and-linen pile greets feet like a fur beneath the bed in this peaceful, white-on-white room. The sheer curtains have a similarly plush, but more delicate, surface.** (Faye Cohen)

# DESIGNER'S TOP TEN

Carpet and textile designer Christine Van Der Hurd offers some pointers on introducing color and texture from the ground up.

**1.** Go with your gut feeling when choosing a carpet. I think color is more important than design; if you don't love the hue, the pattern, however pretty, won't matter.

**2.** Consider whether you want your carpet to be a focal point of the room, or to blend in unobtrusively. Highly patterned, brightly colored carpets obviously belong in the former category.

**3.** If possible, choose your carpet before deciding upon paint, upholstery, and curtains. The colors in your carpet can provide inspiration for the color scheme of an entire room.

**4.** Before making a decision about carpets, think about whether dirt is a factor. Do you have small children or dogs? Do you entertain a lot? More pattern can help to hide daily wear and tear.

**5.** In rooms with lots of pattern and texture, it's generally best to choose a single-color floor covering—but it doesn't have to be beige. Pick out a color you like from the curtains or cushions.

**6.** If you're trying to find a carpet that will work with fabric and colors already in place, consider custom design. It's not necessarily much more expensive than off-the-rack, and you will have a unique, perfectly matched piece.

**7.** Runners on stairs can introduce color and texture to the bland environment of a hall or staircase. A cotton dhurrie runner, for example, could be perfect for a beach house.

**8.** Offices don't have to have wall-to-wall industrial carpeting. An interesting rug that you like to look at can make the workplace far more inviting.

**9.** Children love color, so don't be afraid of using it in their rooms. Choose a carpet that is soft and comfortable to sit on, because they tend to really use the floor while playing. Sometimes the design on a carpet can even feed into activities and games.

**10.** If you don't want a pattern, but like a textured look, consider a natural yarn that takes dye unevenly. Another option is to look for carpets that leave the fabric knots looped, or uncut, which can add wonderful luster and texture.

ABOVE: **A large, subtly varied wool rug adds complementary rustic texture and earthy hues to the wood, rattan, woven, and embroidered furnishings that fill this sitting room.** (Douglas Durkin and Greg Elich)

OPPOSITE: **The small, decorated, allover lattice patterning this carpet is an ideal choice for a space like this, which extends into a dining area. Without borders or medallions, there are no issues with positioning the furniture within the different areas and the flow from room to room appears unified. The soft, pretty pattern suits the dressy French furniture in a way a strictly geometric motif would not.** (John Oetgen)

# RUG OR CARPET?

In casual conversation the terms "rug" and "carpet" are often used interchangeably. Magic carpets aside, it's easier to keep track of the item you are looking for if you think of rugs as woven to a specific size, loose, and portable, and carpets as fixed to the floor, or at any rate, cut to fit the proportions of the room. Carpeting is produced in very-wide widths, which are rolled and sold by the yard, and in tiles. Carpet may be very fine quality, there's nothing inherently inferior about it—the design and fiber content dictate the quality.

RIGHT: **Layered rugs—a flat-woven plaid topped by a folkloric floral pile—feature just two of the patterns skillfully mixed in this room, where a symmetrical arrangement makes everything feel settled and balanced.** (Jeffrey Bilhuber)

## WHAT TO DO NEXT:
# Make a Sample File.

Chances are you need flooring or floor covering for more than one room in your home. To organize your search, make a room-by-room list of the types you need and then a second list organized by type, so you can search for like materials efficiently. Samples are bulky and can be heavy, so set up a box in which to store them. Stone and ceramic tiles and resilient flooring of all types are quite easy to shop for locally and online, and samples may be borrowed or purchased. The accessibility of wood samples varies with the wood; some types are in every local lumberyard, others must be ordered. Because the finish affects the color of wood, you'll want to sample that as well, or at least get a basic idea of the possibilities early on and expect to see samples before the floor is finished. Depending on the complexity of the project and the lead time for ordering, your contractor may ask you to choose flooring early on, but if you can, hold onto all the samples until you are ready to select all the materials for the room. If you do choose early, keep the sample handy for later reference.

Carpeting samples are generally available, as are samples for custom-made rugs, but off-the-rack rugs are an entirely different matter. You may be able to get yarn samples that will at least give you a sense of the colors from some vendors. Swatches are sometimes available, especially for flat-weave styles or from small producers who have a limited line. But unless you wish to base the colors and patterns of other furnishings on an off-the-rack rug and feel confident about purchasing early and can arrange for storage, you may simply have to shop to get an idea of the options, and then make a final selection when you are ready to place the rug in your home. If this is the case, once you've edited the swatches and samples for other items in the room, take them with you when you shop so you can see them next to the rugs you're considering before making any decisions. Here's one saving grace: Many off-the-rack and antique rug dealers will let you try a rug in your home before you commit to purchasing it.

# THE WAVE OF THE FUTURE IS. . .
## DECORATING GREEN

Yes, you can tread lightly on the land and make your interior look fabulous. Home décor products that are environmentally sensitive are increasingly available. It takes some hunting around to find them, but will become easier as interest in them increases and clean technology for producing them matures.

There are varying degrees of "green," but in general a product must be made from a renewable natural material grown organically or harvested with minimal impact to its environment, or from a material recycled in an environmentally responsible way, and the manufacturing process must be nonpolluting, without harmful waste as a byproduct. Energy efficiency during manufacturing and transportation and fair-trade practices are often considered part of the green recipe

LEFT: **Bamboo panels behind this bed convey instant Asian beach chic, add subtle vertical texture, and don't mind the humidity in a steamy climate. Don't miss the framed fern prints—they're sandwiched between glass panes so the bamboo serves as a mat.**
(Barclay Butera)

as well. Green products may be hypoallergenic and biodegradable or recyclable, though not all are.

If new construction or renovation is part of your decorating plan, research green building too—there are many energy efficient structural and mechanical options to consider. If you wish to "live green," purchase energy-efficient appliances and turn off electronic media gear when not in use.

What's in the green decorating market: textiles (fabric and rugs), wallpaper, paint, tiles, and flooring, plus some furniture and decorative accessories. To verify green status, look at labels or product literature and search the Internet to confirm the legitimacy of a certifying organization. Look also for "upcycled" accessories—unwanted items transformed into something desirable (usually art pieces). Another interesting trend is biomimicry—products whose design is informed by structures and patterns found in nature. Examples include fan blades shaped like bird wings for better efficiency and a showerhead spray pattern derived from the whirled arrangement of seeds on a sunflower head.

## Textiles

You'll find the greatest number of green options in the textile category. Organic production of most natural fibers is growing and some, such as hemp, bamboo, and abaca that have been familiar as floor coverings are now used for drapery and upholstery fabric as well. Hunt around and you'll discover both velvet and chintz made of bamboo. Hunt further and you'll find "peace silk," for which the silkworms are allowed to mature and leave their cocoons naturally. Manmade fibers

to watch for include Rayon (made from wood cellulose), Modal (beech cellulose), Tencel (vegetable cellulose), and Ingeo (from fermented corn sugar); these are "natural" products but their manufacture isn't necessarily green. To go underfoot, add recycled paper to the rug category; look for natural latex or cotton backing instead of nonrenewable polyester. Green textiles are made with nontoxic dyes, and technology for cleaner textile manufacturing is constantly evolving. Nontoxic flame retardant finishes are in the works too.

## Wallpaper

For green wall coverings, look for wallpaper made from recycled paper with a biodegradable backing and vegetable-dye printing. You'll find green grass-cloth too. Or use a green fabric.

## Paint

The green news in paint includes water-based products with a soy-based resin and mineral pigments instead of synthetic coloring. Green paints are free of harmful VOC—volatile organic compounds.

## Tiles

Eco-friendly tiles include types made from recycled glass, granite, and marble, recycled metal, or decorative concrete patterns that don't require firing and are therefore considered to have "low-energy" manufacture.

## Flooring

For green flooring, consider retro linoleum (made from linseed oil), bamboo, or cork. See Chapter 9, Floors, for more information. Cork and bamboo may go on your walls too. •

**TEXTILES**
Sophisticated textiles made from natural fibers and nontoxic dyes make it easy to go green indoors. You'll find all manner of weaves and patterns; motifs from nature help to make the point.

**FURNITURE**
This cabinet is built of Kirei board, a lightweight, durable, attractive product made from reclaimed agricultural fiber—not trees. Here it's topped with white laminate.

**ACCESSORIES**
Look for tabletop accessories like these colorful cups and saucers, which have a nontoxic glaze and were fired in an energy-efficient kiln.

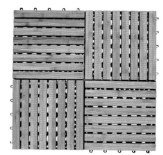

**FLOORING**
These waterproof tiles are made of bamboo strips on recycled plastic bases; just slide together for a new kitchen or patio floor.

# How will you cover your windows?

- ☐ With sumptuous velvet drapes
- ☐ Minimally, I like moonlight
- ☐ In fabric that matches the walls
- ☐ With softly pleated shades
- ☐ Wood blinds, I like classic
- ☐ With lovely plain linen curtains

# 10. WINDOW TREATMENTS

OPPOSITE: **First impressions don't get better than this: 12-foot ceilings, magnificent French doors, drop-dead, lettuce-green silk taffeta draperies falling from ceiling to floor in great, soft folds, and glazed aubergine walls. Enviable space, simple window treatment, elegant fabric, and a sophisticated color palette.** (David Kleinberg)

Dramatic, tailored, voluminous, delicate, layered, swagged, rolled, hard, soft: Which effect will best dress your windows? Are you yearning to cloak them in folds of opulent fabric, curtain them simply with linen or ticking, or cover them with flat but sassy roll-up shades? Have you a period house that cries out for a complex layered treatment with lots of braid and fringe, or a Modernist home where shades that fold away to nothing are all that's wanted? The options for window treatment design are so numerous and invite such creativity, that however you answer, you'll find one that has the right effect. While readymade window treatments are easy to come by in home stores and catalogs, most styles, especially soft ones, can be custom fabricated with the materials and details to give you the look you really want.

To decide what type of treatment to use and the details that will make it suit your décor, think about the role it will play. How important do you wish the treatment to be—prominent or low-key, contrasting or matching the walls, intricately constructed or simple? Will the treatment introduce color or pattern into your decorating scheme, or repeat them from elsewhere? How functional is the treatment—can it be opened and closed, must it provide privacy or filter sunlight, or is it an accent that simply adds interest and helps to tie the look together? Is a top element alone enough, or would you like to have something that hangs to the floor? Will the treatment be visible from outside your home, and if so, how will that affect the look of the façade? Is it important to create harmony from room to room?

# DRAPERIES OR SHADES?
## Fabric at Your Windows.

Would you like your window treatment to soften the walls, create a cocoon, or add a strong vertical element to the room? Draperies (pleated across the top before they are hung) or curtains (flat across the top, with fullness created when they are condensed on the curtain rod) are probably the choice. Would you prefer a strong horizontal accent? Place a valance across the top of your window, choosing a flat style, or one that's pleated or gathered so it has volume. Or perhaps you are thinking of a swag, with the fabric draped into curves across the top of the window. Are you looking for something that can cover the entire window, but doesn't have the mass of drapes or a curtain? Consider a shade, which can be raised or lowered and can be installed inside the window, to reveal the moldings, or outside, to cover them; there are several types, all attractive and versatile.

Fabrication is everything for soft window treatments, as the materials used will turn the basic designs for draperies, curtains, valances, swags, and pleated or rolled shades from dressy to casual as quickly as you can say "cut velvet" or "cheesecloth." Custom fabrication can easily be arranged and allows you to choose and refine every aspect of the design, from the precise proportions to the fabric and trim. When a treatment is made to order, you have the option of playing with the proportions in order to make the ceiling seem higher (place the top of the draperies or curtains at the top of the wall), the window seem taller (place the top of a valance, swag, or shade at some distance above the window), or wider (use a longer rod and hang the drapes so they extend onto the wall beside the window). Plus you can accurately match colors to your palette and use a gorgeous fabric you've fallen in love with, or repeat one chosen for the upholstery, slipcovers, pillows, or bed hangings, or select something that coordinates exactly as you like. Two or more fabrics can be combined as well, making border accents possible and linings that show an asset; also treatments featuring layered components can be easily coordinated.

A good workroom will be able to replicate a design from a photo or sketch, so you can be as creative in your thinking as you like, asking for rigging that creates unusual draped effects, or ornamental cord and tassel trim, eccentric ruching and ruffles, or fancy cockade and rosette embellishments. You needn't be looking for extravagant or dressy effects to take advantages of custom work; simple refinements make a huge difference too. If restraint is more your mode, you can add nuanced borders or tiny bindings, or have your curtains topped with button-tabs or grommets that slide over the curtain pole. Or join the DIY movement and tack some ribbons onto one edge of a pretty tablecloth or bedcover and tie them to a decorative rod for a quick and charming curtain.

LEFT: **Crisp Roman shades are tailored, neat, and as fun or dressy as the fabric they're made in. The awning stripe chosen for these brings together the colors of the kitchen wall and island and even picks up the red of the range knobs.** (Kari Cusack)

OPPOSITE: **Gathered valances over draperies are a classic choice when a soft look is desired; they're more intimate than drapes without a top treatment and less architectural than drapes topped with swags. In this cottage bedroom, they're feminine in a pretty floral chintz, which also skirts the dressing table.** (Justine Cusing)

OPPOSITE: **Made in ecru textured linen chosen to "take the room down a notch," these swagged valances over matching draperies stand out gently against the prominently figured toile fabric that covers the walls. They're edged with the ticking stripe used for the ottoman and throw pillows—a simple unifying touch, and the little stripe looks great pulled closer to the toile.**
(Markham Roberts)

ABOVE: **Pink and aqua striped fabric allows plain curtains to make a pretty statement in this dressy dining room. Because they're not on rings, curtains like these can't be easily drawn closed, so any pattern on the fabric gains density and loses definition as it hangs, condensed, at each side of the window.** (Michael Whaley)

OPPOSITE: **In a nice juxtaposition of curves against angles, double and single swags layered above tied-back panels make a graceful gesture below the peaked ceiling in this sitting room. The plain cream fabric, matching fringe trim, and volume and shadows of the draping allow this pretty treatment to hold its own against the bold sunflower-print wallpaper.** (Marshall Watson)

RIGHT: **A deep ruffle at the lower edge and petite frills along the sides and top give a feminine finish to this soft Roman shade, which tops diminutive drapes hung in the lower portion of the window. White-on-white hues keep this duo light and delicate in the small tub alcove, even when the shade and drapes are closed for privacy.** (William Hoogars)

## RIGID AND BOXED:
# Using a Cornice.

Would you like a top treatment that has a lot of shape and style? Three-dimensional, rigid, and architectural, cornices are sometimes simple boxes and sometimes more complex—pagoda-like shapes or scalloped lower edges are common. They may be stained or painted wood, sometimes with elaborate fretwork or other moldings, or upholstered; inexpensive rigid foam forms to paint or upholster are available with a variety of profiles. A cornice is usually used in combination with a softer treatment, for which the cornice masks the mounting board, track, or rod. Some styles of bed canopies are essentially cornices, often with a skirt attached.

Cornices are generally reserved for formal interiors, but they needn't be. Given the right interpretation, a cornice can be fun and whimsical, or simple and tailored. If you are considering a wide, upholstered cornice, for instance to span a sliding door or a wall of windows, give some thought to how it will be covered so that seams are not obtrusive.

# KEEP IT PRIVATE

Providing decorative character is one role for a window treatment, but protecting your home from prying eyes is equally important. Even if you live in the middle of nowhere, without neighbors, the perception of privacy is comforting and most people want some way to secure at least the bedrooms and bathrooms. Any window treatment that can be drawn over the glass and is opaque can provide the needed privacy, but many treatments only look as though they'll do this. Some are difficult to close because of the way they're constructed or hung, but many more are translucent when lit from behind, which is exactly what happens when you turn on lights inside your home at night. To ensure privacy, use a heavy fabric or line a thin one with a blackout material, or install opaque shades or blinds under the fabric treatment. Many woven wood shades are not opaque—don't rely on them for privacy. Mini blinds, cellular shades, and some accordion pleated and roller shades are opaque; these treatments can be raised high to be unobtrusive during the day if you wish.

Some people prefer to sleep in a room where neither moonlight nor morning sun are permitted to enter. Unless they're sheer or very lightweight, most window treatments will take care of this, but if you require pitch black in the morning, you'll want opaque fabric, blinds, or shutters on your bedroom windows.

LEFT: **Placed far enough in front of the window wall to accommodate the draperies and a light shade that hangs behind them, this cornice is a continuation of the egg-and-dart molding and corbels used around the room; it's perceived more as architecture than as part of the window treatment.** (Phoebe Howard)

OPPOSITE: **A swag with cascades hangs over floor-length panels at the doorway between this bedroom and a conservatory. Wanting to avoid long curtains on short windows, the designer built low cabinets along the adjacent walls and dressed the windows to complement the doorway treatment: Each has a single drapery panel rigged as a tailed shade.** (David Kleinberg)

# TILTED OPEN OR CLOSED?
## Using Window Blinds.

Looking for something simple and stylish that nearly disappears and can filter or totally block the light? Blinds are doubly adjustable window treatments that can, if you like, easily play second fiddle beside other furnishings. They're made with rigid slats that are strung on cords; the slats may be pulled together to expose the window, or released to cover it. Additionally, when the blind is covering the window, the slats can be rotated to slant all the way or part way open, permitting light to pass through, or lie flat, blocking it. Horizontal blinds have slats that are parallel to the floor and pull up; the slats on vertical blinds are perpendicular to the floor and pull to one side. Blinds should not be confused with accordion-pleated or cellular shades, which pull up and stack similarly but do not have individual rotating slats. To add to the name dilemma, some manufacturers refer to their translucent woven wooden shades as blinds—it doesn't matter what you call these products, just be sure you know how they work before you choose them. Motorized and remote controls are available for blinds.

Traditional horizontal blinds with wooden slats and fabric tapes that conceal the cords have been in use for centuries, look good on their own, and are easy to mix with draperies and other fabric treatments. The slats are usually 2 or 2½ inches deep, so they require a window recess at least that deep or should be mounted outside the window. Today wood, vinyl (including faux wood), and aluminum versions are available in a variety of colors; there is quite a range of tape color options too. Mini blinds feature narrower slats so they work well inside a shallow window recess, additionally they condense into a small stack and so are inconspicuous when raised. A matching decorative valance is an option for most horizontal blinds. It's your choice to use a color that matches or contrasts the adjacent window trim or treatment—how prominent would you like the blinds to be?

Because they draw open to one side, vertical blinds are a convenient covering for sliding doors and windows where drapes hung on rings and pulled open or closed by hand might be awkward. They feature 3½-inch deep slats that are weighted at the bottom so they don't blow apart in the wind. There are wood, vinyl, and fabric varieties. The fabric type may be translucent even when the slats are rotated closed, but some manufacturers offer light-blocking inserts for these slats. Vertical blinds come with a top track mounting system and a matching decorative valance is an option.

LEFT: **Well yes, this is not for everyone, but if you have a Victorian home or are looking for something unusual, it could spark your interest. Ornate narrow panels alternate across the rod to make the valance, which hangs in front of simple drapes tied back with large sashes to frame traditional wood louvered blinds.** (Merrill Stenbeck)

OPPOSITE: **Classic Venetian blinds filter light beneath the pulled-back draperies in this cottage bedroom. They're loved for their nostalgic look and they're fun: tilt the vanes closed to enjoy a lazy afternoon nap or keep them slightly open to peek at passersby.** (David Kleinberg)

# INSPIRATIONS

## Bench + Window = **Daydreams**

How romantic: A window alcove with a cushioned bench suggests whispered secrets and hours lost in a great book.

What's the secret? A straight or curved window recess; it's that easy. Not-too-large is better if intimate is the goal. If there's no recess, you can create one by building paired closets or cabinets topped by bookshelves adjacent to a window. Two looks: with the windowsill low enough to grace the cushion top, or with wall enough below the window to lean lots of soft, plump pillows against. •

LEFT: **Contoured to fit a bay window, this banquette has a high back that tucks under the extending windowsill—the perfect place for a teacup while you lean against the cushions to read. Swing-arm lamps and bright-red Roman shades make this spot cozy at night too.** (Jason Bell)

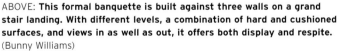

ABOVE: **This formal banquette is built against three walls on a grand stair landing. With different levels, a combination of hard and cushioned surfaces, and views in as well as out, it offers both display and respite.** (Bunny Williams)

RIGHT, TOP: **Take a romantic cue from this jewel box of a room: use deep, rich colors, hang densely gathered Austrian shades at the window, top the bench with a thick cushion and some great silk pillows with fabulous fringe, add a tray with cocktails, and invite a friend.** (Ann Miller)

RIGHT: **Two steps lead up from the sitting room to this tiny room with a captain's bed built under the window and bookshelves tucked into the end wall. If you feel deprived without a space like this, convert a closet to become one.** (Michael S. Smith)

# LOUVERED OR PANELED?
## Using Shutters.

Are you looking something handsome, rigid, and architectural that blends with your window moldings or a paneled wall? One of the two types of shutters may provide just the right effect. Louvered shutters are a traditional choice for homes in warm climates because they can block the hot sunlight while admitting fresh air. Paneled shutters are typical for some older homes, where they once blocked drafts as well as sunlight; they're especially suited to stone buildings with very thick walls, which enable the shutters to fold open against the deep window recess without interfering with draperies or furniture. Often used without another window treatment, shutters may be painted to match the window moldings for a unified effect, or to contrast for livelier one. When walls, moldings, and shutters are all painted a single color, the wall becomes a simple background on which the shutters provide a textural contrast.

Shutters are usually hinged to swing on and off the window like doors, though some slide in tracks; shoji screens fall into the latter category. Those that swing require a clear area in front of the window to be operable, as well as wall space to fold onto, so they can be awkward to combine with other window treatments or use where furniture is close to the window. However, adjustable louvers provide lots of air, light, and a slightly filtered vista, so you can leave louvered shutters closed except while opening or closing the window.

Louvered shutters made of wood, vinyl, or a composite are readily available in standard and semi-custom sizes and shapes. Unique windows or doors may require truly custom construction and you may prefer that anyway, as the best fit comes when the installer measures on site before the shutters are made. Louver sizes range from 1¼ to 4½ inches deep (the deeper ones are known as plantation shutters). Paneled shutters are usually custom-made, although ready-made options exist for exterior use.

RIGHT, TOP: **Tall, simple, and architectural, the arched shutter shares the proportions and cloistered serenity of this alcove and adds a complementary texture to the plastered walls and limestone tub surround.** (Fern Santini)

RIGHT: **The outdoor-style half-shutters that cover the lower part of this arched window were inspired by similar ones seen while visiting homes in Belgium.** (Kay Douglass)

OPPOSITE: **Raised panel shutters blend discreetly with the woodwork in this eighteenth-century Newport home, where the rooms are tiny and already cozy without fabric at the windows.** (John Peixinho)

# SUCH GREAT OPTIONS.
## How Will You Mix Them?

Draperies over sheers. Curtains over shades. A valance over half-height shutters. A cornice over formal draperies. Matching layers. Contrasting fabrics. Same trim on each piece. Spin the mix however you like. What will give you the most attractive look? In a grand room you might wish to use three layers, with blinds or a roller shade next to the window, draperies over the blinds, and a decorative cornice or fancy valance on top. In a casual setting, plain linen curtains over a matchstick shade look fresh and fuss-free; change the fabric to toile and the shade to bamboo, and the look is primmer but fun. A valance over matching drapes is traditional, no matter what fabric you use. A soft, drapey shade beneath a matching valance will be dressy but simple. A swag with tails over matching floor-length panels will be formal if the fabric is, or soignée in lustrous silk, or innocent in gauze. Put the same swag and tails over wood blinds, and you've gone back two hundred years: not-too-fancy and perfect for a home of that era.

If you wish to mix window treatments, ask yourself the same questions you would if using a single treatment: how important should the treatment be, how does it mesh with your walls and other furnishings, how will color and pattern come into the mix? Ask also, what is the purpose of the mix: Is it aesthetic, something that provides stature or nuance to the overall look? Or is privacy part of the equation, in which case you'll want to be sure the layer closest to the window is opaque. Then think about the fabric—what qualities should it have in order to hang or drape as you'd like? What sort of contrast do you want between the elements: texture, color, pattern, scale, or all four?

ABOVE: **In this New York high-rise where there's more than enough glass, the dining area is anchored by an espresso-colored banquette snugged right up against the floor-to-ceiling windows. Striped silk draperies hung in front of natural matchstick shades give the corner an intimate frame.** (Celerie Kemble)

LEFT: **The swag and cascade valances that frame this ocean view are casually elegant, sophisticated, and—look again—faux. They're trompe l'oeil on flat cutouts, painted on both sides so they're believable from the exterior too. Under them are real Roman shades, made in a complementary fabric.** (Albert Hadley)

OPPOSITE: **Softly pleated panels hang like a pretty cloak at this bedroom window; they're mounted at the ceiling in front of the cornice molding and pulled to the side high above the floor. Under them the white shade is finished with a wide blue border—used because very pale colors can look lost if they end against the light coming through a window.** (Charlotte Moss)

# WHAT TO DO NEXT:
## Make a Clipping File.

You'll have to decide what type of window treatments you want before you can purchase readymade options or fabric, so begin your planning by collecting design inspiration. Set up a folder for this, and put into it photos of any window treatments you find appealing. Magazines and interior design books are a great resource for these; check out the DIY category as well for books filled with myriad design ideas. Collect home furnishings and window treatment catalogs too, or search the Internet for online vendors, especially for blinds, cellular shades, and shutters. Try to see the design of the treatments separately from the fabrics they're made in—a great idea might be shown in a fabric you don't care for, but you can borrow the style and change the fabric.

One note to heed while you're researching: Different designers and workrooms refer to the various types of window treatments by different names, with, for example, one person's cloud shade being another's balloon shade and still another's festoon shade—so go by the visual reference, not the label.

Make a list of the rooms for which you need window treatments. Sort the reference in your inspiration file into piles, one for each room. Edit the clippings to select the look you like best for each room. If creativity strikes, make a sketch of your own idea—you can trace a photo to get the basic shape, then draw in your refinements. If you are working with a designer, you'll be set at this point to share your preferences so he or she can further develop them or source the materials. If you are working alone, transfer the reference for each fabric treatment to your fabric swatch file (see page 130). For readymade items, check the available color options against your palette; order samples and swatches if you can. To estimate expenses, check with your workroom to get an idea of fabric quantities and labor costs and refer to the vendor's specifications to price readymade and semi-custom items. Hold onto these materials until you have all the other samples for your décor and are ready to look at everything together on location.

ABOVE: **Lightweight wool London shades complement the tailored but dressed-down look of this window seat. They're soft when raised like this; when lowered for privacy the vertical pleats provide a linear accent.** (Amanda Kyser)

OPPOSITE: **A big, sheer white Roman shade puts a modern filter on the French doors in this dining room. Visually, it's clean and non-competitive; to use the doors, just pull up the shade.** (Michael Canter)

# WHAT WILL MAKE YOUR HOUSE A HOME?

- A look I love

- Comfortable furnishings

- Wonderful hues

- Room for my family & friends

- The kitchen of my dreams

- Attention to the details of style

# PART THREE

# Design, Room by Room

Anyone who desires a beautiful home has the ability to create one. Each of us will define that beauty in a different way, bringing an individual perspective to it in a way that combines the look, colors, and materials we prefer. When you walk into your home, you want to recognize it as yours and be glad to be there, and most likely, you want that first glance to reveal the ambience that flows throughout the house. But your home has both public and private spaces that accommodate different parts of your life and it is logical to plan them individually. There are infinite ways to design each room; for ideas and to see how talented professionals have created rooms that made their owners happy, take a tour through the following chapters.

Which rooms are you designing? Do you like them as spaces or will you want to change them? What is the look you want? Have you thought about the colors, patterns, and materials? Have you begun to collect photo reference and swatches? Design is a puzzle with lots of interrelated elements: the size and proportions of the space, the way it relates to other rooms, the look you want and the elements that will create it, and the purpose, layout, and details of the room itself. You'll not be able to make smart decisions unless you think about these elements individually and all together, so enjoy revisiting Part One and Part Two of this book while you plan the specifics of each room—there's a lot to think about and lots of ideas to consider.

Look through the rooms on the following pages. Have you fallen in love? Take note of the things you like and think about how you can interpret them in your home; there's a guide at the end of each chapter to help you pull your ideas together. Keep the look you love in mind—you'll design a beautiful home that reflects your taste and makes you happy.

# What's key to a welcoming foyer?

- ☐ Gracious proportions
- ☐ Good light, no glare
- ☐ A place for my keys
- ☐ Artwork
- ☐ A glimpse of the rooms beyond
- ☐ The right door chime

# 11. FOYERS & HALLWAYS

OPPOSITE: **Observing layout tradition, a table is centered under the lantern in this large foyer. Because there's no rug here, the designer skirted the table "for a balance of hardness and softness," using a fabric print of oversize leaves, flowers, and fruit that captures the spirit of the house—warm, happy, charming, and a little bit wacky.**
(T. Keller Donovan)

Where are you when you walk in through your front door? Is the space large or small? Is it a room, a hallway, or a corner of the living room? Is there natural light? What sort of welcome does it offer: warmth, tranquility, reserved formality, or the exuberance of your happy family? Do you use the foyer for all your comings and goings, or is it primarily used by guests? Is it an entry room only, or do you pass through it frequently as you move about your home? Do you step into your foyer directly from the weather, or is there a covered porch outside it? Or perhaps you live in an apartment and pass through a shared hallway before entering your home?

Take a look at the foyer you have, note the way it fits into the overall layout of your home, and, acknowledging the size and traffic pattern, ask yourself how you really want to use it. If it is spacious, could it be a gallery, a lobby, or a reading room? Or would you be wise to make it the most efficient welcome center possible given its small footprint? If you have a second entry, how is it used? Is it your default entrance from wherever you park? Is it the passage from the garden or pool? What will make it both efficient and charming? Look at large hallways or stair landings in the same way: How do they relate to the entry and to the other spaces in your home? Are they in the public or private portion of the house? Do they make a promise of pleasant areas beyond? Are they large enough to sit in? Is there natural light? How can you make each a space that you love?

# WELCOME:
## Amenities at the Entry.

Everyone wants a foyer that is welcoming and signals arrival at a distinctive place; when we walk in the door, we want to be glad we're home. We want guests to appreciate the ambience and style with which we live and to feel at home too. How will your foyer accomplish these goals? The answer is only partly aesthetic; while your choice of colors, lighting, and furnishings sets a great part of the mood, the space itself and the way it is integrated with the flow of your home is just as critical and is probably a given.

The size of a foyer establishes the way it can be used and to an extent, the impact it has on anyone entering from outside. Of course, the larger the footprint, the more furnishings can be accommodated and the easier it is to don or doff one's coat without rubbing elbows with others or the closet door, but more important to first impressions are the overall proportions of the room. A very large foyer, or a lofty one that is two stories high, will naturally appear grand; a small entry is naturally more intimate. The first is challenging to decorate because it can feel austere, empty, or overwhelming and dwarf whatever is in it, including you. Very large foyers benefit from elements of architectural interest such as gracious stairways, interior arches, paneling, coffered ceilings, doorways to other rooms, and windows that cast interesting shadows, any of which can provide some texture to the background. Chandeliers or lanterns, sconces, pattern on the walls or floor, or a rug that defines space within the space will also break up the background or add texture, and they're easier to add. Keep an eye on the scale of light fixtures, tables, chairs, or other furniture to see that they have enough visual weight to hold their own.

The challenge of a small, intimate space is to keep it from feeling crowded. Decide what needs to be in a small foyer and keep it in scale—or play with the scale and make a statement, but make sure there's room to pass comfortably.

Pleasant light, a closet, and a table to put things on make any foyer welcoming. Overly bright or glaring light is jarring, inadequate light is annoying. The amount of light you need depends on how large the space is, how dark or reflective the walls and floors are, and what there is to see—art to admire, a mirror for smoothing hair when hats come off, seating arranged for reading or conversation, or simply the way to the next room. An accessible coat closet is a good idea, unless you have a maid who greets you and your guests. And chances are anyone who enters will have a handbag, parcel, bottle of wine, or keys and the mail in need of a quick home, so a table in the entry makes sense. Any entry that gets everyday use can benefit from a place to sit while you change footgear and a place to put wet boots.

LEFT: **With its high window, turning stair, and simple shadowy overtones, this pretty foyer greets you with the look of Vermeer painting. But this is a new home, warmed and kept from looking just-built by walls finished in ocher Venetian plaster (for depth), arches, and vaulted ceilings. The strong, traditional lantern glows poetically when lighted; the glass has been removed to make it feel more contemporary.** (Healing Barsanti)

OPPOSITE: **This entryway is mostly a pass-through space that would have been easy to forget. Instead, it's warm and intriguing, with lots of soft textures coming from an old hand-hooked American rug on the floor, an antique French walnut buffet, and wonderful fisherman's baskets looped over the newel post. At the far end stands an old French grandfather clock "with such beautiful presence," says the designer.** (Barbara Westbrook)

# ROOMS WE LOVE

How does your dream foyer greet you? Is it formal or casual, luxurious or earthy, full of energy or tranquil? Whatever your preference, interpret it in a way that makes a welcoming first impression, reminds you of why you love to be in your home, and introduces your style to everyone who visits. Check the arrangement from all angles—you'll exit through the room as often as you enter and, depending on the layout, perhaps pass through it frequently or see it from other rooms as well. If your foyer leads to a hall or up the stairs, or both, let your style flow throughout. Here are some examples that made us feel welcome.

BELOW: **This gracious stair hall runs from front to back through the house and is wide enough to hold a small sitting area below the second floor landing. The area rug and sheers on the doors add intimacy to the space, where guests can wait, you can read alone, or a private conversation can escape the adjacent living room.** (Jason Bell)

OPPOSITE: **Very old, very simple, astonishingly turquoise: The mix of waxed, sanded original floorboards and an unexpected color on the walls gives this hall charm that bridges two centuries and grabs you when you walk in the door.** (Ruthie Sommers)

ABOVE: The décor in this entry exploits the symmetry of the divided, turning stairs to its satisfying best, with paired elements arranged in perfect opposition and the central mirror carrying the eye up the center. The moldings, railings, and fluted columns add textural interest to the all-white background. And those hydrangeas . . . simply fabulous. (Karen Cohen and Ani Antreasyan)

# INSPIRATIONS

## Where to Put Umbrellas

Wet umbrellas can make a mess of the entryway. Catch the runoff with a stylish receptacle that adds a rain or shine accent to your décor.

Traditional umbrella-stand designs include tall buckets and racks of various heights affixed to a tray base, some tall enough to hold caps and coats too. Choose something that shares the sensibility of your other furnishings—perhaps an antique French enameled iron stand, a fabulous amphora, or an unusual basket. Whatever it is, add a container you can easily empty if one isn't provided. ●

ABOVE: **A big jar in earthy colors adds a subtle, sculptural accent to the restrained décor and graceful curves of this modern foyer.** (Robin Well)

RIGHT: **An urn-shaped rattan basket suits the Asian furnishings in this small entry and picks up the color of the marquetry lattice painted on the wood floor.** (Ashley Whittaker)

# Colorful Opinions: ENTRANCE HALLS

The entry hall is the first thing you see when you walk into a house, so how should it feel—soothing, or knock-your-socks-off? Designers suggest hues that make great first impressions.

**KEITH IRVINE:**
**BENJAMIN MOORE**
**SALSA 2009-20**
Red is the color of excitement, and I tend to go for corally-orange reds. With red, you know you've arrived and you glance in the mirror and realize how great you look and breeze right in.

**JOHN OETGEN:**
**BENJAMIN MOORE**
**PALLADIAN BLUE HC-144**
If you took leaf green and sky blue and put them in a bucket with a lot of air, this what you would get. I even put it on the ceiling. It looks great with black-and-white floors. I'd add a bronze bench with shocking pink upholstery.

**CHRISTOPHER DRAKE:**
**BENJAMIN MOORE**
**SHOWTIME 923**
It's one of those spaces that people go through quickly, so you can afford a higher level of drama. Often there's no natural light, so you need a heavily saturated color like this warm, yolky yellow. Get it in full gloss, because the gloss gives it depth and it's much more simple to apply than glazing.

**EVE ROBINSON:**
**FARROW & BALL**
**DRAB 41**
I like a progression of color. It's good to start dark—this is so moody and has a wonderful earthy tone—and as you move inside, the rooms become lighter, which makes them seem more spacious.

**PATRICIA HEALING:**
**FINE PAINTS OF EUROPE**
**DUTCH CHOCOLATE 6012**
Imagine you're melting dark chocolate in a saucepan—that's the color. It glistens. This is a very high-gloss paint that looks almost like patent leather.

**T. KELLER DONOVAN:**
**BENJAMIN MOORE**
**LINEN WHITE 207**
A hall takes such a beating. Mine looks like the shipping department at Macy's. So I'd choose a cool calm white. Fill a mayonnaise jar with it and keep it in the closet for touch-ups.

**JOHN BARMAN:**
**RALPH LAUREN**
**RACER PINK 1B07**
It's a strong vibrant pink, as masculine as you can get in a pink, with a nice shine to it. In a small entrance hall I like to use deep strong colors to help define the space. Otherwise you lose it.

**STEVEN GAMBREL:**
**PRATT & LAMBERT**
**ARGENT 1322**
Those great eighteenth-century British architects kept the front hallway somber to recall the color of the stone outside, on the facade. I like that idea of bringing the outside in, but stone doesn't necessarily work for me. I tend to use a sky-bluish color that has a pretty heavy dose of gray and green.

**JENNIFER GARRIGUES:**
**FARROW & BALL**
**FOLLY GREEN 76**
Imagine going down a leafy path and opening the door to a lovely green foyer. This is not the usual dark bottle green. It's paler and softer, a really good, goes-anywhere green that feels so very peaceful.

**WHITNEY STEWART:**
**C2**
**QUAHOG 8385**
Here's the thing about entry halls. You want to make it Wow!, but at the same time you have to be neutral because it's the opener for the rest of the home. So what to do? Paint your hall this fabulous gray/taupe, which is still neutral but dark enough to make a statement.

**HERMES MALLEA:**
**DONALD KAUFMAN COLOR COLLECTION**
**DKC-17**
We did a California ranch house where you came into a low, very enclosed front hall before being released into this huge living room—that famous squeeze-and-squirt thing that architects love. So we painted this tight little space an intense barn red. Everything around you was red—walls, ceilings, doors. You were completely encapsulated in red, so you couldn't really tell the dimensions.

**KERRY JOYCE:**
**SHERWIN-WILLIAMS**
**STUDIO MAUVE 0062**
A velvety gray with just the right amount of lavender. If there were any more lavender in it, it would be well beyond my pain threshold, but there isn't, so it's perfect.

**WILLIAM EUBANKS:**
**BENJAMIN MOORE**
**GOLDEN STRAW 2152-50**
I'm attracted to warm colors that kind of wrap their arms around you. This is like candlelight, with a wonderful golden glow. I'll put layers of glaze over it so it's as rich in daytime as it is at night.

# INSPIRATIONS

## A Mirror Adds a New Perspective

A framed mirror makes art of whatever it reflects, adds depth and mystery to a space, and enables surreptitious primping.

Face it: Mirrors are irresistible. They're useful and beautiful in their own right, plus they provide focus and bounce light. Place one above a table in your foyer and create a vignette of interesting objects and reflected space. Choose a frame style that complements your style in proportions that suit the wall space. Quick tip: Any picture framer can make a mirror for you from stock molding. •

LEFT: **Dark, large, and elaborately carved, this ebony and brass Dutch cushion mirror is in perfect balance with the gleaming, carved gate-leg table below it—together they're strong and important against a bleached background.**
(Betsy Brown)

ABOVE: **Be daring—here's an eclectic mix of eighteenth-century pieces that looks very today against the dark wall. The slender Queen Anne mirror holds the center inside the symmetrical arrangement of brighter and more ornate gilt and white elements.** (Robert Godwin)

RIGHT, TOP: **A single, long, dark, Asian table with strong lines, and a large plain mirror have the presence and proportions needed to balance the flagstone surfaces that dominate this entry hall. The mirror reflects the tropical landscape outside too, acting as window to lighten the stone wall.** (Neil Korpinen)

RIGHT: **A modernist brass mirror adds a light, streamlined accent to the darker Asian furnishings in this foyer.** (Garrow Kedigian)

# PULL IT TOGETHER

The vision is in your head. You've formed a clear idea of the way to make your foyer welcoming and you're ready to plan the specifics. Assemble your clipping and swatch files; then spread out the pieces so you can mix and match until you find the right combination. If you'll be using furniture or accessories you already own, take photos of them so you can see them in context with the options for things you plan to add. If you like, make a collage of your choices so you can easily share them with a designer or revisit them yourself. Don't forget, your foyer is probably open to other areas of your home; it's smart to reserve final choices until you can view them in context with adjacent areas. This is the room that introduces your home, so let it display a look you love.

OPPOSITE: **Hats on or off, this foyer welcomes and brings up a smile: It's got vivid colors, an elegant mirror above a dressy chest, a pretty lantern, a place to put umbrellas and a classic black-and-white tile floor that won't mind their drips—all enriched by an array of art and collected accessories.** (Anne Miller)

### Ambience

Choose the key words that describe the look of your dream foyer and its proportions—bright, tranquil, luxurious, elegant, cozy, traditional, expansive, intimate—whatever they may be.

### Color

Choose the overall palette and decide how it will be assorted: which color will be dominant, which play a supporting role? How will you use pattern?

### Walls

What finish do you want for the wall? Paint, perhaps glossy (even glazed) for greater depth? A decorative wall covering? Is there paneling or wainscoting? Is there a stairway with a balustrade that adds texture and color?

### Floor

Would you like a distinctive floor treatment for your foyer or prefer it to match the floor in adjacent rooms? Are you considering pattern and if so, will it include a border or other device that relates to the contours of the room? Will there be a rug on top of the flooring material and on the stairs as well? What about a protective mat right inside the door?

### Lighting fixtures

Provide good, nonglaring general light: A ceiling or pendant fixture will most likely be attractive but may need supplementing if the space is large; make sure there is clearance for a tall person to walk beneath a chandelier or lantern. Use the same or complementary fixtures in the foyer and adjacent halls or stairways. If the ceiling is very high, ask your electrician what's involved with changing light bulbs. Be sure to plan for accent lighting near a mirror or artwork, and lamps if there is a sitting area.

### Window treatments

Natural light is a lovely enhancement for a foyer or hallway but privacy may be a concern, especially for windows near the entry door. Otherwise, if you wish to dress the windows, go for whatever treatment is appropriate for the ambience and choose fabric to support the look.

### Furniture

The size and configuration of your foyer will determine how much, if any, furniture you can include. A side table or cabinet that can receive small packages or the mail is nice; a larger table in the middle of a large space can be attractive.

### Amenities

A mirror, a chair or bench, a lighted coat closet, an umbrella stand, and a mat for wet boots all make guests comfortable and add convenience for you as well. Make sure there's a place for your keys and the dog leash, and don't forget wall space for the alarm controls.

### Accessories

Hang something eye-catching on the walls—a painting, some prints or photos, or an interesting textile. Include greenery such as a potted tree or plant on a stand, or fresh flowers. Display sculptures, ceramics, baskets, or whatever intrigues you on tables, shelves, or a cabinet as appropriate.

### Layout

Make a sketch of the floor plan to scale on graph paper and indicate stairs, doors, windows, and closets. Add the location for key pieces of furniture such as a table or bench. Note the dimensions of the space available for these to make sure all the pieces you are considering will fit so as to allow graceful passage to other areas.

# What are your living room must-haves?

☐ A huge, soft sofa to sink into

☐ Wall space for art

☐ Sleek, low-profile furnishings

☐ An impressive fireplace

☐ A chair by a window

☐ A giant television

# 12. LIVING ROOMS

OPPOSITE: **The friendly, English quality of this Los Angeles living room suits the American family who lives in here. There are lots of gentle, calm greens, and on the walls, pale lavender paint picks up the accent color in the floral fabric that covers the slipper chairs. The designer sprinkled dark accessories through the room to balance the large, dark china cabinet in the corner.** (Mary McDonald)

How much time do you spend in your living room? Do you unwind there every evening, curled up on a favorite chair? Is it part of your everyday life, used for family get-togethers and frequent entertaining? Or do you use it only on formal and special occasions? Do you sit there during the day, or only in the evening?

Be honest when you answer these questions. You want an inviting, comfortable living room that works for the way you live, presenting a face that's as dressy as you need it to be. If you do a lot of formal entertaining, you'll approach the design of your living room differently than if it's the center of your family life or your home is casual. Who will use your living room and how? Guests having cocktails? How will they be dressed, in finery or après beach? Will friends gather there to watch television or a film? Is there a piano? Is it a large room and will you want several conversation areas? If children often will be there, what will make them comfortable? Should there be quiet spaces, so each occupant can be absorbed in a good book? What kind of ambience will suit the way you use your living room, how would you like it to reflect your personal style? And while you're answering: How many sitting rooms are in your home, is there a family room or den in addition to the living room? If so, how will each of these spaces be used, what makes them different?

# PUBLIC PLACE:
## Planning a Living Room.

Whether grand, cozy, glamorous, country-casual, traditional or ultra-modern in style, every living room should be comfortable, gracious, and conducive to conversation. It should also include interesting things to look at—art, objects purchased on your travels, a collection of pottery assembled over the years—that provide a window to your taste. How would you like to arrange and furnish your living room? While you plan, think of how to integrate the way you wish to use the room and the ambience you'd like to create with the nature of the space itself.

What are the physical characteristics of your living room? Is it large? Are the overall proportions grand? Or is it intimate, or somewhere in between? How many people will it accommodate? Is there a fireplace? Are there many windows, does the room open onto a terrace? The answers to these questions will help to determine the amount of furniture you'll need, the scale of the pieces, and their arrangement. If there is a fireplace, will it be the focal point? If not, will you focus on a view or a piece of art? Are the proportions such that the seating furniture will hug the walls, or will it be pulled away from them to the center of the room? Will you use one sofa and several easy chairs, or two sofas? If the space is large enough for more than one conversation area, will you want them furnished differently? How will they be tied together visually and how will people communicate from one to the other? If the room is very small, how will you arrange seating so that people can face one another? Will you use one or more rugs to define different areas within the room?

Think of the seating arrangement as the heart of the furnishings, and then be sure to support it with surfaces to hold drinks and books, and with good light. A coffee table (or two if the conversation area is long) and side tables take care of the first; use a combination of lighting fixtures to provide both soft general light and specific light wherever people gather. If your chairs are not near a wall, can you place floor outlets discreetly under the seating so there are no cords to trip over? If the layout permits, you might consider placing a long narrow table behind the sofa to hold lamps and some objects of interest, or against one wall or under a window. What else spells comfort to you? An ottoman to swing your feet onto or double as a coffee table? Interesting stools that work as moveable seating and side tables? Bookshelves, an intricate secretary or small desk, a wonderful cabinet?

While you're planning, think also about the way the living room fits into the overall layout of your home. How visible is the living room in your normal passage about your home, do you walk through it to reach other areas, can you see it from the entry or the main hallway or the dining room? Or is it set apart, out of your usual path or reached through a narrow doorway? Do your living and dining areas share a single room? If the room is open to another space you'll want to consider how to visually link them: what will be the common elements, what will make the vista from one area to another harmonious, balanced, and inviting? If traffic naturally flows through the living room, for instance from the entry to another room where there is no hall, must the path lie through a seating area or can you skirt it? If the living room is separate, how can you make your overall décor flow into it? In all cases, think about ways to arrange the furnishings so the room, and people in it, can greet you when you enter.

LEFT: **Creamy colors and no pattern on the walls, draperies, and sofa create a unified background and make this room seem much larger than it is. Happy red accessories punch things up and ensure the neutrals don't look dull when the sun is hiding. The paintings are studies for a wallpaper pattern; with gold accents, theyre a bit playful and are purposefully hung without frames.** (Nancy Boszhardt)

OPPOSITE: **Soft, worn blues, greens, browns, and grays on all the surfaces bring the outside into this living room, which has windows to the natural landscape on one side and to a cultivated garden on another. There are wood boards on the walls and ceiling as well as the floor; a lichen-color stain lightens the ceiling, which was first painted a dark hue. "Every single color is hard to put your finger on," says the designer.** (Susan Ferrier)

# LIVING ROOMS WE LOVE

How would you like your living room to make you feel? Relaxed? Elegant? Exotic? Totally up to date? Awed by the proportions and view? Entranced and charmed? Are you drawn to a traditional look; will you acknowledge a specific architectural or regional style? Will it be cozy or open, formal or not-so-formal? Should the colors be bright, neutral, striking, dreamy, rich? Do you want the furniture to be plump, streamlined, or show lots of leg? Will there be contrasting forms and surfaces to keep the eye interested? How will the windows be dressed, how do they play into the background of your setting? However you answer, decide upon a palette and style that create an ambience you love and want to share with family and friends. You'll find lots of options shown here, in living rooms we've enjoyed.

ABOVE: **The owner of this high-rise apartment wanted a look that is sleek but based in tradition. To create it, the designer added glossy black art deco-style doors and furnishings that echo early modernist styles. The palette is silvery and everything has a sheen: either absorbing, as on the silk carpet, or reflecting, as on the highly polished plaster walls.** (Marshall Walker)

LEFT: **Start with a spec house, take the sea and sky as a theme, and go casual as suits a beach environment. This room is fun, easygoing, and uncluttered, features the same fabric in two different colors for come-on-get-happy energy, and enjoys lots of natural light. Under glass on the coffee table is a collage of beloved photos—a space-saving, noncluttering method of display.** (Jonathan Rosen)

OPPOSITE: **The architecture is the star of the décor in this room, where exposed wood, a vaulted ceiling, stone floor, and impressive stucco chimney breast frame just a few mid-century modern furnishings—a look that fulfills the dream of the homeowners to live simply, with minimal possessions and without clutter. A bronze hanger supports the small painting over the fireplace; the coffee table sits on a Lucite base "like a disk of floating caramel."** (Form Architecture and Interiors)

LEFT: **A mix of contemporary and antique furnishings gives an updated look to American country décor. Here wax and the patina of age on the wood furniture, contrasting textures of leather and chenille, the geometric hooked rug, painted wood ceiling, and a few thoughtfully chosen accessories are warm and welcoming. "Things are neither too rustic nor too smooth," says the designer. "A little bit of crud in the most polished houses is wonderful."** (Barbara Westbrook)

ABOVE: **In this sitting area, a large, updated Queen Anne–style mirror flanked by sconces brings light, subtle pattern to the wall above the sofa, adding interest without distracting from the fresh blue-and-white furniture group below.** (T. Keller Donovan)

RIGHT: **In this new, Italian-style palazzo in San Francisco, the fireplace, which has a hand-carved limestone surround, centers the symmetrical design of the living room. Facing each other across a coffee table in front of the mantel, a pair of elegant sofas, soft but trim and tailored, and light in color like the walls, give additional architectural form to the small space, where the chimney breast, doors to the terrace, and archway each has distinct character.** (Paul Wiseman)

# INSPIRATIONS

## Mantel or No? **Fireplace Style**

Lighted or not, it's the focus of your room, so give the fireplace a surround that conveys character and pleases your eye.

Go ahead, paint or stain your floor to make a statement with color or pattern or both—you can be as eccentric or sophisticated as you like. Create a trompe l'oeille effect with faux stone or marble, or opt for a classic graphic pattern like bold checks, stripes, or a border. If you're doing this yourself, consider a stencil to guide an organic motif, or set up a geometric pattern with masking tape. Be sure to seal the finished floor well to protect the paint. •

LEFT: **Choose a classic: Painted to contrast the walls, this traditional fireplace surround in the Neoclassical style is delicate and dressy, with a mantel shelf that echoes the deep cornice molding above it.** (Ken Fulk)

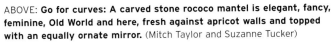

ABOVE: **Go for curves: A carved stone rococo mantel is elegant, fancy, feminine, Old World and here, fresh against apricot walls and topped with an equally ornate mirror.** (Mitch Taylor and Suzanne Tucker)

RIGHT, TOP: **Opt for simplicity: Left completely unframed as suits the casual ambience of the room, this raised fireplace is more graphic than architectural and allows its wall to show off a large, found-object-turned-art.** (David Mitchell)

RIGHT: **Don't compete: With texture and pattern aplenty from the composition of large fieldstones, this imposing chimney breast has sufficient character on its own; embellishment from a mantel could fight or be lost against it.** (Christopher Maya)

# Shopping for . . . **A COMFY SOFA OR CHAIR**

Upholstered furniture is key to the style and comfort of your living room. It's a big investment and not easily returnable. Since you can't see the innards, how do you know what you're getting? Here are the things to consider:

### Frame construction

You won't be able to see it, so ask about the frame. Kiln-dried hardwood is preferred, with doweled joints and corner blocks for stability. Stapled or nailed construction is not as sturdy. Legs that screw on and off are fine; it may be convenient to remove them if the piece has to be moved. On pieces with exposed wood legs, look for feet that are integral, not carved separately. If there are stretchers between the legs, they should be doweled and tight.

### Springs

Hand-tied coil springs under the seat and sometimes in the back are a mark of fine upholstery. Flat zigzag springs that are stapled to the top of the seat frame are less labor intensive to install but won't create the subtle contours possible with coil springs. You can easily tell which is used: Put your hand under the chair or sofa, if you can feel webbing straps across the bottom of the frame, there are coil springs. If you fall in love with an antique chair, check to see if the webbing is taut. If it sags, try to determine if the springs are still securely attached to it. If they are, new webbing can be stretched under the old to support the seat, but if the original webbing is brittle and the springs are loose, the only remedy is to completely strip the chair to the frame, replace the webbing and retie the springs, most likely sacrificing the fabric cover in the process. Dining chairs that have upholstered seats dropped into an exposed frame don't have springs.

### Padding

On a fine sofa or chair, the padding is built up in layers that are contoured to refine the shape. Several different padding materials may be used; a combination of thin foam and cotton and polyester battings is common.

### Cushion filling

Down or a down and feather mix are the squishiest and give the gentlest contours. Foam is firmer and may be more comfortable, especially for a seat cushion. Cushions can be made with a foam core that is wrapped with a down-filled envelope—the best of both worlds. For throw pillows or loose back cushions, nothing beats the look of down, but you'll have to plump them often to revive their shape.

### Cushion style

The seat and back of sofas and chairs are upholstered in two basic ways: with a tight cover or loose cushions. For a tight cover, the fabric is stretched over padding on the seat and inside back and stapled to the frame. Loose cushions are exactly that, covered individually and placed into a frame on which the seat and inside back are fabric-covered but only padded at the edges where they won't be covered by the cushions. The difference is largely aesthetic, and many styles combine a loose cushion seat with a tight back, but there are a couple of things to consider besides the look: First, no one wants to sit on the crack between cushions, so if there are two cushions, figure the sofa seats two unless each cushion is extra long. And second, loose cushions require more fabric

RIGHT: **Early eighteenth-century in style—like an upholstered settee—this tall-back sofa has an upright stance that suits a double-height small room. It suits the owner too, "I'm short, so if a sofa is too deep I feel like a little girl with her feet sticking out." She likes that this sits like a chair; "if it's too cushy you start falling asleep."** (Michael Smith)

OPPOSITE: **If you're eying a bedroom corner as a spot to curl up and read (or nap), a big soft club chair could be just the ticket. This one has a plump seat cushion and pillow back; a cozy throw and a squishy throw pillow invite you to snuggle in.** (Richard H. Lewis)

than tight upholstery, something to bear in mind at the time of purchase and for potential slipcovers or reupholstery.

## Cover

The fabric should be taut over the padding and trims should be straight. If the fabric is patterned, the motifs should continue from top to bottom, matching at horizontal seams. They probably won't match at vertical seams because of the contours of the chair, but they should align horizontally. If the motif is large or isolated, custom dictates that it should be centered on the inside back, above the seat cushion, and the remaining front sections cut so the pattern flows from the back onto the cushion top and then onto the front drop (vertical surface); on each other section the motif should be centered side-to-side but placed to align horizontally with the same motif on adjacent sections. Keep an eye out for vertical stripes that don't align from top to bottom or for checks that slant at cushion edges, hems, or along horizontal seams. Loose cushions always have removable covers; throw pillows may or may not.

## Proportions

Your first thought should be to choose a sofa or chair with the proportions that work for your room, but the size should be right for you to sit in too. If the seat is too deep from front to back, your back won't rest against the chair back; if the seat is too high, your feet will dangle above the floor; if it's too low, your knees will point toward your chin. Of course, people are all different sizes, but especially if you are very tall or very short, the proportions of a sofa or chair can be critical to your comfort. The shape and position of the arms and the slant and height of the back all affect our perception of comfort, which can be quite subjective. If you can, test a floor sample to see if it's comfortable for reading, lounging if appropriate, and chatting.

## Safety

Upholstered furniture bearing a gold UFAC (Upholstered Furniture Action Council) hangtag has been made following industry standards designed to reduce the likelihood of fires caused by smoldering cigarettes dropped onto the upholstery. •

# The Choice Is Yours: **SECTIONAL SOFAS**

We've fallen for the new sectional: stylish, tailored, and sexy. All that room makes it the perfect party piece for a crowd, while lounging solo is like getting a big hug.

ABOVE: Two sitting areas make good use of the shape of this living room: one in the bay window that overlooks San Francisco Bay, the other centered in front of the fireplace. Both sofas face into the room and the armchairs can be swung about, so conversation flows easily, and, with lustrous, dreamy grays with citrus and parchment accents in both areas, so does the eye. (Myra Hoefer)

LEFT: Sparing use of color gives this upstairs sitting room a casual elegance. The designer remarks that most people think this as a blue room, but really, it is ivory, with blue accents found only in the throw pillows and on the ottoman. (Suzanne Kasler)

# INSPIRATIONS

## Cheers! Find Space for a Bar

Whether improvised or built-in, a spill-proof surface to hold bottles, glasses, and ice is all that's needed when drinks are in order.

A sip of this or that will be wanted when your friends gather to toast the evening, the New Year, or the croquet champ. A cabinet that's plumbed with a sink and fitted with a fridge is a fine idea if you've space for it. If not, top a table with a large tray or two to display liquid refreshments and an ice bucket; make sure there are coasters, napkins, and a place for empties. Make the setup permanent or temporary, as suits. •

BELOW: **How appropriate: A 1950s bar table placed behind the sofa holds the liquor here, where the décor is fresh, fun, funky, and "even a bit campy."** (Joe Nye)

# Colorful Opinions: **TAKING THE PLUNGE**

If only you weren't so timid about color, you'd have the rooms you really dream about. Let these designers ease the way—it's not as scary as you think.

**PETER DUNHAM:**
**RALPH LAUREN
OYSTER BAY SS61**
Take this incredible turquoisey blue-green, like you'd see on a cloisonné vase, and paint it on the reverse side of glass. Then use it as a tabletop. You have the effect of color, once removed—even the most color-phobic will usually go for it. And it looks so glossy and deep. Absolutely ravishing.

**ELLIE CULLMAN:**
**BENJAMIN MOORE
SILKEN PINE 2144-50**
Pale green is a kind of universal donor. Even our most beige clients seem to respond well to green, probably because it's a color we see so much in nature. This is a soft, celadony green, like a piece of the palest jade. I'll often use it in a master bedroom.

**MADELINE STUART:**
**FARROW & BALL
LIGHT BLUE 22**
I'm always surprised when clients balk at color, and never surprised when they realize the difference it makes. In a transitional space like a stair hall, you have more freedom, so we tried a grayish-blue— soft, but with great depth. Once the client saw how it enriched the space, the deal was done.

**CHERYL KATZ:**
**BENJAMIN MOORE
COASTAL FOG AC-1**
This is a color for people who think they want all white. It's a warm gray with a little hint of green—a good choice for a living room since it still lets you have a neutral envelope, but it's not boring. Cool it down with icy blues, or warm it up with mustard.

**ANTONIO DA MOTTA:**
**DONALD KAUFMAN
COLOR COLLECTION DKC-17**
A hallway tends to be a dead space, but paint it this warm Etruscan red and it's a blast of life. You don't have to live in it. You're just walking through. But it's a hook. People can get addicted to color after they paint a hallway.

**SCOTT SANDERS:**
**BENJAMIN MOORE**
**CORAL REEF 012**
Don't give guests a white room—they probably have that at home. Take a chance on this bright coral, softer than orange and more hip than pink. Very Palm Beach and lobster salad on a warm day.

**KATHRYN M. IRELAND:**
**FARROW & BALL**
**BORROWED LIGHT 235**
Start with something pale. Then add more color, if you like, with fabric. This is a beautiful, restful blue, very soft on the eye because of all the gray in it. Lends itself particularly well to antiques and faded fabrics. I do a lot of master bedrooms in blue, because both men and women like it.

**TODD KLEIN:**
**BENJAMIN MOORE**
**MAN ON THE MOON OC-106**
The client wanted yellow in the living room but was afraid to commit, so we landed on this wonderful warm cream, the color of a magnolia petal. As the day wanes, it gets deeper and really starts to glow once the lights are turned on. Who doesn't need a little moonglow in their life?

**BARRY DIXON:**
**FARROW & BALL**
**PICTURE GALLERY RED 42**
**AND FOWLER PINK 39**
I took the color of a seashell—actually it was the inside lip of a conch where it goes into this rosy, fleshy tone—and then recreated it with three parts Picture Gallery Red to one part Fowler Pink. If you can find a color somewhere in nature, it often makes people more comfortable.

**KEITH IRVINE:**
**BENJAMIN MOORE**
**UTAH SKY 2065-40**
It's a clean, simple jolt of blue. Simple, like all good American traditions, and I would use it in an entrance hall, against a clear white trim. It's sort of like shock tactics. Get them used to the excitement of a real color here, and then the next injection of color will be a hell of a lot easier.

**SUZANNE LOVELL:**
**DONALD KAUFMAN**
**COLOR COLLECTION DKC-66**
I'd go straight to the library and paint it this deep, luscious purplish brown, like the bark of a tree when it's wet in the rain. A dark color actually expands the space because it erases boundaries. Then the room becomes all about the books and the art.

**NOEL JEFFREY:**
**BENJAMIN MOORE**
**MORNING GLORY 785**
Do this soft blue in a bedroom and it would be like waking up to a clear bright morning. If the person is really nervous about color, paint all the trim white. Do white furniture, white fabrics, white bed linens—then you can have a blue room without hitting them over the head with it.

# INSPIRATIONS

## Mantel + Art = **Focused Display**

The wall above your fireplace is a defined space just waiting to be filled. Honor it with a combination of framed and freestanding art.

The mantelshelf establishes a horizontal boundary of a specific width above your fireplace and is a natural place to rest small objects. Take advantage of both aspects and use the shelf and the area above for a display that balances and complements the fireplace below. If there are additional moldings or paired sconces above the shelf, incorporate them. Go for symmetry or not, both can be effective. Stand back to make sure small items don't look lost. •

LEFT: **Here, a very simple and unexpected mix of objects sits asymmetrically on the mantel. The tall panel at one side, which includes an elaborate relief carving above an inset mirror, has gilt ornament and a pale ground; next to it two small, dark primitive pieces are silhouetted against the butter-colored wall.** (Martha Angus)

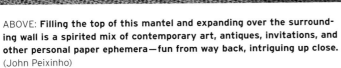

ABOVE: **Filling the top of this mantel and expanding over the surrounding wall is a spirited mix of contemporary art, antiques, invitations, and other personal paper ephemera—fun from way back, intriguing up close.** (John Peixinho)

RIGHT, TOP: **This casual mantel display is balanced but not strictly symmetrical, with non-matching, weightier, darker vessels at the ends, a medium-size painting in the center, and room between to adjust for seasonal flowers or to satisfy a whim.** (Mona Hajj)

RIGHT: **Over the mantel in this dressy room a composition of turquoise cloisonné pieces and an ornate, gilded convex mirror brings some color to the wall, is beautiful, and, with the vertical vases framing the round mirror, subtly echoes the archway at the side.** (John Oetgen)

# FAMILY ROOMS WE LOVE

When someone refers to the family room, you can assume it is a somewhat casual gathering place where relaxation is the preferred activity. Approach the design of a family room the same way you do a more formal living room—ask the same questions of use and size to determine what belongs in it, and then decide upon a look that will make the room a place you want to hang out. Your conversation areas might include a game table, computer station, or crafts area in addition to a spot for chatting and watching the tube. Be sure to plan ahead for your sound system, cable connection, and room darkening window treatments if you need them. Following are some rooms where we'd be happy to while away some leisure time.

BELOW: **First things first: Since everyone who walks into this home loves music, the entry hall is set up with a piano surrounded by stools so the passion can be immediately enjoyed. The big, circular pouf is conducive to collaboration with the musicians—or appreciation or conversation.** (Robert Stilin)

OPPOSITE: **Referred to as "the loft," this sitting room is a previously unused attic, with the ceiling painted white and the floor spiffed and waxed. The furnishings, left from another home in another place, were moved around "until they felt right." In the background, a baby grand piano is tucked under the sloping beams.** (David Jimenez)

# LIVING ROOM OR FAMILY ROOM?

They're both rooms where people gather for conversation and relaxation, perhaps to enjoy music, play a game, or read in companionable silence. Unless you have more than one sitting room in your home, it doesn't matter what you call it as long as it is set up for the way you want to use it. What's the commonly understood distinction? A living room is more formal, a family room or den is less so. More important, a living room is a public space to which guests are invited, while a family room is private.

We think of sitting upright in a living room, lounging before the TV in a family room, with kids given free run. But television and videos are an important part of many people's leisure, and while some interior designers despair of the trend, you'll find a flat-screen TV over the mantel or in a bookcase in a dressy room if it suits the owner's needs. Lots of living rooms glory in their cushy sofas and put-your-feet-up ottomans. Some people place the piano in a less formal room so the kids can practice and other music equipment is nearby. Design-wise, there may be no difference between a casual living room and a family room: You'll decide the ambience you want for each sitting area you have; just be aware of its visual and social impact if you place a television in your living room.

RIGHT: **Tucked beneath rough-hewn post-and-beam construction with painted plank walls, this mezzanine sitting area wears an air of refined rusticity. It's eclectically furnished with a Mission chair, bentwood armchair, and a plump contemporary loveseat. The finely detailed cabinet displays personal treasures and a contrast view of the rough roof; it opens to reveal the television.** (Marshall Watson)

OPPOSITE, TOP: **The place: a family room that's open to the eat-in kitchen. The goal: comfortable, easy, usable, nothing too precious. The device: "Get the interior architecture right" with paneling, cabinets, and moldings, says the designer, "and then fill in with comfortable furnishings." The palette: blue and white, but mixed with beige, and in a variety of textures and patterns. The surprise: he didn't know about the china collection until the clients had moved in.** (James Strickland and Suzanne Rester Watson)

OPPOSITE, BOTTOM: **Calm and relaxing in the grayed palette and uncluttered look of Swedish country style, this large sitting room has two social centers separated by an antique pedestal table and united by a wall of lovely French doors. On the left, the dressed-up, grown-up sitting area is perfect for tea or cards (a fireplace is opposite the painted settee); on the right the dressed-down, sprawling sofa faces an armoire that holds the television.** (Katrin Cargill and Carol Glasser)

RIGHT: **It's young, lively, and upbeat in chartreuse and white, and for true family togetherness, the two TVs are equipped with headphones so each generation can watch what it wants. With the vertical chimney and soaring ceiling, the designer felt a curve was in order—hence the semicircular sofa and oval coffee table. Plus the sofa feels hip and welcoming; an L-shape sofa would close off the room.** (James Radin)

# Shopping for ... **A COFFEE TABLE**

Material and style are closely integrated in coffee table design. Consider both as you decide what you want yours to look like.

### Tradition

There are no antique coffee tables so don't spend time searching for one. Designers hold different opinions on how to resolve this in period-inspired décor. Some will cut down an old table or commission a new one that mimics the lines of the period, others think that's a pretense and prefer to use something modern that complements the other furnishings without echoing them. If you're inclined to go with the first option, check the value of the old piece before you alter it.

### Materials

Wood, glass and mirror, Lucite and various plastics, metal, rattan, and wicker all are options, frequently in combination. Look for style but consider durability, maintenance, and safety, especially if there are children who might fall against sharp edges. Crumbs have a way of getting trapped under glass tops that sit in wood or metal frames and the glass is heavy, so this style may be difficult to keep clean. If drinks and snacks are served on your coffee table, give some

thought to the surface: are you prepared to protect or maintain a fine wood finish? Will crumbs filtering through the woven rattan make you cranky? Does someone you know find it impossible to keep his heels off the coffee table?

## Non-table options

An upholstered ottoman topped with a tray may double as a coffee table and offers extra seating too; aesthetically this option has the advantage of easily pairing with other upholstered furniture. An interesting low wood chest, cabinet, or trunk can also work and will provide some storage as well.

## Extra functionality

Styles with shelves, drawers, and lift tops give some help with organizing magazines, newspapers, and the remote. A lift top may have the sleekest lines but prove awkward to use. A shelf below a glass top becomes a display area, which you may or may not appreciate.

## Contour

How is your conversation area configured? If the area between the sofa and chairs is basically square or round,

choose a coffee table that is also. If the area is longer than it is wide, choose a rectangular or oblong table, or use two small ones. A rounded shape may be easier to walk around in a tight space but there are no rules about the coffee table needing to conform to the shape of the seating area—you can contrast round and square if it pleases you. But do keep the overall proportions balanced. Leggy styles will carry a different visual weight than solid ones. •

ABOVE: **This glass-top, enameled wrought-iron coffee table sits lightly among the bright colors and overscale patterns and furnishings in this family room.** (Diamond Baratta)

OPPOSITE: **Massive, biomorphic, and custom-made, this bronze coffee table centers the grouping of curvy, elegant shapes that furnish the sitting area in this glass-enclosed Manhattan apartment.** (David Easton)

ABOVE: **Inspired by a Belgian aesthetic, this family room is comfortable and inviting but without a lot of furniture. Typical of the style: wide horizontal planks on the wall, unstained light wood, strong, dark light fixtures, and restrained use of color other than the neutrals of the linen upholstery and draperies. The ancient arched doors open to reveal a custom media cabinet.** (Kay Douglass)

OPPOSITE: **Black linen wall covering makes a surprising neutral in this small den, which doubles as a guest room. Everything else in this apartment is serene and calm, but here the designer went for "a shot in the arm" with the marigold velvet sofa and dark walls broken by a grid of ivory moldings, which were applied to make sense of the single, small window, and conceal the closet door.** (Garrow Kedigian)

# The Choice Is Yours: **PILLOWS**

Pillows are to decorating as handbags are to fashion: You can never have too many. Square, round, flat, or boxed, you can glory in the colors, prints, and trims.

# DESIGNER'S TOP TEN

Designer Ernest de la Torre offers these ten rules for using paintings, prints, and photographs to transform a room.

**1.** Art can create the mood for a room, or serve as an exclamation point in a neutral setting.

**2.** Play with size. For dramatic effect, try hanging a large piece of art in a small space such as a powder room or vestibule.

**3.** Don't try to conform to anyone else's taste. Your art should be a reflection of your personal style and interests.

**4.** If you are interested in collecting as an investment, do your homework and only buy from reputable galleries. You can keep tabs on auction results and current prices with Internet sites like www.artnet.com.

**5.** Regarding value, provenance can be more important for some pieces than others, and in the case of prints, condition is all-important.

**6.** Sculpture adds height and a touch of the unexpected. Don't be afraid to juxtapose two artworks from different periods, provided they have a common element.

**7.** Try using gallery-hanging rods. They allow you to rotate your collection effortlessly without ruining the walls.

**8.** Choose frames carefully, the wrong one can overwhelm a piece of art or fail to set it off. Mix frames that differ both stylistically and in color, this gives your collection a sense of having been assembled over time. But stick to one frame style for a single series of works by one artist.

**9.** Create a collage by grouping many small artworks together, linking them through visual forms, theme, or color. The pieces will play off one another to create a single graphic effect.

**10.** Keep track of the artists you are interested in, and learn about their work. A great collection evolves as you do.

LEFT: **Stylized whimsy, saturated colors, and lots of chinoiserie mixed with traditional pieces set an expressive tone in this Newport summerhouse sitting room. It's snappy and fun, and can be dressed up or down. The Chinese screen over the sofa gives the room scale.** (Meg Braff)

# The Choice Is Yours: **OTTOMANS**

A footrest, coffee table, or extra seating . . .
this is the piece that does it all. Take your
pick of large, small, tailored, or voluptuous.

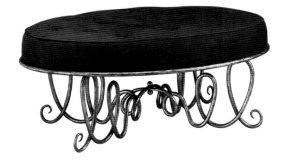

# INSPIRATIONS

## Where to Put Reading Materials

Books and magazines engage your mind, but do they please your eye when scattered about? Find them a home!

Sure, you could be truly disciplined and return them to the library or pitch them after three days, but once you're hooked on a story, you want to return to it at leisure. To keep reading materials organized and tidy, consider a classic magazine caddy or a basket or decorative box in which you can place publications spine-up. If you're a true bibliophile, find a coffee table or end table fitted with a lower shelf on which you can stack or file your current must-reads. •

LEFT AND OPPOSITE: **Neat freaks rejoice—with a bookcase coffee table like one of these you can organize your current reads for quick access and keep the top free for decorative accessories, drinks, or feet propped up while you read.** (Eve Robinson)

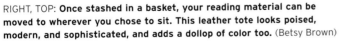

RIGHT, TOP: Once stashed in a basket, your reading material can be moved to wherever you chose to sit. This leather tote looks poised, modern, and sophisticated, and adds a dollop of color too. (Betsy Brown)

RIGHT: It's easy to flip through the titles in a V-shape magazine rack. This one has a jaunty stance and open design. (Michael Canter)

ABOVE: **An aubergine wall, draperies hung at the ceiling, and a circular seating arrangement create an intimate living room in this high-rise apartment. The curvaceous ivory sofa forms an anchor; the colors are sophisticated and lovely, the lampshades and other accessories reflect an individual taste.** (Celerie Kemble)

# TABLESCAPE

This antique Chinese altar table was dressed up by Suzanne Tucker of Tucker & Marks in San Francisco. Here's how you can get the look at home.

**Highlight a large piece of art by framing it, not blocking it, with tall items.**

Combine contemporary and antique elements, your arrangement will have more life.

**Remember the power of pairs. Symmetry makes things feel important.**

Don't forget the floor. It can complete the whole picture.

## Make It Your Own:

**TURTLE BOX**
Isn't he (she?) cute? This stoneware turtle doubles as a stash box.

**DOLPHIN CANDLESTICK**
Cover this shiny brass candlestick with a tall, plain glass hurricane to give it more presence.

**STONE SPHERE**
Concrete spheres have the texture of limestone but come at a fraction of the price.

**PAINTED BASKET**
Instead of natural wicker, try a painted basket in a neutral color.

# PULL IT TOGETHER

Your dream living room is clearly imagined, you can picture it. You're ready to get specific. Take out your clipping and swatch files; add photos of any furnishings you already own that you plan to include. Spread out the pieces on a large table and sort and edit them until you find the right combination. If you like, make a collage of your choices so you can easily revisit them. If you'll be working with a designer, don't worry if you discover holes or feel something isn't quite right; he or she will refine and interpret your thoughts, and source the furnishings.

## Ambience

Choose the key words that describe the look of your dream living room and its proportions—crisp and graphic, soothing, elegant, luxurious, beach-y, traditional with a contemporary twist, in the Swedish country style, lofty, open and expansive, intimate—whatever they may be.

## Color

Choose the overall palette and decide which hues will be most important and which secondary, for instance green-gold and soft white with blue accents. How do you wish to incorporate pattern; is there a rug or fabric that could be the basis for your entire color scheme?

## Walls

How important will the walls be? Plain color? A patterned wall covering? Paneling? If there are moldings, will they match or contrast the wall? How is the fireplace integrated?

## Floor

What will the flooring be? Wood, stone, carpet? Will it provide a strong contrast or a subtle one, how much visual texture will it add? If it isn't topped with a rug, will it have pattern, either painted or created with a mix of materials?

## Rugs

How will you use rugs? A large carpet overall? Area rugs? Layered? Will they provide an assertive or subtle pattern or introduce multiple colors or an obvious texture?

## Window treatments

How prominent do you want the window treatments to be? What style do you want to use? How will they provide night-time privacy or filter the sun?

## Furniture

At the least, you'll need a sofa and one or two easy chairs, plus a coffee table and side tables. Add stools, side chairs, an ottoman, a console table or a desk as space permits. What about an interesting cabinet, a secretary, or an étagère? Consider the contours and proportions of the furniture; try to visualize the way they'll balance and contrast one another and the overall space.

## Lighting fixtures

Use a combination of fixtures to create flattering, welcoming ambient light, bounced off the ceiling if possible. Choose table and floor lamps to light reading and conversation areas.

## Accessories

Think about art and decorative accessories such as pillows from the beginning. They express your personality and interests and can set the tone for the décor or punctuate it. Plan lighting and shelves or pedestals where appropriate.

## Layout

Even if you're not feeling ready to do a real floor plan, it's smart to do something rough that can serve as a reality check for the amount and scale of the furniture. Draw the outline of the room on graph paper; mark the windows, doorways, and fireplace. Make some paper cutouts of the furniture in the same scale and position them. What happens?

OPPOSITE: **With shell motifs happily deployed amid a mix of sun, sand, and blue hues, there's no mistaking this is a beach house living room. A boldly striped rug anchors the conversation area and also leads the eye through the adjacent room and out to the porch, the furnishings have dressy details but are light and delicate, and the birdcages, amber hurricane lamps, and colorful majolica pieces from the owner's collection add a fun and summery touch.** (Paula Perlini)

# Where would you like to dine?

- ☐ In a candlelit manor
- ☐ Under a sparkling chandelier
- ☐ In a quaint, cozy room
- ☐ At a striking glass table
- ☐ Ringed by a painted landscape
- ☐ Surrounded by great art

# 13. DINING ROOMS

OPPOSITE: **Comfortable, cozy, charming by day or night, this small dining room has a round pedestal table encircled by gracious wing chairs. At the end, a bay window is filled with a cushioned bench, on the other sides small bookcases were added—both make the space inviting between meals. The table opens to seat twelve, above it the chandelier is decorated with metal foliage cutouts, and horn handles on the backs make it easy to pull out the chairs.** (Nancy Boszhardt)

Is dinner a daily ceremony in your home, with candles and linen napkins? Is it a family affair, or adults only? Do you entertain frequently? Do you have help for serving, or is dinner family style, with food passed around the table? Is your dining room grand or intimate? Do you eat there during daylight?

In some homes, the dining room is reserved for special occasions, in others it sees daily use. In a small house there may be nowhere else to eat and in some homes by design the dining room is part of the living room or open to the kitchen as well. A dining room that's separate can take on any demeanor you wish to assign it; one that's part of another space must be approached as one part of a whole. What's your situation? How do you use your dining room, do you wish it to be hospitable for both formal and casual meals, or is it used only for entertaining or on holidays? Does it open to the garden or an enticing view, do you love to linger there over brunch or lunch? Is there a fireplace, or might you add one? Is the room large enough for a table that can expand with the number of guests, or are you limited in the number you can seat? What sort of ambience would you like your dining room to have?

# SPACIOUS OR COZY?
## Planning a Dining Room.

Whether you dream of a dining room that's polished and glittering or soft and glowing, the size of the space is the first thing to consider because it defines the scale of the furnishings and of the entertaining that takes place within its walls. A small room will always be intimate but can feel cramped if there's too much furniture or the pieces are too large. A large room can be marvelously gracious, but if there's a sizable void around the table, you may feel uncomfortable in it—this can occur especially if you have an expandable table that is kept small unless guests are present. You can enhance the feeling of intimacy by using darker colors, generous draperies, and larger scale furniture, and depending on the shape of the room, by including a window seat, display cabinets, bookcases, or even a small tea table by the fire or window to balance any space not filled by the dining furniture. Mellow lighting that illuminates the dining table and leaves the corners of the room in shadow will increase intimacy too. If you host large parties, soft window treatments and rugs will help to absorb sound. If your dining room is large and used during the day as well as at night,

you'll probably want to take advantage of the natural light and spacious proportions by day, and use artificial lighting to make it warm and intimate by night.

Whatever the scale of your dining room, you'll want it to be a convivial place where people enjoy being together. The table and chairs will be central to the look; their design can be as impressive or restrained as you wish, and whether they are a matched set or paired with an eye to complementary contrast is up to you. A dining room needs more than a stylish table and chairs and a great color scheme, what else will give yours character? Lighting fixtures, usually a chandelier or lantern over the table, and sometimes sconces on the walls, are a must. A rug is optional; include one if you wish, making sure it is large enough to hold the chairs when they're pushed back so diners can leave the table. Good dining chairs and mellow light will make people comfortable, but what will diners look at while they're sitting at your table? Is there a corner cupboard, a sideboard, an interesting cabinet, or a console that can display interesting objects? Do you have larger pieces of sculpture to honor, either on a pedestal or on the floor? Are there paintings, prints, or photographs for the walls? Or a mirror to reflect the chandelier and animated faces? Fine art or your favorite collectibles are not simply accessories that finish the look, they convey your

LEFT: **Padded benches add a level of family-friendly informality around this 12-foot-long dining table, where lots of chairs would look crowded. Leather upholstery trimmed with nailheads dresses up their garden-shop origins. Of the chocolate brown paint on the walls, the designer says "It immediately connotes a sense coziness that other dark colors don't. It always works."** (Tim Scheerer)

RIGHT: **Subtly varied shades of white bring out the architectural details that quietly define the dining area within this home, where the monochrome palette extends to the floor and keeps the flow from room to room easy and open. The rest of the décor is ship shape and simple: Rush chairs give focus to the white table, a sailboat model presides from the sideboard, and white curtains soften the doorway.** (Jodi Macklin)

RIGHT, BOTTOM: **Hanging like a celestial body above this dining table is a chandelier with a large hand-blown blue glass orb, small crystal balls, and shaded lamps. Complementing the ethereal look are walls hand-painted in a soft freeform pattern, chairs with a chalky gray-blue paint finish and silver-leaf details, and a pair of mirrors with silver-leaf frames.** (Jacqueline Derrey Segura)

interests and they can spark discussion too—which can be an asset if conversation lags.

To plan your dining room, think about the way you use it and the way it relates to the living room and the kitchen. If it's part of or open to these spaces, think about the sight lines—will people sitting on the sofa be able to see over the dining chairs to the kitchen? How will views through the windows or access to French doors be affected by the furniture arrangement? Will you want a sideboard or buffet, and is there room for one? If the space is large or irregularly shaped, you may wish to place the table off-center; how will that affect the overall design? Is there a clear path from the cooking area to the dining room and how far is it—if you are the cook as well as the hostess, will you be able to perform both roles at once? Will diners be able to see into the kitchen, and is this a plus or a minus for you? Is your dining area used for anything else? The kids' homework, games, crafts, or your own office? If so, plan adequate lighting for these activities. Do you need a concealed computer or television in the room? Have you allowed for a sound system so you can dine to music?

# ROOMS WE LOVE

Which visual menu will your dining room present? Traditional style, either formal or relaxed, but with gleaming wood furniture and perhaps muraled walls? A Swedish or French country look? A crisp contemporary composition of metal and glass? Do you prefer a cozy look or one that's open? Are upholstered chairs beckoning you? Will a crystal chandelier be the pièce de résistance, or is the simplicity of wrought iron more your style? What cues does the room itself give you, are there architectural details to set the tone, a nighttime cityscape or a seaside setting to acknowledge? If you've more than one eating area to design, how would you like them to differ? Decide on the look, and then find the colors and furnishings that will make it yours. Start by browsing through the photos of dining rooms we've been happy to visit. (Turn to pages 302 through 305 to see some kitchen breakfast areas.)

## THE RULES OF . . .

### HANGING A CHANDELIER

Follow these guides to hang a dining room or kitchen pendant fixture. For a foyer, make sure there's room to walk below the fixture.

- If a chandelier is too wide, diners may bump their head when rising from the table. Twelve inches narrower than the table is the rule of thumb.
- Allow 30 to 34 inches between the bottom of a chandelier and the tabletop in a room with an 8-foot ceiling. Increase this space by 3 inches for every additional foot of ceiling height.
- Most chandeliers are too heavy to hang from a standard electrical box; if you are replacing a lightweight overhead fixture, a new support system may be required.

RIGHT: **In this dining room, striée wallpaper in deep, beautiful blue expresses the owner's love of a color some people consider too cold to use in such volume. Two small pewter chandeliers are spaced above the long table where one big central one would have hung mid-mirror, and other accessories are paired and displayed symmetrically as well.** (T. Keller Donovan)

OPPOSITE: "The dining room is really the fancy dress part of the house," says the designer of this room. The jade-green background of the hand-painted wallpaper is vibrant and young, brings the delicate floral branch pattern alive, and sets off the buttery draperies. A tiered chandelier cascades with sparkling crystal above the elegant, ebonized walnut table and chairs. (Mary McDonald)

ABOVE: "I love the interest of the upholstered chairs because they break it up," says the designer when asked about the effect of the mismatched chairs that surround this table. With wall space sacrificed to the lovely windows, she bravely hung framed botanical prints right on the wood mullions. (Susan Ferrier)

# Colorful Opinions: **TO DINE BY**

Do you want to feel cozy, casual, glamorous, elegant—or have evenings of all-out fantasy? Designers suggest colors to paint any mood you want.

CHARLOTTE MOSS:
**FARROW & BALL**
**BREAKFAST ROOM GREEN 81**
When you're eating, you want a space that feels fresh, and green reads fresh to me. This is a crisp celadon. With white linens on a wooden table, it reminds me of eating outdoors. I adore eating outdoors. Everything tastes better—even my cooking!

MARTYN LAWRENCE-BULLARD:
**BENJAMIN MOORE**
**ORANGE PARROT 2169-20**
I love pairing this orange with yellow on the ceiling and ivory crown moldings. Doesn't it sound wild? It's a really exotic fun orange that creates drama, yet lets you know the inhabitant is very playful.

ARTHUR DUNNAM:
**BENJAMIN MOORE**
**BRANCHPORT BROWN HC-72**
It's a very dark chocolate brown with a bit of red in it, so there's a warm aspect to it that makes people look good. In high gloss, it really sparkles under candlelight. I think chocolate brown walls particularly suit a city dining room.

**CELERIE KEMBLE:**
**FARROW & BALL
MERE GREEN 219**
We've all had our fill of ruby, sapphire, and emerald. This is like the missing jewel tone we only get in peacock feathers. It's rich and still playful—it can be a formal or sort of decadent color, and it looks very beautiful with accents of white lacquer or dark wood.

**BARCLAY BUTERA:**
**RALPH LAUREN PAINT
CALYPSO VM138**
It's a blue with a certain nobility, something you would have seen in a colonial house in Williamsburg. But it's also a casual and comfortable color. A dining room should be approachable—don't think it's only for holidays and special events.

**BRET WITKE:**
**BENJAMIN MOORE
POWDER SAND 2151-70**
There's a paleness to it, but also a warmth. It's like a blank canvas, so anyone who sits in front of it, or any food, any color, looks really attractive—amazing in fact. Everything pops. The dining room is all about the table and the people sitting at it.

**COLIN COWIE:**
**BENJAMIN MOORE
SHELBURNE BUFF HC-28**
This is a wonderful oatmeal, camel color, and the reason I love it is it's a very neutral background but the gold hue makes everybody look like they just came back from somewhere fabulous. It's a very flattering color.

**JEFFREY BILHUBER:**
**BENJAMIN MOORE
WISPY GREEN 414**
A pale, yellow-based spring green is dazzling to the complexion. Greens bring out the pink in you. Just think what haricots vert do for a good lamb chop—the green is what completes the plate. It's the perfect foil.

**MARIETTE HIMES GOMEZ:**
**BENJAMIN MOORE
SAGE TINT 458**
It's kind of robin's egg blue, and with mahogany furniture and neutral upholstery, it looks great. I see dining rooms as mostly evening spaces, and this has enough life that it doesn't die. The right blue is always soothing.

**MICHAEL BERMAN:**
**RALPH LAUREN PAINT
DESERT BOOT TH35**
Like a blanket of velvet that wraps the walls—it's a really saturated rich brown, very deep, almost aubergine. People in the room almost become the characters of an oil painting. It has the feeling of the background in an eighteenth-century portrait.

**T. KELLER DONOVAN:**
**BENJAMIN MOORE
BROWN SUGAR 2112-20**
I just used it in a dining room in Palm Beach. If you are a chocoholic like me, you just walk in and get hungry. The key word here is chocolicious. It's a really rich, deep, milk-chocolatey color, and we did white brackets with white vases all over the walls.

# Shopping for . . . **A DINING TABLE**

The table takes center stage in your dining room; its shape, proportions, and lines are key to your look. It's your choice to purchase chairs and a sideboard that match the table or not—contrast can be interesting. A good table is big investment, so shop wisely.

### Style

Whether you choose a traditional period style or a contemporary design, the location of the legs and the way it expands, if it does, affect the look and flexibility of the table. The legs should not interfere with diners' legs and should permit the empty chairs to be pushed up to the table—single or double pedestal construction or legs at the corners on a square or rectangular table will give the least interference. Check to be sure you can push in the expected number of chairs on each side and at the end (do this with the chair you'll be using, measuring at its widest point if you can't actually test it). The feet on trestle or sawbuck tables probably won't interfere with the seating, but they can be awkward and it's easy to bump chair legs against them. Drop-leaf tops are supported either by swivel braces, which won't interfere with the seating, or by means of gate legs, which swing out to the center

LEFT: **An elegant mahogany extension table with turned tapered legs and an inlaid accent along the apron commands respect in the center of this formal dining room. The bright pink upholstery on the chairs gives a little wink to tradition.** (John Oetgen)

of the table edge and may interfere. Be aware that you can't push chairs under most drop leafs when they are down. If the table has an apron (the frame that holds the legs and supports the top on many tables), make sure there is enough space between it and the chair seat for your knees. If you use armchairs, check to see if the arms will fit under the apron so the empty chairs can be pushed up to the table.

### Stability

Look for a sturdy table with tight joints and make sure it sits squarely on the floor. Pedestal tables are more wobble-prone than four-legged styles. If the table expands with leaves, check to see that it opens and closes smoothly and easily.

### Material

Dining tables are often made of wood, but other options include glass, rattan, and metal; you'll find many designs featuring a combination of materials too. On a wood table, look for solid-wood construction, with or without veneer. Informal country tables are often made of solid oak, pine, or maple. Veneer over solid wood is a mark of quality (it's an efficient way for costly woods to be used) and generally found on formal tables. When skillfully applied, veneer is stable and durable and can be repaired and refinished should it become necessary. However, inexpensive veneered tables often feature a very thin wood layer applied to particleboard; on these the surface is not durable, may split or delaminate, and cannot be refinished.

### Finish

On a wood table, look for a deep, glowing surface that does not look plastic. If you are purchasing a new table (rather than an antique) ask the vendor about the warranty for the finish and be sure you understand how to maintain and protect it. Nicks and small cracks are not normal for a quality wood table (unless it is described as having a distressed finish), so avoid pieces that claim this as an attribute. On a metal table, avoid rough finishes that could snag clothing or flake.

### Glass tops

Protective glass to be laid on top of another surface can be $1/4$ inch thick and is usually tempered so that if it breaks, it will shatter into many small pieces. For a tabletop that is not laid over another surface, the glass should be at least $3/8$ inch thick; $1/2$ or $3/4$ inch is preferable. To ensure that they remain in tact if they are chipped, these thicker glass tabletops are not tempered; if they were, anything on them would fall when they shattered. The base of a glass table should support at least one third the area of the top.

### Size

"The rules of sizing a table," below, gives the standard number of diners that can be seated at some common table sizes. If you don't know what size table will fit comfortably in your dining area, measure the length and width of the space and subtract $4^1/2$ feet from each dimension; this will give you the maximum size for the table (subtract 7 feet to allow room to walk behind seated diners). Make sure the table will fit through the doorways in your home. •

## THE RULES OF . . .

### SIZING A TABLE

How large should your dining table be? It depends on the size of the room and the number of diners customarily seated. Here are the guidelines:

- Allow at least 26 inches between the table and wall or other furniture; this is tight and with it you might want a chair rail to protect your walls. Allowing $3^1/2$ feet will give enough space for people to walk behind seated diners. If there is a cabinet opposite the table, make sure there is room for you to open the drawers and doors and access the contents.

- Allow 24 to 28 inches per chair, plus 4 to 6 inches between chairs.

- A round or square table 42 inches in diameter will comfortably seat four. One that is 54 to 60 inches in diameter will seat six; to accommodate eight, choose a table 72 inches in diameter.

- The number of chairs you can fit at a rectangular table varies with the width of the table. Assuming one chair will fit at each end, a 60-inch-long rectangular table will seat six; one 80 inches long will seat eight; you need a length of 108 inches to seat ten. If the table is very narrow you may not be able to fit as many place settings.

- An oval table will not comfortably seat as many people as a rectangular one of the same length.

- An octagonal table must be at least 60 inches in diameter to seat eight; anything less seats four, or maybe six at a pinch.

# TIPS FOR SMALL DINING ROOMS

Small is charming. There's no reason to let limited space cramp your dining style.

- Keep the palette light and limited; use contrasting color as an accent in order to bring specific elements into focus.
- Keep the window treatments simple.
- Use a modest chandelier; it will make the table seem larger.
- Consider opening up the ceiling; a tray or vaulted ceiling will make the area seem more spacious and adds the surprise of unexpected proportions.
- Mirrors increase the perception of space, use them on at least two walls.
- Choose a round table. The perimeter of the room will seem larger. Plus, you can always squeeze in an extra place setting, especially if the table has a pedestal base.
- Select chairs with delicate lines. Consider sheer slipcovers. Chairs without arms require less space to maneuver in and out of.

ABOVE: **Fool the eye and have fun: Transparent furnishings make this very small dining room seem larger than it is, cork wall covering adds an interesting texture and helps with acoustics, leaves appliquéd to the linen curtains look as if they've just blown in through the windows, and, declares the designer, "dining rooms can be very boring so you have to have one knockout piece, like this black chandelier with amber crystals."** (Alison Spear)

LEFT: **Set up like a little supper club, this California beach house dining alcove has a bright-orange leather-covered banquette, a small pedestal table, and an exotic, gold-finished vintage Moroccan lantern. Keeping it simple are shirting-stripe curtains, unlined to filter the ocean light, and the beautiful, bare, walnut floor.** (Chad Eisner)

ABOVE: **A huge mirror leaning against the far wall keeps this dining room doubly open to the kitchen and the host-cook. "It's a more human way of living and I think that's what elegance is today—comfort, functionality, and lightness without being formal," says the designer. Three styles of chairs ring the table, one slipcovered in wool with a linen skirt.** (Vicente Wolf)

# Shopping for . . . **DINING CHAIRS**

Style and comfort must partner in the chairs that ring your table.
Be as creative as you like selecting the first and test for the second.

### Style

Options are myriad and while there are sets that share the style of many traditional tables, there are no rules for what style to use—and a mix can be a fine choice too. You'll find everything from delicate to massive, from fine wood to metal and even woven paper, so consider the way the lines and proportions will balance your table and the room. Open-back, leggy styles are visually lighter than upholstered or solid shapes. Look at the stance: The splay of the legs, arms, and back may make a chair look relaxed or formal.

### Comfort

To each his own. Sit in the chair for as long as you can before buying.

### Arms or armless?

It's traditional, but not necessary, to have an armchair at the head of the table. And it's fine to use armchairs all around too—why should the host be more comfortable than the guests? Elderly people will find it easier to get in and out of an armchair.

RIGHT: **Whether for breakfast, lunch, or dinner, these commodious rattan armchairs invite diners to linger. Curved backs keep the chairs from looking crowded in this narrow space and are a nice counterpoint to the straight lines of the architecture, rug, and other furnishings.** (Suzanne Kasler)

OPPOSITE: **A set of contemporary mahogany chairs with cushioned drop-in seats has an orderly presence in this serene room, where a family with two young boys takes three meals a day.** (Christopher Maya)

## Fit

Make sure the chairs fit around your table (see The Rules of Sizing a Table on page 265). If the table is not always fully extended, decide where you'll put the extra chairs.

## Stability

Test to see that the chair is structurally sound by grasping it and twisting it gently; where to grasp depends on the style, but the legs, back, and arms should not flex away from the seat. Antique chairs may look fabulous but be too fragile for real people to sit it for any length of time, especially as people tend to tilt back at the end of meal.

## Seat

Upholstered seats should be firm yet adequately padded— you shouldn't feel the frame through the padding. Generally wood seats should be one piece, not glued up.

## Surface

Upholstery should be pleasing to touch—scratchy isn't nice on bare arms or legs; slippery is annoying. Check that rattan, rush, or similar materials are smoothly secured and won't snag clothing. Check bentwood and old wood for splits that might snag or indicate weakness. Ask about the warranty for the finish, especially with a crackle-paint finish on a country chair, which may be prone to flaking. •

# INSPIRATIONS

## Chair + Slipcover = **Attitude**

A slipcover can bring out (or mask) the personality inherent in every chair and enhance the look of your room too.

Dress it up. Tone it down. Refresh the style. Add some color. Conceal something tired. Protect the upholstery. Change the season. Wash and wear. If you need an excuse for incorporating slipcovers in your dining room, claim one of the preceding. Choose a one- or two-piece design, cover the entire chair or just the seat, make it tailored or sweet, mix fabrics for effect: Dressing a chair is like dressing yourself, what impression would you like to give? •

LEFT: **Treat a strong shape as sculpture: Covered head to toe in plain, dark smoky linen, these high-back chairs sit with monastic composure alongside a large rustic table.** (Kay Douglass)

ABOVE: **Add character: Tall chairs look demure and ready for tea dressed in soft-hued chintz with neat pleated skirts that show just the right amount of leg.** (Justine Cushing)

RIGHT, TOP: **Enhance the impact: Blue-and-white floral garland slipcovers with wonderfully shaped skirts are like "icing on the icing" on these extraordinary antique chairs; they were designed to loosen up the chairs and make them look more casual.** (Diamond Baratta)

RIGHT: **Pair a classic shape with simple design in fabric that makes your point: Plain two-piece covers in three colors of summery striped Indian cotton show off the lines of these dining chairs and capture the spirit of the adjacent garden.** (Myra Hoefer)

# The Choice Is Yours: **VASES**

Take your pick: single posy size or large enough for an armful of blooms. Keep centerpieces low, make side displays as full blown as you like.

ABOVE: **Diminutive in size and light-hearted in concept, this dining area is summer-porch fresh in bright white and soft green, with a delectable still life hung on the paneled wall, a marble-topped curly-based console standing in for a sideboard, a chunky pedestal table lightened up by white paint, and casual wicker side chairs with tied-on cushions.** (Abby Yozell)

# TABLESCAPE

## LUNCH FOR FOUR

House Beautiful editor-at-large Senga Mortimer set this simple romantic table. Dazzling! Here's how to get the look.

**To make flowers really pop, contrast the color of the bouquet with the color of the vase.**

Don't let broken stems go to waste. Put them in short glasses and you'll have more color on your table.

**Mix glass with cut crystal—but only in the same color.**

When choosing table linens, don't stray too far from the overall palette.

## Make It Your Own:

**BLUE GLASS DECANTERS**
Use decanters to serve water. Serving accessories make the meal more of an event.

**HOTEL SILVER**
Vintage hotel silver feels rich and old. Mix and match pieces for more personality.

**BLUE-AND-WHITE NAPKINS**
Pretty, machine-washable cotton floral napkins make everyday meals special.

**BLUE GLASS PLATES**
Glass plates layer readily with old china patterns, making the table feel fresh and contemporary.

# PULL IT TOGETHER

Once you've chosen a look for your dining room, organize and edit your visual resources so you can make a plan and implement it. Pull out your clipping and sample files and spread the contents on a table. Add photos of any furnishings you already own. Sort the pieces until you find a mix that spells *bon appétit*. Make a file or collage of your selection so you can refer to it as needed or share it with a designer. Note anything that's missing or for which your reference isn't quite what you'd like. If you are working with a designer, you'll have his or her insight and resources at your command; if you are working alone, you can continue your search and ask retailers for assistance.

### Ambience

Choose the key words that describe the look you want for your dining room and the proportions of the space—elegant, rustic, urban and hip, candlelit, airy, intimate, petite, grand— whatever they may be.

### Color

Decide upon the palette and determine how the colors will be used. If you'd like pattern, how will it be introduced?

### Walls

Have you a special wall treatment in mind? A mural or a hand-painted decorative effect? Wallpaper? Is there paneling or wainscoting? Is there a fireplace? What color will the walls be?

### Floor

Is the floor wood or stone or perhaps tile? Will it be carpeted? Will it add color, texture or pattern? Will chairs slide easily on it? Are you concerned about spills staining it?

### Rug

Are you planning to place a rug under the table? Doing so can add warmth, tie the look together, and muffle sounds. Multi-color, allover patterns mask spills, stripes can be used to make the room look wider or longer.

### Window treatments

Choose window treatments that provide nighttime privacy. Any style will work, from simple roller shades to fancy swag-topped drapes, so go with whatever suits your décor.

### Lighting fixtures

Choose a chandelier, lantern, or other pendant fixture that complements the ambience you wish to create. Consider two fixtures if the table is long. Add lamps or sconces to wash the walls with gentle light; be sure there is a way to illuminate the sideboard and, if you wish, any display cabinets or art.

### Furniture

At the least, you need a table and chairs. A sideboard can provide storage and extra surface for serving. Other cabinets or a secretary can add interest and display accessories. Consider the style lines, visual weight, and size of the pieces: Your dining furniture will automatically create a composition.

### Accessories

Mirrors enlarge the perceived space and play with the light; choose frames that complement your look. Think about the role you'd like art to play and note the wall space available. Choose decorative serving pieces, knife boxes, decanters, candlesticks or candelabra, topiaries or potted plants.

### Layout

Even if you're not feeling ready to do a real floor plan, it's smart to do something rough that can serve as a reality check for the amount and scale of the furniture. Draw the outline of the room on graph paper; mark the windows and doorways. Make some paper cutouts of the furniture in the same scale and position them. Does everything fit with enough room to walk around?

OPPOSITE: **Dressy traditional style rules in this dining room: The palette of burnished gold, rust, and brown glows warmly, the wall covering is an elegant damask pattern, the furnishings are formal but given a light, contemporary twist with sheer slipcovers on the side chairs, and with the black frame peeking out from its crystal drops, the chandelier adds balance as well as sparkle above the table.** (Kathy Smith)

# MAKING THE MOST OF. . .
# OUTDOOR LIVING SPACES

Think of a porch, patio, or terrace as an extension of your living space that can be as stylish, comfortable, and enjoyable as the interior of your home. When you approach the design of these spaces, begin with the same sort of questions you'd ask about any other part of your home—what is the nature of the space, how do you want to use it, and what would you like it to look like? Then as you pull it together, think about the way the outdoor area relates to the interior, what it looks like from inside and from elsewhere on your property or from the street, and don't get so focused on the furnishings that you forget the locale—take advantage of sunrise, sunset, moonlight, a water view, visiting birds, and the sounds of nature.

LEFT: **Nothing beats a front-porch swing when you need a lazy place to while away the hours, wait for company to call, or keep an eye on the doings of the neighborhood. Add bright pillows for fun and comfort.** (Myra Hoefer)

OPPOSITE: **This enclosed porch wraps a seaside family cottage and is perfectly sized to hold several sitting areas. Comfortable wicker and rattan furniture, summery floral fabrics, and matchstick window shades give this cool green and soft white spot a classic, casual summerhouse look.** (Markham Roberts)

### Public or private?

What is the setting of your home? Is screening your outdoor living spaces an issue? If you're in a neighborhood of individual houses, are front porches part of the social scene? If your home is isolated in a rural setting, are there terraces or porches adjacent to bedrooms or baths where you'd like privacy?

### Adjacent or removed?

It's easy to visualize a porch or deck that's architecturally linked to your home, or a terrace that's simply a step down from an interior living space, but there's no reason to limit the location this way. A separate pergola, gazebo, or terrace can be a destination in your landscape. Is there a pond, stream, pool, glade, or other feature of your property where you'd like to spend time?

### Covered or open?

Is there a roof on your outdoor living space? Or a beamed structure that supports vines? Is the area sunny or shaded? Are there screens or glazed windows? Will you want an awning or umbrellas or window shades? Is this an all-weather porch, or three-season, or for dry weather in summer only? Is there a combination of covered and open space?

## Grand or intimate?

How large is the space and how much of your life can be enjoyably lived on it?

## Sitting, lounging, sleeping, cooking?

What activities will you pursue? Create a layout that flows well, with conversation areas, space to dine, room to party or chat intimately as works for you. Do you envision a complete outdoor kitchen, a simple portable grill, or something in between?

Style and amenity: Choose a look you love to guide your furnishing and color choices. Honor the style of your home and the nature of your landscape, or indulge a fantasy. Consider the effects of rain, snow, wind, and sun—will you need to protect your furnishings or not want to be bothered? Provide lighting for the space and light the landscape too if that will enhance your experience. •

ABOVE: **A large portico makes a gracious outdoor room. This one gives "a nod to old Hollywood" with fluted columns, an iron railing, diamond-pattern tile floor, bold black-and-white striped pillows, and several small tables for intimate meals, cocktails, or tea.** (David Jimenez)

LEFT: **Taking advantage of an amenable climate where more time is spent outside than in, this terrace is truly an outdoor living room: it is set up with comfortable seating arranged around a coffee table and focused on a monumental fireplace. "The key component to beautiful outdoor rooms," says the designer, "is creating drama."** (Jeff Andrews)

OPPOSITE: **It's glorious to dine under or view from afar, and it grows like a weed, so don't hesitate to set your heart on a wisteria canopy if you've a large terrace to shade.** (Myra Hoefer)

# What's key in your dream kitchen?

☐ Commercial equipment
☐ Copious counter space
☐ Room for my friends
☐ An old-fashioned pantry
☐ A sink with a view
☐ A breakfast nook

# 14. KITCHENS

OPPOSITE: **Whimsical details impart a lighthearted air to this kitchen. The hammered zinc stove hood mimics a scalloped fabric canopy, the finial-topped cabinets look like little temples, and the ceiling is papered in a playful bird-cage pattern that picks up the olive-oil color of the subway tile backsplash. Fun touches aside, the center island finishes in a handsome breakfast bar, the range is meant for serious cooking, and a prep sink supplements the cleanup area not in view.** (John Oetgen)

Are you a serious cook? Is food prep a social activity in your home? Do you prefer a room that's crisp and commercial or one that's informal or homey? How much space do you have, and do you plan to increase it? Is your kitchen open to another room or enclosed? What sort of daylight is there?

These are just some of the questions to ask yourself as you plan your kitchen—after all, it's a room that has to work hard as well as look divine, and depending on the way you cook, it may be a private spot or one you share with your spouse, children, or everyone who visits. For every aesthetic choice you make—wood, stainless steel, marble, granite, white, blue, roosters, harlequin—you're likely to have a practical issue to resolve as well—floor plan, fuel, plumbing, access, and budget each comes into play. If you feel your eyes glazing now, relax. You needn't resolve these issues yourself; a professional kitchen designer or an interior designer will bring knowledge as well as creativity to the job. Engaging a pro is likely to be cost-effective and allows you to concentrate on identifying the things that will make you happy when you cook: If you understand what you want you can effectively share them with someone who can bring them to life.

# COOK'S DOMAIN.
## Planning a Kitchen.

Before you spend too much time dreaming about what you want it to look like, take stock of the way you use your kitchen. How large is the room? How many cooks are there? Are they skilled or really just watching? What kind of cooking do you do? Do you bake? Prepare fresh food from scratch? Do you feed a lot of people? Will you need two ovens? Two dishwashers? A refrigerator with lots of drawer space for produce? A stand-alone freezer in addition to the refrigerator freezer compartment? A sizable pantry for whole grains, dried beans, and other staples? What kind of equipment do you need to store—large roasting pans and lobster pots? Pastry tins in every known size and shape, along with cake decorating gear? Electric standing mixer? Espresso machine? Should there be a library area for your cookbook collection? How do you handle recyclables and compost? Is the kitchen a social gathering place for your family and friends? Is it large enough to include an eating area? Does it double as homework central or your flower arranging studio?

Let yourself dream big. Later, if reality imposes limits on your dreams, you can edit them, but if you don't put something on your wish list, you or whoever designs the space won't know to accommodate it. An efficient kitchen is designed with work areas that are ideal for specific tasks and it can be difficult to reconfigure them once the layout is planned and the cabinets ordered; even wiring changes can be tricky or costly once the walls are closed. This is equally true in large and small kitchens; large ones are likely to have more individualized spaces and are more challenging to set up with short traffic routes, small ones have to be tightly organized to accommodate as much as possible.

When you answer the question "how big is the space?" think vertically in addition to noting the square footage. Over-counter cabinets can provide lots of storage, they can also make a room seem closed in or smaller, and to some extent they cut into the usefulness of the counter below. You may like a cozy look or have an inherently spacious room, but if neither is the case and you need the storage space, consider using open shelves or cabinets with glass doors to provide at least some of it; you'll perceive both as lighter and more open than closed cabinets. If daylight is an issue, discuss it with your designer so she can suggest ways to maximize storage without sacrificing windows. Unless the room is very narrow, it's often possible to include an island for storage and work surface and maybe even a breakfast bar.

While a great deal of the style and ambience will come from the specific cabinet and appliance choices you make, accessories are also important to think about early in your planning. For one thing, if you decorate your kitchen with cooking gear, it will look busier than if you keep all the small equipment out of sight—two equally good options, just different in effect. Additionally, you may have things you love that could set the tone in your kitchen—a collection of yellowware, pretty plates, or majolica teapots, framed bistro menus, windowsill herbs, funky potholders from the 1940s—if you do, acknowledge them in the palette and make sure there is a place to display them. And if your kitchen is open to other rooms, you'll want to approach it in tandem with the adjacent spaces to ensure the view into the kitchen shares or complements their aesthetic.

It's easy to spend a great deal of money on a kitchen. Should you have to compromise, ask your designer and contractor for advice on which things are difficult to upgrade later and which easy. It usually makes sense to buy the best cabinets you can afford, with thoughtfully designed interiors; on the other hand, countertops can be changed later. Most appliances come in standard sizes so they too can be upgraded. It may or may not be easy to replace the floor.

ABOVE: **Wide open spaces, a huge island with stools on two sides, and a glass breakfast alcove with the most beautiful banquette make this a place where everyone wants to hang out. There are two distinct work areas instead of just one based on the conventional triangle: On the left is command central for all the cooking; under the hood there's a prep sink next to the range, and at each end a slender refrigerator hides behind cabinet doors. On the right is the cleanup zone, with a big sink under the windows and two dishwashers.** (Sally Markham)

RIGHT: **Opened to the adjacent dining area so as not to isolate the cook, this 1920s Manhattan apartment kitchen goes loftlike with sleek, alternating laminate and stainless steel cabinets standing tall between the windows, a single oversize shade on the pendant light fixture, and a counter-high marble-topped table with turned wood legs extending from the sink island. The slot-back stools are companions to the armchair at the dining table.** (Vicente Wolf)

OPPOSITE: **Pieds-à-terre are not known for spaciousness, and this city pad is no exception. Making the best of a small footprint, the galley kitchen has a refrigerator, freezer, and dishwasher all tucked under the counter on one side, the range is centered on the opposite side (not shown). Instead of upper cabinets, which would close in the space, chunky wood shelves have just the right heft and add some warmth.** (Ina Garten)

# ROOMS WE LOVE

What's your kitchen style? Crisp and contemporary, with sleek, dark cabinets and black granite countertops? Classic white, but with stainless commercial appliances? Like a turn-of-the-century English manor kitchen, with lots of open space, bin-pull hardware, tile or butcher block countertops, and a fireplace surround at the range? Something rustic, with distressed cabinetry and a painted floor? Something Mediterranean, with great multi-color tiles lining the walls and an ornate carved island? However modest or grand your plans, decide on a look that will make you happy while you cook, whether your menu requires starting from scratch or opening takeout containers. As you browse through the photos of kitchens we love, keep two different things in mind: the ambience and the kitchen layout. There are lots of good ideas for both here, and you may wish to mix them in new ways.

OPPOSITE: **Vintage 1930s hanging fixtures, classic cabinetry, and an apron sink belie the age of this new kitchen. The ceiling is 10 feet high, allowing a second tier of top cabinets. Says the designer about the pattern of moldings overhead: "I thought the room would be cozier if I gave it a strong ceiling, one that would minimize its verticality."** (Nancy Boszhardt)

BELOW: **This row house kitchen is tidily outfitted with all the essentials. The owners tried a cabinet island in the middle of the small space but it "looked like a behemoth." The old table that replaced it offers just as much work surface and, being leggy rather than closed in, looks much lighter; previously used by an artist, it's full of scars and no one worries about staining or scratching it.** (Chad Eisner)

LEFT: The ultimate spot for a collector who loves to cook, loves old, and can't buy just one, this kitchen was designed to look as though it had been here for ages and to show off the pottery, milk pails (overhead), and cream pails (on the windowsill) the owner finds irresistible. The massive, hand-carved island was inspired by one seen in France; it features a marble inlay surrounding a cooktop with a pop-up downdraft (an overhead hood would spoil the view). Three tips for display: Quantity is quality; almost anything can be interesting if you have enough examples. Pottery offers an easy way to introduce color. Group objects so you can get a snapshot of the collection with one glance. (Hilary Musser)

ABOVE: Muted colors, strong architectural details, surfaces both aged and polished, and state-of-the-art convenience place this kitchen smartly on the line between rustic and sophisticated. At the back, framed in a massive, hooded stone surround, a commercial range is paired with a wood-burning firepit. Twin islands offer plenty of work space, with sinks at opposite ends. (Susan Ferrier)

LEFT: **Good design makes a virtue of the limited space in this city apartment kitchen, stylishly incorporating a peaceful church-yard view on two sides as well as all the culinary necessities. Sliding glass doors on the upper cabinets reflect the view and seem to enlarge the space (note how the glass turns the corner on the end cupboard); the rod between the tiers supports a rolling ladder for easy access. On the cooking side, everything is stepped out from the wall and left open above the backsplash to take advantage of the window.** (Kathryn Scott)

LEFT, BOTTOM: **At the center of this large, sunny beach-house kitchen stands a rustic worktable with stature to match its setting. It has a mix of open shelves and deep drawers, and has been plumbed with two sinks and topped with a white marble slab. The near sink is accessed from the stove side and features a faucet with a long, flexible neck. The far sink is accessed from the opposite side of the room, where there's a large dining table.** (Waldo Fernandez)

OPPOSITE: **Black cabinets—lower only—have a quiet, graphic stance in this all-white room with a dramatic raised ceiling. The island cabinet sits on delicate legs like a credenza and has elevated trays for sushi, hors d'oeuvres, or display along the nonworking edge. Along the wall the cabinets are topped with stainless steel with an integral sink; small, black floating shelves and an interesting internal pivoting window call attention to the room's lofty proportions.** (Mallory Marshall)

OPPOSITE: **A mix of old and new makes things interesting. Huge, fun, and all marble, a vintage ice cream counter has been recycled and paired with stainless steel open shelves on industrial brackets to provide storage in this contemporary kitchen. White subway tile puts a classic finish on the wall; an antique farm table and vintage chairs provide a complementary breakfast area.** (Joan Schindler)

RIGHT, TOP AND BOTTOM: **This kitchen/family room combo is all about being multipurpose, with a seamless blend of space. To play down the culinary area, cabinets are stained nearly black to disappear and merge with the floor and, viewed from the sitting area, the island looks like a console. Great ideas here: The cabinets are topped with Carrara marble— "simple, inexpensive, and reminds me of those candy shops where they knead fudge," says the designer/owner, who likes the contrast of light against dark, and the two drafting tables that create the island topped with frosted glass. "Nothing stains it, not even red wine."** (Eldon Wong)

ABOVE: **Although there's a lot going on in this busy kitchen, it seems composed. To balance the handmade blue-and-white tiles above the range and the upholstery of the chairs in the adjacent breakfast area, the oak cabinets were cerused (limed) to turn them a quiet beige, the wood floors were ebonized, and honed black marble was used for the counters and backsplashes. Curtains in the glass doors keep the upper cabinets neat but light.** (Alessandra Branca)

ABOVE: **Where's the kitchen? Dominating this modern room, and most certainly not found at the kitchen cabinet shop, is a pair of arched, tall, rustic cupboards with heavy wrought-iron hinges. They add character and color and help to make this a living space with a culinary department rather than the reverse.** (Kay Douglass)

RIGHT: **Inspiration: Classic English butler's pantry. Recipe: New cabinets, typical bin pulls and cupboard latches, new appliances, and everything else is old. The source: Internet searches uncovered salvaged marble countertops, a recycled gnarly wood counter for the island, reclaimed flooring and subway tile. The fun: putting it all together.** (Brenda Kelly Kramer)

# KITCHEN ISLANDS:
## Extra Space, Extra Style.

Space permitting, an island may be just the spot for a sink, cooktop, dishwasher, or stools for snackers and helpers. If you've a large open area, a commodious island will be endlessly useful, but if your space is small, an island that's just as large as possible will still be an asset. You can tie the design to your cabinetry and incorporate appliances, seating, or a sink, or introduce a contrast with a table-like look, an industrial wire configuration, or fine carved wood—or just choose a different color. Top your island with wood, stone, tile, or a synthetic material. You'll never regret the convenience and social center it adds to your workspace.

ABOVE: **Create a center of attention with architectural details such as the turned columns that frame this island; make it work for you too, with a kneehole for stools and a good size prep sink near, but not at, one corner.** (Healing Barsanti)

LEFT: **To keep it light and have storage too, go for a table island fitted with shelves and drawers. This kitchen enjoys two, pushed together as one.** (Robin Bell)

OPPOSITE: **Repeat the cabinet style and palette to maintain the overall mood when introducing a large island. In this new Vermont farmhouse a spare aesthetic and whitewashed palette with black accents set a peaceful tone.** (Susan Tully)

# THE RULES OF . . .

## KITCHEN CLEARANCE

Here are some standards that make a kitchen easy to move in and keep the accoutrements accessible.

- The minimum width of the aisle between work counters is 42 inches; this allows space to open appliances and cabinet doors and drawers and access the contents. For two cooks, allow at least 48 inches.

- Allow at least 32 inches between a table and wall; this is tight. Thirty-six inches allows someone to edge past a seated diner; 44 inches is enough for someone to walk past.

- Standard countertop height is 36 inches. Eating counters paired with stools may be as high as 42 inches; paired with chairs they should be 30 inches high (standard table height).

- Ideal height for the bottom of an upper cabinet is 54 inches above the floor (18 inches above the countertop).

- The ideal height for a top shelf is 72 inches above the floor.

LEFT: **Get ready to multitask at this island—there's room for several cooks to work at once, a dishwasher, and a prep sink. Marble tops one end (it won't get funky from the water and can't be beat for rolling out pastry) and butcher block tops the other.** (Carol Lalli)

RIGHT: **Indulge your inner minimalist and go streamlined. This large island offers nothing but glorious open space—for the cook, the kids' homework, and brunch. Sexy white stools beckon in front of the multiple grays and square edges.** (Alexander Adducci)

# Colorful Opinions: **A SUNNY KITCHEN**

You're ready to break away from the white, but what color should you choose for your kitchen? We asked the experts to help out.

**PAULA PERLINI:**
**BENJAMIN MOORE**
**WARM SIENNA 1203**
Might as well make it cozy. Everybody comes in anyway, you can't beat them out with a spoon. Plates would look great on a wall against this warm cayenne, and I'd do teak countertops and cork on the floor—very soft and warm to bare feet.

**JOANNE HUDSON:**
**SHERWIN-WILLIAMS**
**WHOLE WHEAT SW6121**
It's the color of golden brown sugar. Very appetizing, with a lot of warmth. I'd use it on the walls with white trim, custard-colored cabinets, and a terra-cotta floor.

WEDGEWOOD GRAY

**CLARE DONOHUE:**
**BENJAMIN MOORE**
**WEDGEWOOD GRAY HC-146 AND**
**WOODLAWN BLUE HC-147**
Wedgewood Gray for the walls and Woodlawn Gray for the ceiling; they have that robin's egg vibe. I always hedge my bets toward grayed-down shades, because bright colors that look so happy in the paint store can look bizarre in real life. If you're nervous, start by painting the back wall inside the cabinets.

WOODLAWN BLUE

**BEVERLY ELLSLEY:**
**BENJAMIN MOORE**
**GOLDEN HONEY 297**
Kitchens often have so little wall space you have to make the color count. This is sunshine in a can. I like yellow with a little bit of brown in it, as opposed to a yellow with green. Looks wonderful with wood.

**MARK CUTLER:**
**FINE PAINTS OF EUROPE**
**P1130**
I have one of those little green boxes from Ladurée, that Paris pastry shop, on my desk. Turns out my client has one too and we re-created that Ladurée green on her kitchen island. It's an incredibly complex color, a weird combination of yellow and green with this red undertone. Beautiful.

**PHILIP GORRIVAN:**
**BENJAMIN MOORE**
**RAZZLE DAZZLE 1348**
Pick one wall. Apply two coats of Rust-Oleum Magnetic primer, paint this yummy raspberry color, and then put up your children's artwork, school schedules, and birthday invites with magnets.

**BARCLAY BUTERA:**
**RALPH LAUREN**
**CREAM STONE UL54 AND**
**WEATHERED BROWN UL44**
Home Depot Expo Design Center has some great cabinet options. Paint them Cream Stone, a muted off-white, more gray than yellow. Then use rich, taupey Weathered Brown on the walls for contrast. It makes the kitchen a little more masculine, a little more sophisticated.

**SANDRA NUNNERLEY:**
**BENJAMIN MOORE**
**WOLF GRAY 2127-40**
I'm so tired of those off-white cabinets. I'd paint them this dark Swedish gray-blue, and make the room very Gustavian, with chalky white walls, Carrara marble countertops, and stainless steel appliances.

**MICK DE GIULIO:**
**BENJAMIN MOORE**
**GREAT BARRINGTON GREEN**
**HC-122**
Especially in a small kitchen, people don't think of dark colors as an option, but that's exactly where you need the drama. This is a lovely gray-green, not too dark and very soft, kind of like moss. Very elegant with white cabinets.

**ANN MCGUIRE:**
**VALSPAR**
**SPRING SQUASH 2008-1B**
You're taking a chance with orange, but it can be fabulous. It's playful during the day for kids doing projects, and at night, with the lamps lit, it glows. Start with one wall—that may be enough.

**JASON BELL:**
**PRATT & LAMBERT**
**TAMPICO 1411**
In an old kitchen where the cabinets, counters, and appliances were all mismatched shades of white, we needed a distraction. So we painted just the doors, not the frames, of the cabinets this teal-green aquamarine and replaced the cheap white plastic knobs with vintage hardware. Last touch—a black-and-white tile floor.

**ERICA BROBERG:**
**BENJAMIN MOORE**
**MERLOT RED 2006-10**
Red is energizing, invigorating, and this is the perfect red, not too orange and not too blue. It works equally well in sunny or dark rooms and really sets off the cabinets, which we order primed and then paint on-site with a nice, brushed finish.

# BREAKFAST IN STYLE:
## Eat-In Kitchens.

If there's room for an eating area in your kitchen, choose a table and chairs that complement the cabinet style—or work the other way, and, for instance, select dressy cabinets because you know the dining furniture is on the formal side. If you opt for a chandelier or other pendant light to give character to the eating area, don't let it visually compete with the fixtures in the work area. Site the table to take advantage of windows or glass doors. And yes, you can have both an island snack bar and a separate table.

LEFT: **With so many squares and rectangles in the tin ceiling and kitchen cabinets, and a traffic pattern that demands access from every side, a round table was in order for this room. The octagon was discovered while searching for one, and suits the space even better. The white slipcovered chairs have a complementary geometry—and they're extremely comfortable.** (Jacqueline Derrey Segura)

OPPOSITE: **A formal table and chairs tucked into the pantry side of the large, English-style kitchen on page 295 make informal meals feel special.** (Brenda Kelly Kramer)

ABOVE: **Breakfast, lunch, or dinner for eight is no problem in this large, open kitchen/dining area, where a long table embraced by low-back chairs suits the space. The driftwood finish on the table is perfect for the beach locale; all the whites make the space airy. Open shelves on the blue tiled wall at the back keep the room from dead-ending in a phalanx of cabinets.** (Jodi Macklin)

OPPOSITE: **Country home, country kitchen, country table: Nestled between French doors and a work station, this hefty trestle table partners well with more delicate bistro chairs. Pretty floor too.** (Karen Cohen and Ani Antreasyan)

# CABINETS ARE KEY.
## What Style Will You Use?

Traditional panel doors? Victorian beadboard? Totally plain? Rustic? Glass inserts? Cabinets are the principal furniture in a kitchen; their design details, the material they're made from, and the color used have greater impact on the overall look than anything else.

There are two basic types of cabinets: frameless (sometimes called Eurostyle) and framed. The doors and drawers on frameless cabinets abut and appear nearly seamless. The case structure of framed cabinets is more apparent; the doors and drawers are either inset to be flush with the frame, or overlapped on it. Doors and drawers for both types may be paneled or plain; the plainer they are, the sleeker the look.

Both framed and frameless cabinets can be found in many materials, colors, and finishes. Pulls and knobs have a lot of impact on the overall effect too. Check out the interior options before you order—pull-out interior shelves, full-extension drawer hardware, trash receptacle drawers, utensil dividers, and all manner of nifty conveniences are available. Also decide if you want matching panels to conceal your refrigerator or dishwasher. Many vendors offer stock cabinets, which come in standard sizes that can be configured however you need, others have stock designs but can customize the sizes; independent cabinetmakers will build to suit your design.

LEFT: **Grooved recessed panel doors have a retro country charm that pairs well with beadboard walls and an apron sink. These happen to be vintage, freshened with soft white paint and new hardware and updated with a marble countertop and new basin; new ones aren't hard to come by.** (Eldon Wong)

OPPOSITE, LEFT TOP: **Plan ahead for open shelves that store your stuff as neatly as these, which incorporate a plate rack section and look great with the patterned tiles peeking from behind the dishes too. The lower cabinets have classic raised panel doors with bead detail and small decorative pulls.** (Erin Martin)

OPPOSITE, RIGHT TOP: **If you're looking for subtle and serene that are plain and simple but not boring, consider the Zen appeal of oak slab drawers, limed to wash out the color and topped by softly figured Carrara marble, plus basic white shelves that float on white walls. White dishes required—colors will punch up this look.** (Betsy Brown)

OPPOSITE, LEFT BOTTOM: **These Eurostyle cabinets stack up sleekly to make a nearly seamless wall, their long bar handles adding silvery punctuation to the dark oak finish. In the back on the left is an appliance garage—a stainless steel tambour door that rolls up to reveal a niche topped with small drawers and a shelf above the counter.** (Carol Lalli)

OPPOSITE, RIGHT BOTTOM: **These cabinets line the walls in a hallway butler's pantry. On the top, window-like divided-light glass doors slide sideways to give access; on the bottom, the swing-out doors are faced with fake drawer fronts (complete with bin pull hardware) because the horizontal lines are pleasing in the space—but cabinets with shelves suit the owner's needs better than drawers.** (Joan Schindler)

# The Choice Is Yours: **KNOBS**

A twist of a screw, and you've got a whole new look. See what a difference a knob makes—it can change the entire personality of a room.

# AUXILIARY SPACE?
## Create a Pantry.

Designate a closet, small ell, or even an adjacent room to supplement your kitchen. Pantries are at least partially concealed from the main work area, so utilitarian features can rule with ease; this is the ideal place to store staples and oversize or infrequently needed pans and appliances. Depending on the space available and your needs, set up yours for storage only or put in a sink and relegate the cleanup station or the coffee bar to it as well; if your culinary habits warrant it, you can even outfit a pantry with a second cooktop or oven. If the primary purpose of a pantry is to store tableware, locate it near the dining room.

LEFT: **Who would think a plain simple cupboard would hold such a surprise? It's like a walk-in closet, with an entire baking station inside along with storage for staples. Good ideas: the metal rack mounted on each door and pullout shelves fitted with removable willow baskets under the marble counter.** (Mick de Giulio)

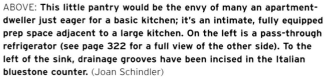

ABOVE: **This little pantry would be the envy of many an apartment-dweller just eager for a basic kitchen; it's an intimate, fully equipped prep space adjacent to a large kitchen. On the left is a pass-through refrigerator (see page 322 for a full view of the other side). To the left of the sink, drainage grooves have been incised in the Italian bluestone counter.** (Joan Schindler)

RIGHT, TOP: **Form, function, and finish: Great looks were very much part of the plan in this butler's pantry. Flanking the sink cabinet are an undercounter refrigerator and ice maker, just visible on the left is a large wine cooler, and on the right, storing china and glassware, are stock stainless steel medical cabinets installed over custom drawers. The cabinets at the end are jelly-bean green, the backsplash over the stainless counter is bamboo suspended in polymer.** (Sally Markham)

RIGHT: **Tucked in the corner of a passageway, this pantry serves as coffee center and light clean-up station (the large cabinet door on the right conceals a dishwasher). With beadboard wainscoting and ceiling, classic cabinets, and tiny hexagonal floor tiles, it has a graceful old-fashioned charm; note the marble washstand-style backsplash separating the sink from the lower windowsill.** (Judith Barrett)

RIGHT: **This sunny and capacious country pantry supplements the kitchen on page 288 with a second sink and microwave oven. Set up as a coffee station, it's large enough for all manner of prep and planning tasks and the white, tumbled subway tile walls are a bright background for the owner's colorful collections. The sink is nickel silver, the countertop a 2-inch thick slab of white marble.** (Hilary Musser)

# SUCH GREAT COUNTERTOPS.
## Which Will You Choose?

Go for a surface and color that complement your kitchen ambience. Wood countertops generally look homey or Old World; metal appears slick and industrial; tile, solid color or figured, is charming; and the diverse stone options add sophisticated and classic style. Solid synthetic materials (such as Corian) and plastic laminates (such as Formica) can be handsome and easy to care for. Concrete and glass are other great-looking options. In truth, there are so many surface finish and color options for each type that, depending on the specifics, any of these materials can be used to dress a kitchen up or down. So visit showrooms and look at photos for ideas. With the possible exception of concrete, which is colored and poured to order, you can get samples of anything that appeals to you to consider at your leisure. All countertops require a certain amount of custom work, either to be cut to size on- or off-site or to be totally fabricated to order, so don't worry about standard sizes when you are planning.

Appearance is important, but for countertops, it's not the only thing that counts. Inquire about the maintenance requirements for any countertop you're considering. Stone, tile, concrete, and solid synthetics won't be damaged by hot pans, but wood and laminates may be; wood and some stones are porous and must be sealed or waxed to protect them from stains; wood is sensitive to moisture; stone, concrete, and solid synthetics are heavy; tile can chip and the grout must be sealed; metal scratches easily. And remember, unless you're into the rustic look of beat-up butcher block, no counter material should be used for cutting— you'll ruin it or it will ruin your knife.

ABOVE: **Concrete countertops look similar to some natural stones, but they are not patterned (so never busy) and can be custom colored. They're cast to order, either on-site or at a factory; once cured they are honed or polished and sealed to resist staining. A matching sink can be integrated if you like (including a countertop vessel for a vanity), or you can use any standard basin. The unusual 2-inch thickness of this one complements the overall proportions of the large kitchen it adorns.** (Shannon Bowers)

LEFT: **Limestone gives a mellow look that suits this English-style kitchen. It's porous and many people like to seal it to preclude staining, but the owner here prefers it left natural. "I like the fact that it isn't static,"** he says, **though he admits to having it cleaned from time to time. Two other mellow touches here: the grout on the backsplash of handmade tiles is tinted to match the countertop and the faucet is silver-plated.** (Michael S. Smith)

OPPOSITE: **If you think metal countertops are limited to laboratory installation, check out the one in this retro country kitchen. It's zinc, which oxidizes naturally to a rich, monochromatic patina that contrasts gently with the stainless steel apron sink used here; it can be polished if you prefer shiny. Pewter, copper, zinc, and stainless steel are other metal countertop options. They all scratch easily, so be prepared to coddle them or love the worn-in look.** (Ruthie Sommers)

ABOVE: **Lavastone countertops can be made in any color, for instance, the brilliant turquoise matched to this harlequin tile backsplash. This material is a glazed natural stone, the colors are clear and shiny, and the finish is impervious to hot or cold—maybe that's why the French use it for road signs.** (Diamond Baratta)

ABOVE: **Butcher block is a classic countertop option that's durable, relatively inexpensive, and adds a warm look. You can choose a food-safe oil finish (sand and re-oil if damaged) or a varnish. Maple is the standard; red oak, cherry, and walnut are other readily available choices. Of this island, the designers say "everyone loves to pile in around the 10-foot maple island and chat and drink and slice and dice"; snowy marble on the other white cabinets keeps the overall effect light and in the Swedish style.** (Katrin Cargill and Carol Glasser)

RIGHT: **Admire these snappy black-edged white-tile counters? They're "the cheapest tiles we could find" applied over the original laminate counters as part of a budget redo that also included painting old oak cabinets bright white. A matching backsplash that runs up to the top cabinets adds to the graphic look.** (Craig Schumacher and Philip Kirk)

# SINKS AND FAUCETS.
## Take Your Pick.

Round, oblong, square, trough shaped, with a single, double, or triple bowl, there's a sink for every size and shape space. Enameled cast iron, stainless steel and other metals, acrylic, and various resins are common options; slab or carved stone sinks can be found or custom-made. Styles range from classic to country (apron-front) to ultra modern; options include under-mount (installed under the counter and not appropriate to use with laminate counters), drop-in (inserted on top of the counter) and tile-in. The right one is the one that complements your kitchen style, is appropriately sized, and works with the counter material you've selected—so you have lots of good choices for each sink that you need.

Faucets are stylish the way jewelry is, some flatter one sort of kitchen, some another. Look for shape, proportion, and finish; pay attention to small design details on the faucet and the control handles, they make a lot of difference and are easy to overlook. Gooseneck and pullout styles are convenient for filling tall pots. Coordinating sprayers and soap dispensers are available for some faucets. Fall in love with whichever style speaks to you, but be sure to match it to the sink, which will be predrilled to accommodate a specific faucet configuration. Of course, you might set your heart on an old-fashioned wall-mounted faucet and then choose your sink because of it.

ABOVE: **Color and material options for undermounted sinks are myriad; here the warm antique copper patina of the sink and bronze finish of the faucet and its accessories look mellow against the taupe limestone counter. A single large basin like this will hold a big baking pan or conceal a small dish drainer; multi-bowl styles are another option.** (Sandra Bird)

LEFT: **A self-rimming prep sink is a good idea for a wood countertop—preventing cutout edges from water discolored over time. Old parquet flooring tops this island ("If you can walk on it for 200 years, why can't you use it as a countertop?" comments the designer, who notes that it solves the problem of where to put seams on a large counter); the weathered copper finish on the small sink and faucet complements the warm wood tones.** (Beverly Ellsley)

RIGHT: **Stainless steel sinks have a sleek, clean look; this one is integral with its counter, which extends over the dishwasher on the right. Metal sinks are light-weight and, depending on the metal, may be quite inexpensive; better ones are backed with a soft material to help absorb the sound of utensils clattering against them. There's an ingenious floating breakfast bar in the window of this kitchen too.** (Todd Klein)

ABOVE: **A high lip and backsplash add to the old-fashioned charm of a country apron sink and keep the adjacent wall and counter dry.**

LEFT: **Use an undermounted sink to keep the lines of a countertop sleek and make cleanup easy. This white one repeats the cabinet color and looks fresh with the semi-polished bluestone around it; the silvery tone of the simple, old-fashioned faucet and sprayer is classic, soft against the figured stone background, and matches the cabinet hardware too.** (Mona Hajj)

# COOK'S ESSENTIALS:
## Major Appliances.

Appliances are essential. Without them, your home dining pleasure will be at the mercy of the local takeout restaurants. Three overall categories exist: residential, semi-commercial, and commercial. Commercial appliances look great and have terrific features, but they are costly to purchase and operate, often require more space, may be noisy, and don't necessarily make you a better cook—unless you enjoy using them so much that you spend more time in the kitchen. Style-wise, commercial and semi-commercial appliances tend to have signature looks that don't date the way residential styles do. To decide what to install, think about the kind of cooking you do and your budget. A good designer knows how to accommodate whatever you wish to use, but he or she is probably not an expert on BTUs and operating noise levels, so do your homework by visiting some appliance centers and talking with the salespeople so you are well informed on the practical as well as aesthetic considerations. This is a good time to check the operating efficiency and impact of each appliance on the environment too. It's fine to mix appliances from different manufacturers; if you are considering this, think about their aesthetic compatibility (check the handle styles) and consider adding door panels to match your cabinets. Once you have an idea of what you like, talk with your designer; you are unlikely to have the knowledge, skill, or patience to fit the pieces together—besides, he'll have access to resources you do not.

Which appliances should a great kitchen include? Refrigerator, stove, and dishwasher go without saying, most people want a microwave oven too. Check refrigerator models to be sure the drawers and shelves accommodate the kind of food you store, some hold more veggies than others. You might want to check out undercounter refrigerator drawers to supplement or replace the main unit. For cooking, decide between a one-piece range and a separate cooktop and wall oven (your layout may decide this for you, sometimes one option is more workable than the other). Few residential ranges include two ovens, so if this is important to you, go with separate pieces or plan to supplement the range with a countertop oven or a dual microwave/convection oven. Whichever way you go, investigate the options for an exhaust hood, which is not always possible over an island cooktop. Check dishwasher interiors to see that the dishes you own will fit in the racks—large plates and stemware can be problematic in some. Consider smaller, drawer dishwashers if you would like to do small loads. Nice extras (or expert's essentials) include warming drawers, a steam oven, a wine cooler, trash compactor, and a wood-fired grill and a wood-fired pizza oven (not really appliances, but still something to plan for). When you shop, open and close all appliances to see that the doors feel sturdy and substantial, the seals look businesslike, and any racks or shelves operate smoothly. If you've lots of space, you can have two of anything if it suits your needs and makes you happy.

LEFT: **If you are a sophisticated chef, you'll appreciate the specialized equipment in this kitchen: Set into a niche in the wall beyond the unusually deep commercial refrigerator/freezer are a steam oven, convection oven, and warming drawer.** (Architect: Peter Fisher)

OPPOSITE: **Undeniably handsome, a large stainless steel range like this is designed for serious cooks. This model is standard cabinet-depth, has two ovens, six burners, a griddle, lots of power even with propane (an important thing to check if that's your fuel), and a tall backguard with a shelf; a number of manufacturers and other sizes and configurations exist. Note the pot filler faucet on the wall to the left. A good exhaust hood is a must for a stove like this; here one hides inside the paneled overhang.** (Architect: Peter Fisher)

LEFT: **This substantial cooktop sits neatly surrounded by heat-proof white marble in the middle of a massive, handmade island. Control knobs on the front mean you don't pass your arm over the lighted burners when adjusting the heat. Wall ovens are nearby, opposite the island end.** (Hilary Musser)

LEFT, BOTTOM: **The quiet star of a wonderful kitchen, this pass-through refrigerator is an eight-door, double-front custom model that also can be accessed from a smaller prep room behind it. (See the full kitchen on page 164.)** (Joan Schindler)

BELOW: **Enameled cast-iron Aga cookers are unique in the way they work (always on, always ready, no control dials), come in more than two dozen colors and several sizes, and have a classic look of their own. This one seems suitably old-fashioned for its classic country kitchen setting.** (Susan Tully)

# DON'T FORGET:
## Small Appliances.

Toaster. Espresso machine. Coffee maker. Blender. Food processor. Juicer. Standing mixer. Classic designs exist for all of these and sharp new models are available for many. If small appliances are part of your culinary gear, decide whether you want to see them all the time or store them out of sight. Seems obvious, but these can eat up a lot of cabinet or counter space, so it makes sense to think about where they'll live from the outset. You might want to include an appliance garage (a cabinet with a tambour door that rolls down in front of countertop appliances). Or if you know you need cabinet storage for certain items, you can commission pullout shelves that pop up to just below countertop level for the food processor or mixer, or simply make sure that the cupboard where you'll store the blender is convenient to where you'll use it. On the other hand, if you think you've more counter space than you can possibly use, it may prompt you to acquire that espresso machine after all.

ABOVE: **A two-drawer dishwasher like the one next to the sink in this kitchen is an efficient choice for a one- or two-person home or one where all the coffee cups are dirty long before the plates are. At the end of the counter is a wine cooler. The mirror above the sink is the next best thing to a window on this interior wall.** (Phoebe Howard)

RIGHT: **Small appliances such as a coffee maker, toaster, blender, or stand mixer can be awkward or even too heavy to move in and out of a cabinet. If you don't wish to look at them sitting on your counter, consider an appliance garage—a cabinet with a tambour door that slides down to the counter to cover them. This one also conceals a shelf for the microwave, with small hanging bins on the underside.** (Carol Lalli)

# LIGHTING FIXTURES:
## Use a Mix.

Kitchen light should be bright and well focused for work and cleanup, and yet subtle and inviting for socializing. Make sure all your work areas are adequately lighted—the sinks, cooktop or range, and all the counters. If there is a pantry area without workspace, don't neglect it; you'll need to see the cabinet interiors. Because a kitchen is used in daylight and at night, multiple fixtures controlled individually or in strategic groups, and on dimmers if it suits their function, will give you the flexibility to light the entire room or just the coffee station, as you wish.

Most kitchens require a variety of fixture types; which you need depends on the size of the room, the ceiling height, and the look you prefer. Ceiling lights, either recessed or on tracks, can provide a lot of illumination and depending on their type, will be relatively unobtrusive or quite stylish. Pendant lights provide good light and instant character over an island or table; as you shop for them, remember they're likely to be one of the first things you notice in the room, whether lit on not, and choose a style, size, and color that create the effect you want. Many stove hoods incorporate lights in easy-to-clean housing. If you like, install under-cabinet fixtures to light the countertops; most cabinets are constructed to conceal these, but it's smart to check for this. If there's a reading area or desk in your kitchen, you can use a table lamp if it suits the look. Talk to your designer about lighting; it isn't always easy to plan.

ABOVE: **The island in the middle of this eat-in kitchen is long and the room is large, prompting the designer to want a "huge gesture" over the island. He had two double-size lanterns custom made; their dark color balances the green below.** (T. Keller Donovan)

LEFT: **Hidden behind the mantel over this stove is an exhaust hood. Its built-in lamps keep the cooking area bright and bring out the detail of the whimsical trompe l'oeil wall painting.** (Jamie Gottschall)

OPPOSITE: **There wasn't room in this house for both a large kitchen and a dining room, so this room serves as both. Unobtrusive recessed ceiling lights illuminate the work areas and large table and have no impact on sightlines.** (Betsy Brown)

ABOVE: **Caged sconces designed for exterior use add an industrial accent to the tiled wall above this counter—no broken glass if that flexible pre-rinse spray faucet gets away from you.** (Judith Barrett)

OPPOSITE: **The French factory lights that illuminate this honed granite countertop have ribbed lenses that "just glow." Their graphic, workaday look suits the utilitarian room with its surprising red wall, crisp metal and frosted glass cabinets, and floating shelf.** (Amanda Kyser)

# DESIGNER'S TOP TEN

Designer Gary Paul reveals how to make your kitchen function to the max and still look stylish.

**1.** Zone the kitchen according to functions and account for every task. This includes food preparation, eating, cleanup and storage. Don't forget areas for taking a coffee break, surfing the Net, dining alone, or entertaining a group. A good design will accommodate all of these functions.

**2.** Create a kitchen for entertaining. I always imagine the cook is giving a star performance and that dicing onions, stirring, and sautéing are equivalent to the delivery of a monologue or an aria. The idea is to enchant the audience until dinner is served.

**3.** If you're considering construction, I recommend installing new windows, which give focus to the interior as well as providing light and outside views.

**4.** I like honed stone for countertops, it's softer to the touch and less glaring than highly polished stone. Glass or high-glazed ceramic backsplash tiles bounce light and add color and pattern.

**5.** Don't be afraid to embellish on a theme. For a house located on a former chicken farm, I commissioned a chandelier depicting hens laying eggs.

**6.** Display your collections. Majolica plates, ironstone jugs, decorative cookie jars, and teapots all personalize your space.

**7.** Raise the ceiling. Varied ceiling heights create and define separate areas within one space. In one project I opened the kitchen ceiling to expose the pitched roof above. Dormer windows were added, and now the morning sun floods the room.

**8.** Regarding flooring, weigh the good and the bad: ceramic tiles have a luxurious glaze but are hard on the feet; wood is soft to walk on but requires more maintenance.

**9.** It's your home—keep the lighting warm and inviting.

**10.** Think green when possible.

OPPOSITE AND ABOVE: **A little Italian, a little French country, this California kitchen enjoys a mix of Old World materials, warm colors, and great amenity. In the middle is a large column full of electrical wires and plumbing pipes that could not be relocated; instead the designer worked around it, putting the range on one side, a buffet for the dining table, a desk, and a baking area each on the other sides, and wrapping the whole with a galvanized metal hood modeled after one she saw in Paris. There are several work areas in the room, each spaced so as not to bump into the others, with a total of three sinks. Opposite the drawers in the freestanding worktable is a wood-burning pizza oven in a tiled chimney—it's just visible in the photo of the desk.** (Sandra Bird)

# PULL IT TOGETHER

Your kitchen is clear in your mind and you can't wait to start cooking. It's time to plan the specifics. Pull out your clipping and sample files, including any cabinet and appliance brochures, and spread the contents on a table. Select the pieces you like the best and check the mix to see if it's close to your dream look. Unless you're in a do-it-yourself mode, don't worry if you don't have the perfect reference for each element—your goal is to create an annotated collage of ideas that you can share with the design pros who will bring your kitchen to life. If there's something eluding you, just note it as a question to be discussed with your designer.

## Ambience

Choose the key words that describe your dream kitchen—classic, retro, country, urbane, professional, charming, all white, bright, gleaming, efficient—whatever they may be.

## Layout

It's probably too early for a real floor plan, but do give some thought to the overall size and shape of your room. There's no point in planning a giant island in a ten-foot-wide room. Make a scale drawing on graph paper if you'd like to rough out a plan.

## Color

Think of the overall palette, for instance, all natural wood tones, and also the color of specific elements like the floor, walls, cabinets, and appliances. Consider what role pattern should play.

## Cabinets

What style do you like? What color? Will they all be alike, or will you use a mix of open and closed storage? Will there be an island? What style knobs will you use?

## Countertops

What material do you favor? Will you use a mix? Does the color work with your cabinets and floor? If using natural or faux stone, look at a large sample so you can judge the busyness and impact of the pattern.

## Appliances

Which do you want in addition to stove, refrigerator, and dishwasher? Have you chosen the style and finish? Will you install door panels to match your cabinets?

## Sinks and faucets

How many sinks do you need? Have you chosen the size, style, and material for each? Do they work with your countertop? Does the faucet complement your look and work the way you like?

## Floor

What material will give you the look you're after? Can it be laid in a pattern and do you wish to use it that way? Will it be comfortable to stand on and easy to clean?

## Lighting fixtures

Will you use decorative or unobtrusive fixtures? Consider the color, finish, and scale of whatever you choose as well as the style. Will they take energy-efficient bulbs? Will they work with dimmers?

## Walls

How much wall shows? Do you favor paint or wallpaper, or have some other treatment in mind? Will you use tile for backsplashes or wainscoting?

## Window treatments

They're optional in a kitchen. Use them for privacy or to complete your look. If they're near cooking stations, keep them simple and easy to clean.

OPPOSITE: **Lots of daylight, charcoal cabinets, a blue enamel range, and a rustic wood island, painted red, give this kitchen a comfortable country ambience that softens the state-of-the-art setup. The cabinets are brushed steel, an expanse of stainless steel fitted with utensil racks gives a professional finish to the wall between the upper and lower cabinets, stove, and exhaust hood, and wall ovens ensure that a variety of roasting and baking can be accommodated simultaneously. The deep windowsill adds a handy shelf above the sink and counter. Factory-style overhead lights balance the dark tones below.** (Paul Siskin)

# MAKING THE MOST OF. . .
# OPEN-PLAN LIVING SPACES

How pleasant it is to have kitchen, dining, and sitting rooms all in one open space—and how challenging too. Open plan living spaces are great for social interaction and for dispelling any sense of cramped quarters, however, when you decorate one, you've got to think about a lot all at once. If you find this a bit daunting, take comfort: Many professional designers feel the same way. One we know mentioned a "not-so-great room"; others acknowledged it's sometimes difficult to get the right scale, balance, and harmony of disparate furnishings in a very large room. On the other hand, perhaps there are fewer color and style decisions to make. Think about the function of each area and the flow within and between them, and choose a look you love that works for all three.

LEFT AND OPPOSITE: **In this beach house great hall, the kitchen, dining area, and living room flow together. Facing each other across the fireplace are two conversation areas with matching sofas. Around the dining table, two styles of chairs preclude a conference room look; above it hangs an oversize but airy chandelier. The large-scale furnishings make the space masculine and stable, and remove the opportunity to "put out a lot of little things" that might distract the eye. "I think of it as a treasure ship," says the designer. "Some things in it are crusty-looking and mysterious. It's a romantic attitude." Two steps up, in an ell open to the kitchen, is a second, smaller, sitting room that's often used for breakfast.** (Susan Ferrier)

## Loft-like:

Most open-plan living spaces will have a loft-like feeling simply because they are open. Think about the natural light in any large space—are there enough windows to bring light into the interior? How does the open space relate to the rest of your home? Is it also the foyer and hallway, as it often is in a true loft? If so, how will you accommodate the entry and pass-through aspects in your layout?

## Ceiling height:

In many open-plan spaces the ceiling is raised—sometimes two stories high—over some or all of the area. This increases the sense of spaciousness, but can feel cold or echo-y or make the furnishings look lonely. Think about a ceiling treatment such as decorative rafters or a painted or paneled finish. Choose pendant light fixtures that have weight and character—often a darker finish helps them to balance the things below—and remember they'll be viewed from several vantage points. If there is an interior balcony looking down on

your large room, consider its appearance when viewed from the room below.

## Sightlines:

You'll probably want to keep chair backs fairly low unless they're against a wall and avoid tall cabinets between areas so you don't inadvertently close up the space or make it difficult for the cook to see and be seen. However, you may wish to design the kitchen in a way that masks the after-dinner mess from the rest of the space. What are the focal points and where will you hang art?

## Proportions:

Sketch the basic configuration of the areas and try to visualize whether a long dining table or a square or round one will be most complementary and balanced. Do the same to plan the sitting area—is it basically square or more comfortable as a rectangle? Will you want a pair of sofas, a sectional piece that can form an L, or just a standard single sofa? What about easy chairs, are pairs in order? Will there be more than one sitting area? Often these large spaces can accommodate a small conversation or reading area as well as the main social one. Think about the scale of the various pieces and how much visual weight is wanted to make each area balance all the others. •

ABOVE AND RIGHT: **Kitchen, dining, and sitting areas are arranged one-two-three in a straight line in this long, airy, tailored space. A high ceiling and clerestory windows add drama to the sitting and dining areas. The kitchen gets a feeling of separation from a lower ceiling and projecting end walls built out to enclose the work stations on each side; hanging cabinets in the middle provide extra storage without blocking the view. Tall mirrors at each end (over the fireplace and above the sink) toss the light and details back and forth. An area rug punctuated by bright red chairs defines the symmetrical sitting area.** (Jeffrey Weisman and Andrew Weisman)

# What's your favorite reading spot?

- ☐ In front of a blazing fire
- ☐ With my elbows on the table
- ☐ Wherever the computer is
- ☐ Sitting cross-legged in a big chair
- ☐ In a chair by an open window
- ☐ Lying on the sofa

# 15. LIBRARIES, STUDIES & OFFICES

OPPOSITE: **Paired with a stylish wing chair and placed near the window so its glass top can catch and reflect the light, this English architect's table serves as desk, and occasionally, dining table in a corner of an apartment living room, where traditional paneling, soothing neutral colors touched with gold highlights, and fine art mix to create a look of easy elegance.** (Phoebe Howard)

Are you an inveterate reader or collector of books? Are you so engaged that you have a room for enjoying them? Do you run the business of your home from a room set aside for that purpose? Do you run a business from your home? Is the computer key to your daily life, for correspondence, research, managing wealth, playing games, creating graphics, or editing videos? Is there a student in your family who needs a quiet, organized place to study? Do you need studio space for a creative pursuit?

If you've answered "yes" to any of these questions, what is your library or office like? Is it private and discrete, or is it part of another room, perhaps an ell or simply a corner? Is the room used as a den or media room too, for watching the tube, hanging out, meditating, or whatever you do for leisure? Does your family join you? If you have a library, is it a reading room, a social center, host to your book group, part of the office? Is it dignified or relaxed? Do you share your office with your spouse? Do you meet with clients there, or have an employee, and if so, is there an exterior door? What sort of atmosphere do you want it to have, should it be corporate, trendy, serene, or energized? Is there a cultural norm for the business you pursue? Are these rooms primarily used during the day, or at night? What sort of space do these rooms occupy, are they large, flooded with daylight, tucked under the eaves, perhaps in a walkout basement? The nature of the space and the requirements of the activities you pursue in it will guide the way you set it up, but it's part of your home, you can give it any look you like.

# QUIET PLACES:
## Rooms for Work and Study.

There are as many ways to design an office as there are people who run one—every person has her own way of working and needs specific furnishings, and every business, even the business of keeping in touch with friends, organizing a local charity, or doing homework, thrives on its owner's vision and comfort. Libraries are a bit more straightforward; depending on how you wish to use yours, it will be similar to a living room or family room, or a mix of living room, dining room, and office, but with lots of bookshelves. Library and office spaces share a need for comfortable seating, good light, a table or desk, and a way to organize and contain a lot of stuff. Chances are you'll have a computer and some sort of sound system, and possibly a television as well.

Whether you call a room a library, office, den, or study, its furnishings most certainly include comfortable reading chairs, and perhaps a sofa, an ottoman, and a coffee table. There might be a fireplace too. You'll find ideas for and information about these in Chapter 12, Living Rooms. If there's room for a library table—either a classic one, with drawers under the top, or a simpler one—refer to Chapter 13, Dining Rooms, for some tips on shopping for a table and chairs. Is relaxation part of the plan, would you like a chaise? Is your family devoted to board or card games, will you need a table for them? Is your library also a music room? How much wall space will you allocate to shelves, is this room also an art gallery? Will the shelves be built in, or freestanding, and will there be cabinets below them? If they're wood, do you plan for it to be clear finished, or painted? How formal is the architecture, do you plan impressive shelves that set the tone for the room? Are they linked to other architectural features such as wainscoting, a coffered ceiling, the mantelpiece? Are there lots of windows, or doors that open to the garden? How formal do you wish your library to be? Think about the way you'll use it and the nature of the space it occupies—are they naturally compatible or will you make physical changes to the space in order to achieve the ambience you want?

If you plan to include a more traditional office in your home, list the features you want to include. How businesslike should it be? Do you need lots of filing drawers? Do you want a desk as well as a computer station and if so, are you thinking of a suite of furnishings, perhaps designed to fit together and flow around the room, or of individual pieces?

If you use a lot of computer equipment, should it all be in easy reach? Are you okay with it being visible, or would you prefer to conceal as much as possible in cabinets or a closet? Do you need counter or table space to spread out your work? How much of the space will be devoted to relaxation or socializing? Which activities would you like close to the windows?

Early in your office planning, think about the aesthetics as well as the setup. Do you wish to continue the ambience used elsewhere in your home, or shift gears to create a professional space? What about the energy level? Do you want lots of things on display, or a spare look that will be calming? Would you like a curtained space that wraps you in solitude, or one that's light and airy? Do you require peace and quiet to be productive, or do you welcome proximity to your kids' playroom or the distraction of a bird feeder outside the window? Does the nature of your work suggest or even contribute to the décor? For instance, if you are a designer or architect, will you want a way to display sketches, samples, and other visual inspiration, perhaps on walls you can pin into? Will photos or prints of your work be framed and hung on the walls? If you are a writer, teacher, or attorney, do you have a large reference library? Have you an area of expertise or a charity endeavor that's provided a collection of artifacts and memorabilia that you love to keep in sight?

When you design a library or office that is self-contained you have the option of making it look however you want it to. When they're part of another room, decide how you'll mesh your aspirations to accommodate all the activities and create one look that makes sense and thrills you.

OPPOSITE: **Viewed from a dark, imposing living room, this library is like a light, bright painting. Two pedestal tables provide ample room to enjoy the books; at mealtimes, the books are returned to their shelves so the tables can be used for dining. The large mirror on the end wall expands the lovely effect.** (David Kleinberg)

# ROOMS WE LOVE

Where do you want to be when you read, write, pay your bills, and organize your life or conduct your business? In a private-club library, resplendent with formal woodwork and commodious chairs? In a spare, elegant drawing room? In a cozy den with a roaring fire? Somewhere exotic, hung with ethnic textiles or native baskets and masks? Should the space look studious or businesslike in order to remind you of its purpose or would you rather it be more subtle, simply a beautiful room arranged to accommodate solitary pursuits? If your office will be part of another room, can you create it with a gorgeous secretary that adds the finishing touch to the overall décor? Will a laptop computer, a cell phone, and a great looking lamp be all you need to convert a side table and chair to your headquarters? However you designate the space, choose a look that makes you happy, with colors you love. You'll find options both relaxing and charged with productivity here, in photos of studies where we'd be glad to spend time.

BELOW: **Tranquil in cream and brown, with French doors opening to a balcony, elegant furnishings that include a desk, comfortable seating, and built-in bookshelves, this master-bedroom study is a retreat to envy. The glass chandelier, pretty bergère, irresistible heart chair, and hints of blush pink in the carpet add a feminine touch to the tailored décor.** (Sally Markham)

OPPOSITE: **Don't think of "library" as a synonym for "staid"; a book room can be as adventurous as the spirits that use it. The intense mustard yellow of this book nook makes a vivid, wide-awake background for ethnic textiles, Asian figures, and reading materials.** (Allegra and Ashley Hicks)

ABOVE LEFT: **Lady-like in pink and taupe, this office area features two classic bookcases on cupboards, trimmed with the same crown molding that frames the walls and separated by a wide shelf over a drawer. The desk is simply a glass slab set on sleek metal sawhorses, and is paired with an elegant wooden swivel armchair on wheels. Giving it a personal spin is the generous, crisscross ribbon memo board displaying many beloved photos.** (Ruthie Sommers)

ABOVE: **Two chairs, a table, and a laptop do an office make. This one is the entire interior of a converted garden shed, made lovely with a bay window, vaulted ceiling, cupola skylight, Oriental rug, and tiered chandelier. Built-in shelves hold books, pottery, paintings, and the printer.** (Jill Morris)

LEFT: **A vaguely Moorish stencil (inspired by a favorite fabric) makes a witty frame around this interior designer's home office and gives some structure to the masses of magazine pictures "that seem to grow on my walls." Against the back wall is a chinoiserie cabinet; the desk is a Parsons table freshened with avocado-green auto paint—"a great color that's about to sneak in the back door after being banished for overstaying its welcome years ago."** (Betsy Brown)

OPPOSITE: **If a connection with nature helps you to collect your thoughts, set up a desk on an all-weather porch. Here an old, concrete and marble garden table, blotter, lamp, and creatively slipcovered chair sit ready for the words to come.** (Nancy Boszhardt)

RIGHT: **Working theory: A rustic trestle table with antique, rush-seat armchairs acts as desk for a couple who bring their laptops to this study on weekends. Truth be told: Anyone wanting to escape with a good book heads to the wing chair and puts his feet up on the ottoman. The look: Casual American Country, with board paneling painted soft green, an amazing antique geometric hooked rug with folk art flavor, and botanical prints evenly spaced around for continuity.** (Barbara Westbrook)

ABOVE: An irregular shape, large fireplace, arched doorway, complex traditional woodwork, plump sofa and chair, and deep colors offset by cream make this little library cozy and inviting. The bookcases may look as though they've been there forever, but their adjustable shelves indicate otherwise and make space for the small TV. (Jason Bell)

# TABLESCAPE

## DISPLAY YOUR COLLECTION

Kansas City designer David Jimenez has a penchant for artfully arranged surfaces. Why not follow his cues?

**Layer and lean framed photographs against the wall instead of hanging them, to keep the arrangement tight.**

Keep your palette simple. Nothing is more powerful than black and white—with one hit of color.

**A tray makes anything look richer.**

Use a vase with a strong silhouette. Fill it with one type of stem or flower, for impact.

## Make It Your Own:

**CRYSTAL SPHERE**
Always include one thing that reflects light. This solid crystal sphere also adds a strong shape.

**LACQUER BOXES**
Color is the spark that brings this arrangement to life. Forms that echo each other create interesting rhythms.

**TALL VASE**
Proportion is all. This understated ceramic vase with chinoiserie accents would look best filled with tall stems.

**FRAMED PRINT**
Look for interesting prints or photos produced in multiples—they're less expensive than one-of-a-kind artwork.

# Colorful Opinions: **NEUTRALS**

What neutral do you find yourself always using? Designers reveal the colors that keep them loyal.

**CHRISTOPHER MAYA:**
**BENJAMIN MOORE**
**GLASS SLIPPER 1632**
I love grayish blue as a backdrop—the blue of a washed-out sky just after a storm. I'm sitting here in my office right now with this color on the walls. I have Swedish painted grayish-blue chairs, an eighteenth-century mahogany desk, a shiny chrome lamp, a painting done in black oils, and red curtains! Almost anything looks great with this blue. That's what neutrals are all about, aren't they?

**CHRISTOPHER RIDOLFI:**
**BENJAMIN MOORE**
**GRANT BEIGE HC-83**
My standby is Grant Beige. It's like a favorite pair of worn khakis. It works with modern spaces and traditional ones, fares equally well with the light of Texas or the East Coast. If you want to keep your palette clean with whites, creams, and accents of black, it becomes very architectural, or you can warm it up with soft reds, blues, and greens.

**DD ALLEN:**
**C2 BELLA DONNA C2-316W**
I've been using Bella Donna a lot. It's a smoky lavender gray, the color of a twilight sky. I used it on the parlor floor of a brownstone, and it looked flat-out sophisticated. I'm in the

bedroom of my country house right now, which is painted this color. Bella Donna is a sexy, adult color, but it can go a lot of different ways.

**MATTHEW PATRICK SMYTH:**
**BENJAMIN MOORE**
**LINEN WHITE**
When in doubt, Linen White. You can phone that in. It might seem like a cop-out, but it works beautifully. I use it when people are unsure. They want something light and airy, but not stark white. No matter what light you put it in, it looks good.

**JENNIFER GARRIGUES:**
**BENJAMIN MOORE**
**MESQUITE 501**
Mesquite is a flattering light moss green without much yellow. I love it because it doesn't shout "I'm green!" Instead, it says, "I'm a very beautiful color."

MARY MCDONALD:
**DUNN-EDWARDS**
**COCONUT SKIN 1055**
I could paint every room in the house Coconut Skin, a deep mocha brown with some milk in it. It's cozy and comforting without being kidsy: grounding with pastels, weighty with bright colors. Even with a funky, kitschy color like lime green, you've got an elegant combination.

STEVEN GAMBREL:
**BENJAMIN MOORE**
**HORIZON 1478**
I always come back to Horizon, a pale gray that doesn't turn blue or green on you. It's a sophisticated, perfect background to so many interiors. Blues, of course, look beautiful against this gray, but so do pinks, lavenders, and the legs of sofas and chairs that have been stained a driftwood color.

ELLEN KENNON:
**FULL SPECTRUM PAINTS**
**MUSHROOM**
I'll do entire houses in Mushroom, which is pretty darned fabulous. It's a beige, but it changes drastically—one minute it is putty and the next it's rosier. Chameleon-like and mysterious, it takes on the properties of the colors around it. You want to put your hand out and touch the wall because it doesn't look solid. It's almost cloudlike.

MARIETTE HIMES GOMEZ:
**FARROW & BALL**
**STRING 8 AND GREEN GROUND**
Khaki and celadon are my picks. These are colors, but they're still very neutral in their integrity. Each one is softly beautiful. They don't scream. They don't dictate —you can put them with anything.

MALLORY MARSHALL:
**BENJAMIN MOORE**
**WENGE AF-180**
Wenge is a rich blackish brown, the color of that bitter chocolate with 70% cacao that everyone's calling health food now. A neutral should get along great with every color in the fan deck, and this one is like the nicest girl in the sixth grade. It goes with silvery greens. It looks beautiful with creamy yellows. It is wonderful with red. And if you're really having color mood swings, it will support lilac.

GERRIE BREMERMANN:
**BENJAMIN MOORE**
**PAPAYA 957**
The most enduring color I've found is Papaya, which looks like homemade vanilla ice cream with a little caramel in it. My whole apartment is Papaya! I love it with the blues, greens, and blue-greens of the sea and sky, and with various soft warm pinks. There's nothing edgy about it, which suits me fine. I like pretty furniture, pretty people, pretty books, pretty music, and I like a room to be beautiful.

JEFFREY BILHUBER:
**BENJAMIN MOORE**
**PALE VISTA 2029-60**
I use spring green as a neutral. It's the color of buds and bulbs popping out of the ground after a long winter—a reassuring color, great in a bedroom. I think the coolness is therapeutic.

ABOVE: **In an excellent use of an interior alcove, bookshelves extending from the baseboard nearly to the ceiling keep this small library in easy reach. A small antique English chandelier and classic library lamps—a charming alternative to directional can lights—illuminate the titles. Books on the top shelves can be reached via a small stepladder; anyone wishing to sit and browse a volume can flip the ladder top down to transform it into a chair.** (Madeline Stuart)

OPPOSITE: **Say "elegant private library" and visions of a Gilded Age novel with a room like this are likely to come to mind: Coffered ceiling, elegant pilasters framing the bookshelves, large table in a bay window, comfortable formal seating, rich but quiet colors. Giving this brand new room an unexpected finish is the triangle pattern-striped rug that "makes it youthful, makes it today," says the designer.** (Bunny Williams)

# DESIGNER'S TOP TEN

"Books are the best decoration," declared the legendary Billy Baldwin. Most interior designers agree. Books bring warmth, color, and character to a room, and incorporating them into a space can be as simple as adding a pair of freestanding bookcases or even just stacking them neatly on the floor. Custom cabinetry or antique étagères can make for more sophisticated arrangements, but there are clever storage options in every price range. Mini-libraries work in almost every room of the house, and best of all, Baldwin pointed out, "when you decorate with books, no room color is wrong."

**1.** Bookcases can camouflage a multitude of sins: surround a poorly placed door or window with books to create symmetry and balance.

**2.** Capitalize on unused nooks and crannies—under a staircase, below a window seat, or in a seldom-used closet with the door removed—by building in book storage.

**3.** Think creatively about the height and shape of bookshelves: tall floor-to-ceiling units, long and low horizontal shelves, and freestanding étagères can add structure to a room.

**4.** To preclude sagging, shelves should measure no wider than 40 inches.

**5.** Incorporate art and decorative accessories into a wall of books to create visual interest, but be ruthless about your selection. Too much clutter can look messy or tacky.

**6.** Paint interior surfaces of bookshelves in rich colors to add depth and contrast.

**7.** If you don't own a library's worth of books, improvise: cover a cabinet door with faux book spines or use wallpaper patterned with book motifs.

**8.** Stack books horizontally as well as vertically.

**9.** For tall bookshelves, splurge on a library ladder, the kind that rolls along a brass rod affixed to the bookcase.

**10.** If space is tight, go for bypass bookcase units that stack two or three deep in front of the wall and roll sideways.

# INSPIRATIONS

## Secretaries = **Stylish Focus**

Function takes on glorious form in the secretary, a combination desk and bookcase with cubbyholes and class.

Conveniently vertical and not-too-big, secretaries have that magical allure of secret drawers and tasseled-key closure, with a flip-down writing surface that flips up too, to hide unfinished business. Pick an antique form or one that's suave and modern, and use it to introduce the patina of polished wood, a jolt of incredible rich color, or a painted pattern to a space where you need something really special. •

LEFT: **A piece with tailored lines like this can look antique or modern depending on its setting and finish; this one is new and gets its jewel-box hue and dazzling sheen from ordinary glossy exterior house paint.** (Christopher Maya)

ABOVE: "I want one fantastic piece, like this," said the client, displaying a photo of an antique with a price equal to the entire design budget. Here you see a more affordable reproduction, complete with rich gold chinoiserie motifs on a black ground; it's now the focal point of her **living room.** (Michael Whaley)

RIGHT, TOP: Dated 1740, this stunning secretary comes from the Veneto (environs of Venice) and is painted with scenes representing the family for whom it was made. (Paul Wiseman)

RIGHT: Soft, old, cream-colored paint and quirky lines place this provincial Alsatian secretary comfortably at home in a contemporary room where sisal blankets the floor and embroidered linen covers the chairs. (Alessandra Branca)

## POWER SOURCE

We live in an increasingly wireless world, but if the equipment in your office requires electric, cable, or telephone connections, plan for them. Nothing is more irritating (or potentially dangerous) than long cords trailing around the room. If your computer is cabled to the printer, fax machine, an uninterruptible power source (UPS), or any other gear, take that into account when you plan the office layout. Most desks are more comfortable to work at if there is a lamp near the computer; if you are planning to work at a laptop computer on a table in the middle of the room, install a floor outlet for the lamp.

ABOVE: **Set up for a good read or a good chat, this library has a pair of built-in bookcases that each turn a corner to form a niche for a comfortable sofa. Leather-covered cushions transform the ends of the coffee table into ottomans—put your feet up or invite friends to drop down.** (David Easton)

OPPOSITE, TOP: **Here's a great idea for what to do with the cramped space below a dormer window in a sloped ceiling: Span it with a built-in counter, add your computer, a lamp, and a chair.** (T. Keller Donovan)

OPPOSITE, BOTTOM: **Two narrow tables arranged in an L frame this office area; the "desk" extends into the middle of the room so the sitter doesn't stare straight at the wall. Against the wall are small storage devices that don't interfere with the artwork.** (Stephen Brady)

# The Choice Is Yours: **DESKS**

There's a style that's just right for your office, a corner of your bedroom, under a kitchen window . . . wherever you love to work.

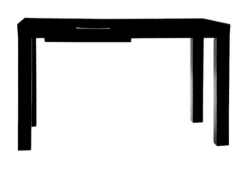

# "CORNER" OFFICE ...
## in 10 Square Feet.

If your office needs are modest or you're really pressed for space, think creatively about outfitting a corner with a desk and shelving in a style that complements the look of the room. Use furniture designed for this purpose, such as a secretary or a ready-to-assemble shelving ensemble, or have something customized: You can outfit an armoire or have a bookcase with a desk shelf built.

ABOVE: **Forget makeshift: give yourself a professional workspace even if it is only a closet. This one is wood paneled, and fitted with bookshelves, a desk counter, and a readymade file cabinet.** (Peter Forbes)

LEFT: **This ladder-like combination desk and bookcase is simple, light but not fragile, fun to look at, and suits the exposed wood framing of this home. All that's missing is closed storage.** (Douglas Durkin and Greg Elich)

OPPOSITE: **A secretary does the desk/storage plan for you and is not too big for a bedroom corner. This contemporary one is plain, looks modern, and has compartments to organize and conceal whatever you like.** (David Jimenez)

# INSPIRATIONS

## Creatives at Home: **Studios**

Not every work space is an office. Artists have studios. If you are a passionate creative, you deserve one too.

Whether creativity is an avocation or your livelihood, pursue it in a room that invites your muse to visit. You'll know best what you like to look at; whatever it is, surround yourself with it. Give yourself good lighting and the work surface and equipment you need. Provide an area where you can relax—or wow your patrons. •

ABOVE: **Work and play do mix if they have a shared aesthetic. This dressmaker's atelier is all business on one side, and ready to relax on the other. Common ground: neutral palette, red and black accents, modern furnishings, wire storage, no clutter.** (Chantal Dussouchaud)

RIGHT: **If space is tight, one great piece of furniture like this old office timekeeper's desk can stand in for the studio you wish you had room for. Must-have supplements: small intriguing or recycled stackable storage bins for the top, large baskets for underneath.** (Stephen Brady)

OPPOSITE: **This old farm table in front of a corkboard idea collage serves as desk and planning center for an artist/designer; easy chairs welcome his clients or friends. Personal quirks: the old mantel propped against the wall for casual display of large canvases, circus-like striped curtains, great lamps (his self-described fetish).** (Craig Schumacher and Philip Kirk)

# PULL IT TOGETHER

It's clear in your mind. You know what you want your library or office to be. Assemble your clipping and swatch files so you can begin to plan the specifics of each room. Spread out the contents; sort, mix, and match the pieces until you come up with a group that is close to your dream look. If you like, make a collage for each room so you can revisit your choices later or share them with a designer. If you find you're missing something, note it; discuss it with your designer, or with salespeople if you're working on your own.

### Ambience
Choose the key words that describe your dream library or office—hushed, traditional, private club, offbeat, tranquil, stimulating, corporate, arty—whatever they may be.

### Color
Think of the overall palette, for instance blue and antique gold with white and dark wood accents. Which will be the principal color? How will you use pattern?

### Walls and shelves
Will the walls be mostly covered with built-in or freestanding shelves? Will they be paneled? Do you need bulletin boards?

### Floor
What will the flooring be? Wood, stone, carpet? Will it provide a strong contrast or a subtle one, how much visual texture will it add? If it isn't topped with a rug, will it have pattern, either painted or created with a mix of materials?

### Rugs
How will you use rugs? A large carpet overall? Area rugs? Layered? Will they provide an assertive or subtle pattern or introduce multiple colors or an obvious texture?

### Lighting fixtures
Use a combination of fixtures to create flattering, welcoming ambient light, bounced off the ceiling if possible. Choose table or floor lamps, as appropriate for the space, to light reading, desk, and conversation areas.

### Window treatments
Do you favor draperies or something that takes less space? How will the treatment provide nighttime privacy or filter the sun? Do you need something to keep the glare off your computer screen?

### Furniture
For a library, at the least you need comfortable reading chairs and a coffee table or side table. For an office, you need a desk and chair. If you wish, include the basics of one room in the other. Will you want a sofa, a large table, or a secretary? A chaise? Will you want anything special for displaying your books? A decorative screen to divide the room?

### Storage
In addition to bookshelves, include cabinets and cupboards suitable for the materials you'll be storing.

### Accessories
Think about art and decorative accessories such as pillows from the beginning. They express your personality and interests and can set the tone for the décor or punctuate it. Choose desk accessories that enhance the look. Don't forget a vase for flowers.

### Layout
Even if you're not feeling ready to do a real floor plan, it's smart to do something rough that can serve as a reality check for the amount and scale of the furniture. Draw the outline of the room on graph paper; mark the windows and doorways. Make some paper cutouts of the furniture in the same scale and position them. Does everything fit with room to walk around? Will your office be conveniently organized?

OPPOSITE: **Elegant, bold, sumptuous, with a great view from the well-appointed desk, this study sits in a high-rise glass-box apartment that's been warmed, wrapped, and made cozy with rich colors and textures. The desk, wing chair, and ottoman are contemporary, feminine takes on classic forms; a tall cabinet with glass doors doubles as book-and curio-case. The figured rug and marvelous frescoed panels add pattern to the textured sisal carpet and faux shagreen wall covering.** (Celerie Kemble)

# What are your bedroom must-haves?

☐ An ornamented bed frame
☐ Sumptuous linens
☐ Tranquility
☐ A personal reading light
☐ A window seat
☐ Headphones for the TV

## 16. BEDROOMS

OPPOSITE: **Both the client and designer fell in love with the steel blue color of this elegant bed. "It's serene," says the designer. When added to the bisque walls and carpet and bits of gold that accent the décor, "the whole thing becomes like a watercolor. Along with the blend of different period antiques, the lighting, and art in the room, it creates such a relaxed mood."** (Fern Santini)

Do you spend much time in your bedroom other than when you're in bed? Do you linger there to read by the window, watch TV from an easy chair, or talk at length with your spouse? Is breakfast-in-bed part of your weekend routine? What sort of dressing area is there, a separate room, a dressing table, none? Do you use part of the room as an office or to entertain family or close friends? What about the other bedrooms in your home, how do they function for your kids and guests?

Almost everyone wants a bedroom that's a private sanctuary and retreat. What will make yours such a place? While you think about a great bed, beautiful linens, and soft carpets, think too about the way you really use the room so you can set it up to meet your needs and satisfy your yearning for a place in which to relax, or at least get a good night's sleep. You may decide your exercise bike or the computer are simply not compatible with your vision of a soothing sanctuary; is there somewhere else to put them? Do the same for the other bedrooms—who uses them? Do you have young children, teens, or grown kids still living at home? How much of their life takes place in their bedroom? How often are your guest rooms used and by whom? Do you use one as an office until company visits? How can you make each bedroom gracious?

# PLACE FOR REPOSE:
## Planning a Bedroom.

How big is your bedroom? Is it inherently snug or spacious? Has it an ell, a change of level, or some other nook or cranny? Is the ceiling high, sloped, or low? Is there a fireplace? How is the room situated? On the ground floor or upstairs? Does it open to a terrace or balcony? Has it a private or shared bath, and is the bath reached from within the bedroom or entered from the hall? Is there a dressing room? A walk-in closet? Take stock of your bedroom space—do you love it or want to change something about it?

Whether you dream of opulent or simple bedroom décor, the size of the room will determine how much furniture you can use, its scale, and how it can be arranged. No matter how spare or delicate the furnishings, a small room will be intimate; you can make it cozy too, by softening it with textiles, pattern, and well-chosen accessories, or get carried away with your decorating and end up feeling crowded. If your bedroom is large, you can enjoy its capaciousness, or make it feel more intimate by zoning it—say with a sitting area, place for handling correspondence, and maybe another for taking tea—and by using a bed with hangings, draperies at the windows, and perhaps a bookcase wall.

How would you like to store clothing? Will you have adequate closet space? Enough to incorporate shelves and drawers for items that don't hang? Will you build a wall's worth of cupboards, perhaps flanking windows so you can work in a window seat? Or will freestanding chests of drawers be

used? Do you live in an antique house where there are no closets at all, making an armoire essential?

Make a list of the furnishings you want in your bedroom, including storage pieces, and decide how they'll be arranged. As you shop for them, keep their scale and the size of the room in mind—several different kinds of furniture might be required or desired and you want to create a lovely room, not a warehouse of functional items. If your home is small, don't neglect to measure the doorways and hallways to make sure your new purchases will make it into the room.

Both artificial and natural light are important to plan for. You'll need light for reading in bed and in any sitting areas, ambient light for moving about, task light at a dressing table, accent light for art or bookshelves, good light inside closets. Nightlights are reassuring for small fry and guests. How you deal with natural light, allowing it free entry or blocking it, has a lot to do with individual preference as well as the situation of the room. Do you love to fall asleep in the moonlight and wake up to the dawn, or is a dark room essential for you to sleep soundly? What are the privacy issues, how close are your neighbors? If your aesthetic preference is for diaphanous window treatments but you need something opaque for privacy or room darkening, add unobtrusive shades or blinds.

There are often human challenges involved in bedroom décor. If you share the room with a partner, do the two of you agree about aesthetic choices and have similar habits and rituals? Is setting up your bedroom going to require a lot of compromise? Don't ignore this as an issue; talk about it together, and with your designer if you work with one. Somehow it's easier to reach consensus about the public part of your home; the bedroom truly is a personal space, how will yours accommodate two personalities? If you are planning your children's rooms, you'll know best how much input is appropriate for them to have. Things to consider: the child's age and how long you see the décor lasting. It's not likely a baby's room will work for a child in grammar school, but with good planning, a tween's room might make it through high school with a change of paint, bed linens, and small accessories. Are you planning to stay in the house long enough for this to be a concern?

LEFT AND OPPOSITE: **A pair of club chairs with matching ottomans offers a comfortable, put-your-feet-up spot for conversation in the window alcove of this glamorous bedroom, where a cream-and-taupe palette and soft textures accented with shimmering details unite furnishings of disparate styles.** (Marshall Watson)

# ROOMS WE LOVE

What's the ambience you dream of for your bedroom? Romantic, with pretty colors and patterned walls and a delicately carved or curtained bed? Country casual, with a graphic hooked rug, a quilt on a cannonball bed, and the coolest antique blanket chest? Something dreamy and tranquil, with a watery palette and shimmering surfaces? Is tailored more your style? Something spare, streamlined, crisp, and very modern? Should it be open or cozy, dressy or informal? Do you long for opulence or the exotic, or is a main criteria that your dog find it as comfy as you do? Are there architectural features that give you a head start on making the room special, charming, or elegant? However you answer, decide upon the palette and style that create the bedroom you long for, where you can refresh and nurture yourself. You'll find many ideas here, in photos of rooms we'd be happy to dream in.

ABOVE: **An antique door serves as headboard in this bedroom, adding interest, taking minimal space, and demonstrating the value of repurposing. Its character is nicely matched to the rustic chandelier. With no footboard, a pair of scroll-back chairs adds a flourish at the end of the bed.** (Kay Douglass)

LEFT: **A pomegranate-red niche framed in bold white molding anchors the bed in this richly hued room. The upholstery on the bed is the same velvet that covers the wall, but embossed with a moiré pattern that gives a color cue to the pastel pink lamps. Paired by wood tone and scale rather than form, a small desk and pedestal table flank the bed.** (Diamond Baratta)

OPPOSITE: **Scripted for romance in the California wine country, this room looks out on a view so marvelous it makes you believe there's nothing wrong in the world. What we see looking in: powder-blue plaster walls, a new iron canopy bed made unique with an antique French needlepoint headboard, Louis VIX-style consoles serving as bedside tables, and a pretty settee upholstered in sky blue. Says the designer "Things at the end of a bed make me feel cozy and protected."** (Erin Marin)

LEFT: **Who needs room to move around when repose looks this sweet? An exuberant, rose-on-white block-print wallpaper wraps the soffits for a cozy feeling, the bed has lots of character, fresh country stripes soften footsteps, and a big floral print flows over the small upholstered chair. Finishing touches, thoughtfully chosen and lightly applied, include shams with a striped ribbon lattice, the folky bird print covering the small pillow, soft brush fringe trimming the upholstered chair, and the small paintings hung next to the bed.** (Healing Barsand)

ABOVE: Smallish windows keep the natural light shadowy in this master bedroom, so pale blues and greens were chosen to mix with white to keep the mood gentle and light. At the desk, a chair covered in leopard print adds a touch of the unexpected and picks up the warm tones of the painting. The awning stripe fabric is crisp but not formal—just the right balance for a home on the water. (Kari Cusack)

RIGHT: Juxtaposed textures and a bit of age mixed with lots of new give great energy to this master bedroom. Nickel wall lamps flank a skeletal steel bed, a fun rawhide chair tucks under the aged farm table, lacquer Parsons tables pose on the shag rug. The nautical blue-and-white palette speaks of the home's seaside locale. (Jodi Macklin)

ABOVE: "I always do the master bedroom to the woman's taste, because it is her place. He can come visit, but it's all about the woman," says the designer when asked about the pink-and-cream palette in this pretty room. Velvet upholstery, lace-trimmed pillows, and an Aubusson rug create a soft, relaxed but dressy ambience within the high, board-and-batten wainscoted walls. (Mona Hajj)

OPPOSITE: Romantic, nostalgic, and beyond cozy in a small lakeside cottage—what a fresh and lovely room in which to awaken. The simple iron bed is topped with a classic, blue-and-white patchwork quilt and bandana print pillows, the floor is painted lagoon blue and gleams like the water outside the window. (David Reed)

# EXPERT INSIGHT

## CREATING A HOLISTIC BEDROOM

Interior designer Ellen Kennon of Saint Francisville, Louisiana, brings a holistic approach to bedroom design, creating spaces that are rejuvenating sanctuaries.

**What are major mistakes homeowners make in designing their bedrooms?**

People try to make the master bedroom too multi-functional. It's a really important part of life—sleeping and dreaming, planning your future, rehashing your past—the bedroom is a very sacred space. Using stimulating colors and patterns that are not restful doesn't help either.

**How do you feel about ancillary activities in the bedroom, like watching TV or doing paperwork?**

The bedroom should be your sanctuary—a "womb" instead

of a room. If space constraints prohibit you from having a separate home office, then you should use an enclosed armoire-type computer cabinet. I have to admit, I personally like a TV in my bedroom, but I keep it behind closet doors opposite the bed.

## What colors work best in a bedroom? Which should be avoided?

Pale blues induce sleep and reduce inflammation. Pale pinks are emotionally healing. Greens are physically healing. And browns are nurturing and grounding. I would avoid reds because they raise your blood pressure and generally make it harder to relax and sleep. Some brighter yellows are also too stimulating and should be avoided.

## How should the bed relate to the room's design and layout?

The bed should be placed opposite the entry door so that you have a full view of the door. It should not be in front of a window. You should also avoid placing the head of the bed right under a window, which can create an uncomfortable situation.

## What kind of lighting fixtures do you like for a bedroom?

The more variety, the better—table lamps, sconces, floor lamps. I avoid overhead down lights because they cast ghoulish shadows. I like to include good bedside lamps with dimmers so that they can be used for reading as well as atmosphere. I also like scented candles on bedside tables.

## What elements best define the bedroom?

Color is the most powerful element to work with. It affects emotion, physical wellbeing, and promotes certain activities. Comfort is equally important. A great mattress, sensuous bed linens, and good down pillows make the room inviting and facilitate a really good sleep.

## How do you deal with the issue of bright natural light?

Simple curtains that are interlined with flannel so that they block the light. I like them simple but very full—at least three times the window width. Think "ball gown."

## How do you deal with bedroom storage?

I don't use dressers. I prefer to store folded clothes inside of the closet and keep the bedroom floor space more open so that it can breathe. Decorative boxes are great for storing bedside amenities like sleep masks, lotions, aspirin, etc.—especially if your bedside tables have no storage. Just remember, if there is one room in the house that should be your sanctuary, it's the bedroom. •

ABOVE: **Hung with simple curtains, this bed is a sanctuary within a bedroom retreat. Smooth linens, a pale blue coverlet, and soft, plump pillows facilitate sleep. The gently curved upholstered headboard is very simple: "no tufting, no nailheads, no nothing," says the designer, who feels most people try to make these too complicated.** (Phoebe Howard)

OPPOSITE: **The wall covering and very full, simple curtains in this dreamy room are an iridescent silk that goes from blue to green; it keeps the room quiet and brings movement—like watching the ocean change colors as the day goes by. A tall padded headboard and swing-arm sconces make reading in bed comfortable, and piles of soft pillows induce sleep.** (Vicente Wolf)

# The Choice Is Yours: **NIGHTSTANDS**

Each one has such distinctive character. Which one would you like to sleep next to?

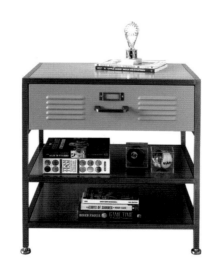

# INSPIRATIONS

## Bedside Fireplace: **So Romantic**

A fireplace near the bed warms your feet, your soul, and your heart. Besides, flickering flames are so seductive.

Walk into a bedroom where there's a fireplace and you're instantly charmed. If the room is small, the fireplace makes it extra cozy, if it's large, you have your choice of placing the bed nearby or creating a sitting area in front of the hearth. If you don't have a real fireplace, fake one by leaning a mantel against the wall and filling the opening with a decorative screen or faux painting. •

LEFT: **The feminine take: "I looked at this fireplace and thought, I want to see this through a bed," explains the designer. "I want to be pulled into the bed and beyond." Hence the four-poster bed with hangings in the middle of the room. On the far side of the bed is a writing table set up for tea.** (Charlotte Moss)

ABOVE: **The calm, quiet take: A raised hearth puts flames at pillow height; this bed is positioned to enjoy them at their seductive, toe-toasting best.** (Ken Fulk)

RIGHT, TOP: **The fun take: True, it's not the same as a working fireplace, but a mantel propped against the wall lends a touch of romance nonetheless. This one dresses up a whitewashed attic bedroom in a very old house and fakes the glow of flames with a screen woven of sheet metal.** (Eldon Wong)

RIGHT: **The classic take: In an historic or newly constructed period home, a bedroom fireplace is a natural. In this cozy room, the flames may be enjoyed from the pillows or the little sitting area at the foot of the bed.** (Keith Irvine)

# Colorful Opinions: **THE BEST BLUE**

From light and airy to deep and mysterious . . . they're all beautiful. Top designers share their favorite shades of blue.

## RALPH HARVARD:
**SHERWIN-WILLIAMS/ DURON COLORS OF HISTORIC CHARLESTON VERDITER BLUE DCR078 NRH**

An intense eighteenth-century blue-green with a great history. They used to make it by pouring acids on copper and using the verdigris as the pigment for the paint. A living room would be a killer with this on the walls, dead-white trim, and mahogany or black-painted furniture. I'm fair and blue-eyed and we go for these incredibly sharp colors. You couldn't sell this to a brown-eyed person.

## WHITNEY STEWART:
**C2 ELECTRIC 275**

Forget all those pale shades. What you want is an evening blue, an Yves Klein blue. Deeper than deep. You see it on Byzantine ceilings, in Jean Paul Gaultier's stripes. It's contemplative, meditative, mysterious. When I want to be enveloped, blue is the only color that will do it for me.

## THOMAS JAYNE:
**BENJAMIN MOORE HEAVENLY BLUE 709**

This is the color of the sky in Old Master paintings, when the varnish has yellowed. It has a luminous quality. You

could paint the whole room or just the floor—you'd feel as if you were floating. Be careful about blue in a north-facing room—it can get chilly. And it's hard to mix more than two blues together. They start to fight.

## WILLIAM DIAMOND:
**SHERWIN-WILLIAMS SASSY BLUE 1241**

Blue is my secret agent color. I'm always sneaking it in these days. I guess it's like a bit of sky peeking out, which makes everything work. Blue is lightness and air. I used to use white to lighten things up, but now I'm using blue. It gives breath to everything.

**MARKHAM ROBERTS:**
**PARKER PAINT**
**WATERSIDE 7573M**
This bright, pretty turquoise reminds me of summers on Lake Michigan when I was a child, skipping stones and looking up at the sky and feeling the sun on my body. Blue calms me and reenergizes me—just as the ocean always does.

**JOHN YUNIS:**
**BENJAMIN MOORE**
**AQUARIUS 788**
I've never met a blue I didn't like. Everything from the darkest to the lightest—and this is in the middle, with a hint of aquamarine. A blue living room would be glamorous, especially with bottle-green silk velvet upholstery and a touch of silver or gold on a chair, or tiebacks for a curtain. And the walls should be slick, which gives a room sparkle. It can never be too glossy for me.

**ELISSA CULLMAN:**
**BENJAMIN MOORE**
**BLUE WAVE 2065-50**
Blue is tricky. It can go gray and sad. But not this warm Mediterranean blue. It's the blue in all those Pucci prints, a bright, happy, not-a-cloud-in-the-sky blue, as if you're in vacation mode and having lobster and rosé at Tetou on the beach near Cannes. I love it in a bedroom, where you would crisp it up with a navy-and-white striped fabric and one of those great Elizabeth Eakins plaid rugs.

**ROBIN BELL:**
**BENJAMIN MOORE**
**PADDINGTON BLUE 791**
This is a peacock blue, a very happy, exuberant blue that would set off all the objects of a room. I'd use it with a high-gloss finish with lots of white moldings, and maybe pull in marigold or puce. Blue is one of the best colors around for crispness and contrast. After all, what looks better than a naval officer in his dress blues?

**ERIC COHLER:**
**FARROW & BALL**
**CHINESE BLUE 90**
This is not too hot, not too cold, with a lot of green, which makes it feel grounded. Blue is so regenerative. There's the idea of water, renewal. It's powerful, regal—think of bluebloods, blue ribbons. And it looks great with most other colors, especially browns and camels and beiges.

**ROGER DE CABROL:**
**BENJAMIN MOORE**
**PATRIOT BLUE 2064-20**
I don't like baby blue or sky blue—I like dark, strong cobalt blue. It reminds me of Europe, in the sense of luxuriousness and the privacy it creates in a room. It shields you. I'd use it in a study or library, and then snap it up with furniture from the 1940s or 1950s and a faux-zebra rug.

**JAMIE DRAKE:**
**BENJAMIN MOORE**
**WINDMILL WINGS 2067-60**
Blue is America's favorite color. It's certainly the most telegenic. That's why politicians wear blue shirts and why the White House pressroom is blue. It's cool. It's calming. It's all about blue skies and fresh air. This is an ethereal blue, with a touch of red that gives it a lavender cast. I love it with ivory and cyclamen pink.

**DAVID KLEINBERG:**
**BENJAMIN MOORE**
**COLONY GREEN 694**
I grew up in a house that was all turquoise, and for years I couldn't look at blue. But this color is so terrifically pretty and filled with joy—sort of like you were inside a robin's egg looking out into the light. I'd use it in a bedroom with white lacquered trim, a four-poster bed lacquered white, and crisp white bed linens.

# INSPIRATIONS

## Curtained Bed: **How Alluring**

Fall for their mystery, romance, and charm—bed hangings create an inner sanctuary in your private retreat.

Arrange a beautiful fabric in a canopy that drapes, ruffles, or sits tight around the top of your bed frame, hang the simplest curtains at each corner, pull some yardage through a ring suspended from the ceiling, or have a cornice built over the head of your bed and hang the fabric from it. Choose the most gorgeous heavy silk, a graphic toile or gingham, or a swathe of delicate voile, or show off an unusual hand-woven textile. Add an elegant braid, a stylized appliqué, or fun tassel fringe. It's like dress-up, you can choose any style you like. •

LEFT: **No bed posts? No problem. This canopy frame is suspended from the ceiling; its Indian voile valance and curtains are soft architecture that creates a room within a room and keeps the bed from being overwhelmed by the barn-like space.** (Jeffrey Bilhuber)

ABOVE: **Fabrics printed and hand-embroidered in ethnic patterns complement the rustic aesthetic of this Hawaii bedroom. The bed is massive; semi-sheer hanging panels soften its architectural effect and give it a sense of intimacy.** (Douglas Durkin and Greg Elich)

RIGHT, TOP: **Demure and wonderfully proportioned, these simple curtained crowns welcome guests in an ultra-feminine room reminiscent of a bedchamber in the South of France.** (Karyl Pierce Paxton)

RIGHT: **A beautiful hand-embroidered panel from India hangs at the head of this drop-dead mirrored bed. It's a fabulous bed beyond most of our reach, but if you love the graphic effect, you can borrow the panel idea and pair it with a metal or wood canopy bed and a cloth valance.** (Bunny Williams)

# Shopping for . . . **A BED FRAME**

It's the focal point of your bedroom. You've decided on the style. You know the size. What else matters? Indeed, bed sizes are standard and with myriad style options, the choice is yours. But there are practical things to consider that will ensure that choice is the right one for you and your bedroom.

## Bedding height and headboard position

Why does this matter? The top of the mattress should be at a level that makes it easy for you to get in and out of bed and should not obscure the headboard. But the bed frame is only part of this story: Mattresses and box springs come in a variety of thicknesses. It's smart to shop for everything at once so you can discuss the impact of the bedding thickness with the bed frame retailer before you commit to any of the components. Better bed frames are made-to-order (this is true even if the vendor has stock designs you choose among), on these the box-spring support brackets and headboard can be positioned to accommodate your preferred bedding.

Two more caveats here: If the support brackets extend below the bottom of the side rails, they and the box spring will show unless concealed by a bed skirt. And if the top of the box spring is below the top of the side rails, the bottom of the mattress will be too, making it awkward to tuck in the sheets.

## Scale

A bed consumes a fair amount of a room's volume. Depending on its style and specific design details, a bed frame may appear delicate, massive, or somewhere in between (a no-frills metal frame won't show at all). Think about the proportions of your room and choose a frame that is in scale with the space and the architectural details. Massive posts may overwhelm a small room; a canopy crowded against the ceiling won't be graceful.

## True size

What's standard is the width and length of the mattress and box spring. Because these sit inside the frame, the frame itself is at least a few inches larger in each dimension. The headboard, footboard, and posts may add more to the size than you anticipate at first. For instance the scrolled ends lengthen a sleigh bed, a headboard with a storage unit adds length and probably width as well. To see the true size in your room, tape or chalk the footprint of the frame on the floor.

## Stability

The frame should be steady and sturdy. Don't be shy about shaking the floor model, if there is one, to check the joints. King-size bed frames have center slats to support the two-piece box spring; if your queen bed requires a split box spring (to fit through the stairwell or doors), make sure the frame can be made with a center slat too. Any wheels should lock.

## Delivery

White Glove service will assemble the bed in the bedroom; common carrier just carries the boxes into your entry hall. •

ABOVE: **A stylish easy chair, a platform bed wrapped in taupe and white and topped with big plump pillows, and a simply striped shag rug provide the essentials here: a place to sit, a place to sleep, and something nice to greet bare feet. Add the lamps and side tables and one important piece of art, color it all in natural sandy hues, and peace ensues.** (Form Architecture and Interiors)

RIGHT: **Casual country style gets an update with the chunky proportions of this pencil post bed. Custom-made to fit under the eaves, it has three-quarter height tapered square posts and a classic headboard and footboard.** (Barbara Westbrook)

OPPOSITE: **Tailored traditional style turns upbeat sophisticate, dressed here in chartreuse and white with chocolate accents. The upholstered headboard goes graphic with stripes, acres of white linens are unpretentiously seductive, and smart cube stools give a sleek finish at the foot of the bed.** (Jacqueline Derrey Segura)

# INSPIRATIONS

## Padded Headboard = **Soft Style**

Nearly any contour you can dream of can be cut out, padded, and covered with fabric to head your bed.

Since you can have one made in any style from severely rectilinear to voluptuously curvy, an upholstered headboard is an excellent choice for any bedroom. Choose a tailored effect with a smooth edge, or one that's finished with a chubby roll. Go for a quilted or tufted surface, or a tightly stretched expanse of fabric. For a delicate look, choose a bed with a framed headboard that's meant to be upholstered. Then prop up all your pillows and sit up in comfort to read or sip your morning coffee. •

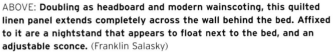

ABOVE: **Doubling as headboard and modern wainscoting, this quilted linen panel extends completely across the wall behind the bed. Affixed to it are a nightstand that appears to float next to the bed, and an adjustable sconce.** (Franklin Salasky)

RIGHT, TOP: **Tufting and a big ruched roll at the edge give substance to this headboard and signal comfort. Colors from the fabric are picked up in the pillows, coverlet, chair, and bench.** (Michael Whaley)

RIGHT: **History is full of ideas: This stylized headboard echoes the profile of an elaborately carved bedstead, here outlined, cut, padded, and covered; the same fabric is used for the bed skirt.** (Bunny Williams)

OPPOSITE: **A carved frame gives a light, delicate finish to upholstery at the head and foot of a bed. Choose an uncomplicated fabric to let the frame details shine—velvet, chenille, simple damask, a subtle silk stripe are luxurious but won't compete.** (Christopher Maya)

OPPOSITE: **Spare, graphic country style proves enduringly modern in chocolate and white. Adding casual sophistication here are horizontal planking with narrow grooves, the vintage geometric hooked rug, and a large embroidered folkloric pillow. If your ceilings are low, take this for inspiration—the roof was raised so the bed would fit comfortably.** (David Mitchell)

ABOVE: **A restricted palette of blue-green and gray is soothing and calm in this bedroom; velvet, damask, and linen fabrics give the hues watery depth. A grid of framed botanical prints continues behind the headboard: "I like to layer things," says the designer, remarking that when things overlap they relate and seem attached, not separate.** (Susan Ferrier)

# PRITVATE LUXURY:
## A Bedroom Sitting Area.

Since your bedroom will be a beautiful place, designed to make you happy, it would be a shame if you never enjoyed it except to sleep. If there's room, create a sitting area where you can read, talk quietly with a confidant, and daydream. Add a chaise, a couple of easy chairs, a settee, a coffee table or ottoman—whatever complements the space, the design, and your idea of comfort. When you choose furnishings, think of the room as a single environment and select a palette and style that work for both the sleeping and sitting areas. Arrange your sitting area to face the bed or be perpendicular to it in front of a window or fireplace, which way to go depends on the shape and size of the room and your preference.

LEFT: **A settee with plump pillows makes an inviting, cozy spot for reading or tea, especially in a warm, coral-colored room. This high-arm settee is an eighteenth-century French antique and shares the sensibility of the new bed, which is modeled on an original from the same period.** (Albert Hadley)

OPPOSITE: **Sit up, lean back, stretch out—a big, cushy window seat is irresistible. Lucky are the people who have a bedroom with a huge bay window that can accommodate a built-in bench. This one is simply adorned with lots of creamy hues that don't compete with the view or the pretty curtained bed.** (Albert Hadley)

# The Choice Is Yours: **BENCHES**

Add books and a breakfast tray. They're so civilized (and sexy) at the end of a bed.

# INSPIRATIONS

## Bed Linens: **What's Your Look?**

They caress your skin and sooth your eye—top your bed with textiles chosen for their color, texture, and style.

Tailored, feminine, luxurious, whimsical, exotic, soft, cuddly, cozy, crisp, smooth. Embellished with borders, ruffles, embroidery, a monogram, a pieced and quilted design. Layered for drama, warmth, elegance, or fun. Look for readymade linens with the look you want, or have them custom made using fabrics and dressmaker details that give unique style. You notice the way a bed is dressed first thing when you walk into your bedroom, so don't let the linens be an afterthought. •

LEFT: **New traditional: White linens scalloped onto blue borders give a crisp graphic edge to the yards of ivory muslin sweetly gathered into the classic canopy, curtains, and skirt on this reeded four-poster bed.** (Markham Roberts)

ABOVE: **Sumptuous and subtle: Shimmering, luxurious, champagne-colored silk and fur give a sophisticated finish to this elegant carved bed painted and aged in a similar hue. Color and sheen are the story here; the bedclothes are plain except for the petite pleated ruffle at the edge of the duvet.** (Karyl Pierce Paxton)

RIGHT, TOP: **Easy elegance: Tailored plain white sheets, an ecru spread with a wide satin border, a whole-cloth quilt with a suble swirled pattern, and plump throw pillows in a large print signify comfort and warmth on in this modern décor.** (David Easton)

RIGHT: **Ultimate indulgence: Surrounded by hangings lined in apricot silk "the color of candlelight," these lustrous custom-made linens with a silky, satiny touch and elegant appliqué motifs "make you want to take off your clothes and roll in the bed."** (Celerie Kemble)

# ROOMS TO STAY IN:
## Planning for Guests.

Extend to your guests the same comfort you appreciate: a pleasant room, a good bed with a reading light, a place to sit, and a place to put overnight bags and clothes. For a room with two beds, make sure each has a light. Provide adjustable window treatments. Add amenities that anyone would love—flowers, some books, some music, something to drink, and intriguing things to look at. Use the same sensibility you employ in the rest of your home so visiting friends and family feel part of your life, but skip the very personal—no family photos. Remember that guests will be in unfamiliar territory, make sure they know where the light switches and towels are. If the room is large enough, include a sitting area; guests will be more comfortable if they have a place to relax alone, and so will you.

ABOVE: **A crazy, bright, orange-and-white wallpaper may seem an unexpected choice for a bedroom, especially in a very old house with low ceilings and aged wide floorboards, but it makes this room fun and happy—just how guests should feel.** (Ruthie Sommers)

OPPOSITE: **Tiny room, wonderful deep window, old plaster walls and beamed ceiling, spare aesthetic perked up by a small chrome bench with a bright yellow top and a splashy red throw: this monastic room lacks nothing for charm or tranquil comfort.** (Eldon Wong)

ABOVE: **Who wouldn't feel special invited to stay in a room with these beds? Custom-made and wonderfully hand-painted and gilded, they were inspired by French antiques. They're beautifully dressed too, with simple button-cuff coverlets and pretty floral pillows. Behind them, the wall is glazed and glows softly; between them, a gilt-trimmed vase holds fresh flowers.** (Marshall Watson)

ABOVE: **This alcove barely accommodates a bed and two side tables, but it's pretty as can be, with a vintage iron bed, rag rug, and worn bench mixing with fresh lace-trimmed linens, painted white floor, and softly gathered lamp shades in classic country cottage style. Sweet dreams.** (Valerie Smith)

OPPOSITE, TOP AND BOTTOM: **Comfort, amenity, and charm all around— visitors might be reluctant to leave such an appealing bed-sitting room. The toile print is rather fun (check out the scalloped hem on the sofa too), the plaid makes a great companion to it, and you can safely leave chocolates for your guests since the brown throw won't show stains.** (T. Keller Donovan)

# DESIGNER'S TOP TEN

Designer Monique Gibson reveals how to bring a touch of charismatic glamour to any bedroom.

**1.** Re-cover existing furniture in a more glamorous fabric, such as cashmere, silk, velvet, or wool sateen. All of these feel wonderful and upholster exceedingly well.

**2.** Look for sensuous shapes when selecting furniture. The curve of an arm or chair back can create a touch of glamour.

**3.** Choose colors that are appealing to you and evoke the mood you want to experience. For a bedroom, it's important to select hues that complement your own coloring.

**4.** Small windows have no glamour quotient, but redesigned curtains can make them look larger. Simply place the rod under the crown molding instead of above the window and allow the draperies to meet at the top. Then tie them back loosely so that an ample amount of fabric frames the view.

**5.** Add a chaise longue. It's probably the most glamorous piece of furniture every created.

**6.** Add a little sparkle with a pair of glass lamps, a Venetian mirror, or a mirrored coffee table. But be careful not to go overboard.

**7.** Fill several small vases with fresh flowers and place them in the bathroom, on the bedside table, everywhere you spend time.

**8.** Candles add an instant touch of glamour. The scents are appealing, and the movement of the flickering light is visually wonderful.

**9.** Reconsider your lighting. Something as simple as changing the bulb wattage can create an entirely different mood. Also think about adding or removing lamps, or maybe installing art lights above a favorite painting.

**10.** Make something routine glamorous by adding something special to it. Bring out the good china for breakfast in bed, or eat your cereal with a silver spoon for a change!

# INSPIRATIONS

## Keep It Tidy: **Make It Stylish**

Clutter isn't soothing, so outfit your bedroom with storage pieces that encourage tidiness and please your eye.

Choose conventional dressers, armoires, and blanket chests with classy lines or an appealing decorative finish (think about what you can display on top as well as hide inside). If closets are scarce, add built-in cupboards in keeping with your architecture. And even if your closets are adequate, give some thought to the door style and finish so you aren't staring at a dull expanse of sliders. You can opt for the unexpected too, almost anything small makes a good bedside table. •

LEFT: **The large antique three-door armoire in this big dressing room is so much more interesting to look at than a closet, offers copious storage, makes an elegant complement to the double pedestal table, and has a terrific beveled oval mirror in which to check your garb.** (David Jimenez)

ABOVE: **In homage to Shaker craftsmanship, these cherry wood cabinets may be the ultimate wall of storage. With graduated drawers and different height compartments, they have been thoughtfully planned to hold specific types of clothing.** (Susan Tully)

RIGHT, TOP: **The decoration on this inherited red lacquer desk is charming, the color comes to life against the ballet-slipper pink wall, and with room to hide necessaries and display small treasures and a lamp, it makes a fine and personal bedside table.** (Myra Hoefer)

RIGHT: **Painted storage furniture is decorative as well as functional; this delicately ornamented chest of drawers harmonizes lightly with the gray-blue and ivory hues and dressy furnishings used throughout the room. Bold pattern and contrast color could be fun in a different situation.** (Suzanne Kasler)

# ROOMS TO GROW IN:
## Designing for Your Kids.

Where does your child wish to live? In a tugboat, a jungle, a castle, on the moon, or in the hippest spot in town? Is she hooked on romantic linens or pop stars? Does his life revolve around cars or action movies? Many design pros waive the principle of whole-house continuity when they reach the children's rooms. And why not, the kids have personality to express and lives that don't always mirror yours. The meaning of "sanctuary" in a child's room is different from in the master suite; where you want to get away from work and social responsibilities, your child needs his own territory for study and entertaining friends as well as sleeping. You can have fun together deciding on a look. Decide which furnishings will be needed and try to zone the room for different activities. If you're reluctant to invest in trendy or age-specific furnishings that your child will outgrow, focus on classic or plain items to which you can give a new look by changing linens, accessories, and paint over time.

LEFT: **Blue, pink, yellow, white, flowers, stripes, plaid: Two young sisters sleep, laugh, and read in this room. It's a happy space, with nothing built in, so it can easily be updated as they grow up. Overhead a chandelier with wire baskets holds shells collected at the nearby beach.** (Ruby Beets)

ABOVE AND OPPOSITE: **Hot pink, lively, a bit theatrical, the tempo for this room was set by the girl who loves being in it. On one side a black wrought-iron daybed serves as sofa and sleeping spot, on the other a quirky niche holds bookshelves and a cushioned banquette for lounging. Mirrors bounce the bright colors and patterns around the room; a Lucite coffee table and chair, flokati rugs, and giant floor cushions add to the fun.** (Sally Markham)

ABOVE: Complete with faux bois wallpaper, antler trophies found on eBay, rattan accessories, and stag print fabric, this bedroom plays up the hunting lodge ambience that pervades the house. The would-be big-game hunter who sleeps here is 7. Says the designer, "I wanted it to be masculine but not juvenile. I don't think a room needs to be designed so specifically for a child that it can't be used for guests in a pinch." (Tom Scheerer)

LEFT: The vision: An elegant yacht, with a 1930s-style bed upholstered in white piqué and nailhead trim looking out a large porthole. The colors: Dreamy lavenders, royal blue, oyster, and white, chosen to flatter an older redheaded girl. The furnishings: A mix of French and contemporary, with pretty linens, very full curtains, a skirted vanity. The result: feminine, opulent, fantasy-filled, yet restrained. (Myra Hoefer)

# PULL IT TOGETHER

Your dream bedroom is clear in your mind. You're ready to plan the specifics. Pull out your clipping and swatch files; sort, mix, and match the pieces until you have a selection that is close to the look you want. If you're doing more than one bedroom, edit a set of samples for each. If you like, make a collage so you can revisit your choices later or share them with a designer. If you find you're missing something, note it; discuss it with your designer, or with salespeople if you're working on your own.

## Ambience

Choose the key words that describe your dream bedroom— sanctuary, tranquil, traditional, hip, glamorous, open and airy, snug—whatever they may be.

## Color

Think of the overall palette. Which will be the principal hue and where will you use it? What role will pattern play?

## Walls

What sort of background will the walls provide? Plain color or pattern? Are there lots of windows? If one wall is devoted to closets, how will you finish them?

## Window treatments

Will the window treatments blend with the walls or contrast them? Will they be simple or voluminous? Is there a door to a terrace? Will you use draperies, shades, blinds, or shutters for privacy?

## Floor

What are the floors like? How important will they be, will they contrast the walls or be mostly covered?

## Rugs

Your feet will be bare; what kind of floor covering will give you the look you want? A large carpet overall? Area rugs or small rugs at the bedside? Will they provide an assertive or subtle pattern or introduce multiple colors or obvious texture? Might you layer them?

## Storage

Plan shelves and hanging storage inside closets. Choose dressers or chests with the character you like, in a suitable scale. Is there a dressing room? How will you design it? Do you have room for bookshelves?

## Lighting fixtures

Keep ambient light soft and soothing; use a chandelier if it suits your fancy. Provide reading light at the bed and in any sitting areas—what style fixtures will make you smile? Make sure closets are lit.

## Furniture

A bed, of course, with side tables. Storage furniture if necessary. Include a chair or two, upholstered if there is enough room. Add an ottoman or coffee table if there's a sitting area; a table or desk if you like. Would you like a bench at the foot of the bed? Is there a window seat?

## Accessories

What sort of bed linens complement your look? A mirror is never out of place; choose a great frame. Add artwork, family photos, and any collectibles you wish. What about television or a sound system?

## Kid's rooms

Provide a study center with a place for a computer. Decide how to accommodate and display teddy bears, dolls, model trains, musical instruments, or whatever "friends" and gear your child holds dear.

## Layout

Even if you're not feeling ready to do a real floor plan, it's smart to do something rough that can serve as a reality check for the amount and scale of the furniture. Draw the outline of the room on graph paper; mark the windows, doorways, and closets. Make some paper cutouts of the furniture in the same scale and position them. Is there room to move about comfortably?

OPPOSITE: **In an antique home, this bedroom has a traditional look with a modern spin. Creamy coffee, eggshell, and teal hues balance the dark, time-mellowed floorboards and overhead beams to make the space soothing. The reproduction bed wears a classic canopy made in an iridescent synthetic fabric; the bedclothes are simple and modern in style. The texture of the large wool rug echoes the subtle grid pattern of the canopy lining. Antique silver candlesticks converted to lamps sit on mismatched tables at the bedside.** (Robert Goodwin)

# A STUDIO APARTMENT

Studio apartments are almost always small, but the limited space is not the most challenging aspect of living in one. That comes from the lack of a bedroom door. So if you are a studio resident, think of the positive adjectives that can describe "small": charming, snug, quaint, jewel-box—and be assured they really can apply to a living space where the bed must be in, or visible from, the sitting/dining room. Choose whatever look you like for a studio—opulent, elegant, tranquil, jazzed, modernist, traditional, sophisticated; consider how cozy or spare you prefer the overall ambience to be; and then edit your vision to fit your space.

### Zone it

The shape and overall size affects the setup of your studio. Can you separate the living and sleeping quarters? Is there room for a bed as well as a sofa, or will you need a daybed or sleep sofa? Is there an ell that can be the "bedroom"? Will the dining table double as a desk? Which part of your life does the entry door open into? If the kitchen is not a separate room, read "Open-Plan Living Spaces" on page 332.

### Play with the space

Use mirrors to make the space feel larger and brighter. If there's room, consider a folding screen, sliding panel, or curtain to separate one area from another—even a narrow panel that suggests an alcove could make a difference. Look up too, if the ceilings are very tall, there could be room for a loft area or overhead storage.

ABOVE AND RIGHT: **The sleeping area in this small, L-shaped studio is little more than a hallway between the foyer and the combined living/dining area and is always on view from both. It looks pulled together, dressy, and not overtly "bedroomy," with a high headboard and footboard on the daybed providing a sense of enclosure and privacy. At the other end, the room is blessed with a window wall and the sofa is turned away from the dining table to define and separate different activities.** (Elizabeth Orenstein)

## Storage

Assess the closet space and any other built-in storage. Will you supplement it? What about bookshelves? When you pull together your furnishings, be creative about what can go in what—a secretary, armoire, or credenza can be used for clothing, linens, pantry, or office supplies as you like. Look for dual-purpose pieces such as a captain's bed, bench, or ottoman that has a storage compartment.

## Scale, balance, and harmony

Sketch the floor plan and think through the furnishings plan. Everything will be visible at once and space may be an issue; be especially aware of the scale of the pieces and their visual weight when choosing a style; be thoughtful about furniture shapes, legs, side and back views; and choose fabrics, finishes, and colors that complement the whole. Designers hold different views on how, when, or whether to use large pieces in a small space or whether colors can be saturated or patterns bold, so look at photos to see what appeals to you. •

LEFT: **There's no pretense of large quarters here—it's one-room living, enjoying a bay window and focused on the mantel. The look is light and modern, with a small sofa serving as footboard to the bed, chairs that are fun to look at, and a sleek freestanding closet tucked into the recess next to the fireplace.** (Frank Roop)

# What's key in your dream bathroom?

- ☐ A huge soaking tub
- ☐ Rain showerheads
- ☐ A tub with a view
- ☐ A shower for two
- ☐ Trendy basins
- ☐ Flattering light

# 17. BATHROOMS

Is your bathroom a place of ritual? Do you speed through your grooming routine or linger in the room, alone or with a partner? Do you prefer a look that's meditative or one that's crisp, perhaps almost clinical? How much space do you have and is the bath en suite with your bedroom? Which other bathrooms are you decorating? A guest bath, one for a child, or a powder room? How should they differ from yours?

Bathrooms in contemporary homes are often generously proportioned, numerous, and lavishly appointed. Older homes don't always have such space to devote to grooming, but that's no reason to sacrifice style. What's your situation? Are you starting fresh, with a room that's brand new or about to be gutted? Are you redecorating but using existing fixtures? Will you reconfigure the layout? If it's a master bath, will two people use it at once? What with plumbing, lighting, fixture, and fitting specifications, not to mention building codes, there's a lot of technical know-how involved in bathroom design, and whether you wish to pamper yourself with glamour, Old World charm, minimalist modernism, or country simplicity, you'll be dealing with more than the look if you're doing anything extensive. There's no need to figure it out yourself: if you engage a professional bathroom designer or an interior designer, she will listen to your vision, assess your budget, add a layer of creative insight, and figure out how to make your dream bathroom real.

# PRIVACY RULES:
## Planning a Bathroom.

Set aside your style preferences for a moment and begin your bathroom design with an assessment of the space: how large is the room? Although fixtures come in various sizes to suit different spaces, you can probably tell by standing inside an existing room if you're facing a crisis of dimensions or if there's room to play with. If your home is not yet built, the floor plan will indicate the bathroom layout and you can consult with your architect and interior designer if you wish to alter it.

Bearing in mind what you've discovered about the size, start to dream. Make a wish list of the features you'd like to include: Toilet of course. Soaking tub? Walk-in shower? Tub with shower? One or two basins, in a vanity or not? Bidet? A grooming station you can sit at? A comfortable chair or bench? Is this your master bath, or a child's bath, or guest bath? Your wish list might be the same for each, or it could be different. What do you think: Are your dreams in line with the space, maybe possible, or obviously impossible? No matter how you answer, hold onto your wish list. It's smart to adjust your thoughts realistically, but a good designer may be able to find space you didn't know you had, and she won't know you need it if you haven't thought about the features you'd love to put in it.

How do you envision the background of your bathroom? Are you dreaming of gleaming marble walls and floor? Of painted wainscoting and a natural wood floor? Of colorful ceramic tiles laid in a geometric pattern, or of classic white subway tiles on the walls and tiny hexagonal tiles on the floor? Nearly everything that goes into a bathroom becomes part of the structure and the materials chosen can have a great influence on the look of the room, so it's important to think about the look you want and the effect of different surfaces early on. Many of the materials used are hard—tile, stone, metal, and the plumbing fixtures themselves—with colors and sheen or texture often integral with the material. While there are many options, remember that tile comes in fewer colors than paint, natural stone in fewer still, and materials and colors for plumbing fixtures are even more limited. Your choice of materials could become the basis for your palette.

Fixtures, faucets, showerheads, water controls, and accessories such as towel bars provide the style lines in a bathroom. You'll see lots of options in this book and there are many publications and online resources devoted to them, but nothing beats a visit to a showroom for giving you a true sense of scale, shape, and finish. Go shopping; even if the brand you'd like doesn't have a local showroom, visit whatever is available to sense the impact of different options. Most fittings (faucets, showerheads, and controls) come in complementary sets for all the fixtures in the room; if you want something special you may wish to select pieces from different lines within a brand or from different manufacturers.

Every bathroom needs some kind of horizontal surface and at least a minimal amount of storage for toiletries. A vanity takes care of both; if you wish to include one, you have the option of something built-in, either from a line of kitchen cabinets or custom made, or of a freestanding unit, perhaps with legs that give the look of a piece of furniture. In any case, a vanity should be topped with something water-resistant. (There is information about cabinets and countertops in Chapter 14, Kitchens.) If a vanity doesn't appeal to you, consider a sink with an integral flat surround, a shelf mounted on the wall, a side table or cabinet, and a medicine cabinet.

Most bathrooms require window treatments for privacy. If you have a view from the tub or French doors that lead to a terrace, you'll be the best judge of the privacy needs as indicated by the proximity of neighbors and the landscaping. Remember that sheer and translucent treatments that filter the natural light will appear transparent to anyone outdoors when the room lights are on.

While you're planning, give some thought to the effects of moisture—it takes a toll over time, especially on textiles, paint and wallpaper, and these may need freshening more frequently than hard materials like tile. Some people are reluctant to display fine art in a bathroom, others enjoy it; if you decide to display art, try to position it away from the steamy shower.

OPPOSITE: **Here's a dramatic use of space for anyone whose bathroom is large: A shower enclosure, glass on the front and back and marble-cased on the sides, stands in the middle of the room to show the full impact of the large tub platform and window wall at the end. The shower is set up for two, has a marble bench across the back, and is lighted by a skylight. Heated towel bars are nearby on each wall.** (Albert Hadley and Harry Heissmann)

# ROOMS WE LOVE

Once a utilitarian space devoted to hygiene, the bathroom has become a place of relaxation and pleasure. What sort of ambience will make you feel pampered? Romantic, with a chaise and candle sconces? Classic, with a claw foot tub and old-fashioned pedestal sink? Very modern, with a custom-made hammered metal tub, or graphic shapes silhouetted against plain walls? Do you long for opulence, with surfaces that shimmer under a crystal chandelier and touches of gold leaf? Or is your preference for an unpretentious look, with lots of fresh air, to suit an informal country house? Or something rustic, with distressed woodwork? Is a spa look, with everything in watery colors and arranged for leisurely indulgence, the one you'll love? However modest or grand your bathroom may be, choose a look that will satisfy your need to unwind and set it up so you'll feel fresh and ready to meet the world. Take your inspiration from these photos of bathrooms we'd love to linger in.

ABOVE: **This bath exudes the warmth and elegance of pale earthy hues, a molding-trimmed panel fronting the tub, a dressy bench, and hand-painted velvet curtains. When the curtains are closed for privacy the mood becomes beautiful and serene.** (Kathy Smith)

LEFT: **A floor of Cararra marble slabs and waterproof white plaster on all the walls, including the shower, give this master bath "a monolithic feel," says the designer, adding, "The effect is Zen and peaceful." A full-length shower curtain hung on a ceiling track, limed oak cabinets, and a frameless mirror complete the look.** (Betsy Brown)

OPPOSITE: **Why not? A nineteenth-century English secretary adds an impressive focal point next to the tub in this master bath. The owner spends a lot of time in this room and the secretary is a special piece she loves to look at, so she placed it here, where she can enjoy it often.** (Paolo Moschino)

OPPOSITE: **A bathroom bay window begs for a soaking tub; this one has the nostalgic appeal of vintage style (the tub, tub filler, and hand-held sprayer all are new) enhanced by an antique stained-glass pendant light and tiny hexagonal tiles on the floor. Privacy as-you-like-it comes from top-down Roman shades with matching valances.** (Ken Fulk)

ABOVE: **This spare country bath has simple charm and offers an idea for what to do in an antique home where indoor plumbing isn't "authentic." The freestanding basin set on an old workbench calls up visions of a large washbowl; the faucet mounted on the mirror adds a witty touch. Unbleached linen Roman shades bring a rustic touch to the windows.** (Kay Douglass)

# THE RULES OF . . .

## BATHROOM CLEARANCE

Here are some standards that make a bathroom easy and safe to move in.

- A minimum space of 21 inches is required by code in front of a sink, toilet, bidet, or tub; 24 inches is required in front of a shower. Thirty inches or more is preferred.

- Allow at least 20 inches from the center of a sink to the side wall or a tall cabinet or shower. For a double vanity, center the basins at least 36 inches apart; two freestanding or wall-hung sinks must be separated by at least 4 inches.

- A shower interior must be at least 30 inches square excluding any seat or bench; 36 inches or more is recommended.

- The minimum distance from the centerline of a toilet or bidet to the side wall or another object is 15 inches; 18 inches or more is preferred. A toilet compartment must be at least 36 by 66 inches and the door must swing out.

RIGHT, TOP: **A curved wall faced with vertical boards sets the stage in this bath, where sinuous lines shape the vanity and the tub snugs the wall. Black-and-white granite, polished on the counter-top, honed on the floor, and stain-less steel, hammered and mellow for the tub and smooth and shiny on the vanity are unexpected complements to the painted wall.** (Diamond Baratta)

RIGHT, BOTTOM: **The tub and van-ity area in this inviting master bath are furnished much as any other part of a home might be, with a dressy chair, pretty side table, a painting, and surfaces for vases of flowers.** (Jill Morris)

OPPOSITE: **You can walk from this bathroom right out onto a teak wood deck; to link the aesthetic between the two, teak is the only surface material used indoors. It gleams beautifully around this tub and is also used wherever else one might put tile or stone.** (Waldo Fernandez)

# EXPERT INSIGHT

## KEYS TO PERFECT BATHROOM DESIGN

Jerry Jacobs, principal of Jerry Jacobs Design in Tiburon, California, shares his techniques for bringing style to the most functional of rooms.

### What are the keys to a perfectly designed bathroom?

It's a matter of what the bathroom is for: A powder room is your introduction to guests, your master bath is perhaps the most generous in terms of design and comfort, and in between is the utilitarian guest bath. But the primary consideration is precision. In the bathroom you have to be very accurate with dimensions because plumbing is unforgiving. So the prime consideration is planning.

### Where do you start in bathroom design?

The first question I ask is "What color do you like?" They all work. I don't discriminate with colors, they can all be beautiful. But you know, it depends on what you're trying to achieve—that's what you'll focus on in the design.

### Getting back to focus, what are the potential focal points?

The vanity is the most important piece because it's the one that's not necessarily functional or related to health; plus the mirror above it expands the space. Sometimes you open the door to the bathroom and the first thing you see is the toilet. What you should see is the vanity.

### What are the biggest challenges you face in designing a bathroom?

Usually it's a size issue. A small room and a small budget.

### So how do you deal with the space constraints in a bathroom?

The mirror, of course. I did a bathroom that I called "Hall of Mirrors." All the walls had a percentage of mirrors, from wainscot to 6 or 7 feet. The point was not only enlarging the small space—which the mirrors did—but having fun as well.

### How do you feel about art in the bathroom?

I'm okay with it. The more time you're going to spend there—like in a master bathroom with a huge bathtub where you're going to relax—you have to enjoy your walls. That's why you have art. The humidity in a bathroom can be controlled by ventilation. In a powder room, it's practically nil.

### What types of lighting do you think work best in the bathroom?

The most desirable is natural light. It's the best kind of lighting. But, of course, you also need good artificial light. The vanity lighting is most important because it lets you know how you look. Because of the shadows created, it's much better to have light on either side of your face, not above it. But you need good general light—relatively simple lighting works.

### What do you think are the best ways to create a sense of luxury in the bathroom?

The materials. If the entire space is covered with finishes and fixtures of a high quality, you feel like the room is a jewel, totally contained and private. That's the luxurious aspect. If you start cutting costs then it looks like a regular bathroom. But if you go all the way, you have the sense of a jewel. •

ABOVE: **A charming vanity is the first thing you see from the doorway to this guest bath—it's so much nicer to look at than a toilet. Nice touch for visitors: towels neatly stacked and readily visible through the mesh cabinet doors.** (Barbara Westbrook)

OPPOSITE: **A large mirror seems to double the size of this small bath and maximizes the already copious daylight. Gold leaf is an elegant choice for the frame and picks up the soft gold in the mosaic floor.** (Kerry Joyce)

# Colorful Opinions: **BATHROOMS**

Whether your style is ready-set-go or long soaks in the tub, these designers will bathe you in just the right color.

**ATHALIE DERSE:**
**PRATT & LAMBERT**
**ANTIQUE WHITE 2207**
I want a color that's subtle and refreshing at the same time. This looks like an old celadon that would have been popular back in the 1940s. First thing in the morning, I don't want anything jolting that's going to give me a headache.

**RONALD BRICKE:**
**PRATT & LAMBERT**
**AUTUMN CROCUS 1141**
Imagine waking up and walking into the brightest, sunniest day. This is a bright lavender blue, moderately intense, very cheerful. Some people will say, "Oh, I don't like lavender," but this does not come off like lavender. It's clean, fresh—guaranteed to perk you up.

**ANNE CARSON:**
**BENJAMIN MOORE**
**BRILLIANT WHITE**
In a bathroom, there's nothing better than clean, fresh, pure white. This is a very clear, soothing white, not too bright and not too creamy. You never get tired of it, it never looks dated, and you can easily change the look by changing the artwork.

**MICHAEL FORMICA:**
**BENJAMIN MOORE**
**CALIFORNIA BLUE 2060-20**
It's a strange color, sort of an old-fashioned blueprint blue. I actually like dark bathrooms with very controlled artificial light. That way you can really hone in on the problems when doing your toilette. Besides, I think dark walls are sexy.

**DAVID MANN:**
**RALPH LAUREN PAINT**
**ARCHITECTURAL CREAM UL55**
This is kind of a pale khaki gray. It approximates the kind of light you get on a cloudy day, which makes all the other colors around look deep and true, more intense. We generally use white fixtures, and it really sets them off and makes them look absolutely clean.

ROBIN BELL:
**FARROW & BALL
DIMITY 2008**
This is a beautiful, cloudlike off-white with just the right amount of pink in it, so people look nice—but not so flattering that you walk out the door thinking you look terrific when you really don't.

THAD HAYES:
**DONALD KAUFMAN
DKC-64**
It's a dark gray-brown-green; you name it, it's in there. It's almost like a clay mud color—really rich and really beautiful. Very dramatic with dark or light stone and nickel features.

STEPHANIE STOKES:
**BENJAMIN MOORE
FRESH DEW 435**
This is in the mint, pine family. It's a pale wash of green that reminds me of the water off Corsica in the summer. Since I spend a lot of time soaking in my Jacuzzi, I can't imagine anything better.

BETSY BROWN:
**PRATT & LAMBERT
WENDIGO 2293**
This is really, really dark, almost black. It's not a color that introduces anything, you're barely aware of it all, you see what's in the room.

JARRETT HEDBORG:
**BENJAMIN MOORE
TANGERINE DREAM 2012-30**
It ain't white, honey. It's a wonderful, glowing Luis Barragan color, an orange that doesn't look silly. The dirty little secret about these big white California Spanish houses is that inside they feel dark and gray. So I sit the clients down, tie them up, and tell them this is what we're going to do and it will make you look 10 years younger. That usually gets them to say "yes."

BARBARA SALLICK:
**BENJAMIN MOORE
SILVER SATIN OC-26**
Historically, white is the color of health and hygiene. But it has to be the right white, something soft and warm like Silver Satin that can complement a range of materials—marble, tile, porcelain, metal. A really bright white would not be attractive on your skin.

PRISCILLLA ULMANN:
**FARROW & BALL
YELLOW GROUND 218**
This is a rich egg-yolk yellow, a classic English color. I used it in my own bathroom, which doesn't have any windows, and it brings in the sunlight that's not there.

RALPH HARVARD:
**PRATT & LAMBERT
PELHAM GRAY LIGHT CW 819**
It's a very evasive gray from the Colonial Williamsburg line that changes color in different lights. I hate to call it a gray, because people think of gray as chilly, and this is very warm. It can look 1930s chic or 1810 countrified or twenty-first–century cool.

# SO ALLURING.
## Which Sink Will You Choose?

When it comes to washing your hands, porcelain, enameled cast iron, glass, copper, zinc, stone, painted ceramic, and even crystal are among the options for a basin. Properly called a "lavatory," the bathroom sink can be a prominent stylistic element or so plain you don't pay much attention to it. There are four basic types—pedestal, wall-mounted, console, and vanity. Each comes in many styles, shapes, materials, colors, and sizes, so play one up or down as suits the look you're after. Various styles require different faucet configurations, so look for them together, choosing a faucet and controls that work with your basin choice and have a shape and finish you love.

Pedestal sinks are often chosen for traditional or old-fashioned baths, but they come with sleek modern silhouettes as well as in classic styles that have pretty fluted or footed bases and generous molded surrounds and integral backsplashes. They're most often porcelain; the more modern types come in whatever colors are current as well as standard white. Viewed from the front, the pedestal masks the water and drain pipes, though you get a glimpse of them in the side view. Pedestal sinks are a good choice where space is limited—they have considerably less mass than a vanity with a comparable basin.

Wall-mounted sinks are generally used in small spaces; you can even find them shaped to fit in a corner. Among smart contemporary shapes available are generously sized basins with the look of elegant utility sinks and others that look like small floating bowls or sleek wading pools, so don't assume these are limited to retro looks of the last century. The pipes below a wall-mounted sink are always on view.

Console lavatories combine features of pedestal and wall-mounted styles. The basin often has a tabletop or counter surround, and is supported on two, or occasionally four, legs, sometimes with towel bars attached. Style and material options vary widely, with both classic and modern types to be found. The pipes are always exposed, though the larger tops minimize their visibility.

From a practical perspective, vanity cabinets play the dual role of supporting a sink and providing storage but aesthetically, they bring plenty of style to the room as well. If you choose to use one, its character will be your first concern, and the basin that goes with it is part of its style (see The Choice Is Yours: Vanities, page 430). There are simple basins that mount under the counter, drop into it, or can be tiled in, some materials can be fashioned as counters with integral basins, and there is also a terrific array of sculptural vessels that sit like bowls on top of the counter.

LEFT: **A thick marble slab with an undermounted basin tops this streamlined vanity. The asymmetrical design allows for maximum counter space on one side of the off-center sink, making it a smart choice for a small space like this powder room.** (Nancy Corzine)

OPPOSITE: **To increase the sense of space and openness in this bath, which was designed to be like one in a luxury hotel, cabinets were omitted from the double vanity; instead you see the marble undermounted sinks and the nickel frame. To make up for the lost storage, the medicine cabinets are 4 inches deep. With lots of marble and polished nickel, the look is clean, white, crisp, and efficient. Hurricane lamps, more often used in a hall or dining room, light the mirrors.** (Phoebe Howard)

# INSPIRATIONS

## Powder Rooms that Pamper

What does it take to make a half-bath gracious, surprising, and stylish? Just a bit of something special.

Claim the small size of a half-bath as the perfect excuse and indulge your whim for that unusual basin, glorious light fixture, fabulous mirror, or hand-painted wall. There's no humidity to worry about in a powder room, so a fine painting would be nice too. Make sure there's somewhere for a visitor to place her handbag, and add scented soap, candles, lovely or fun hand towels, and other thoughtful amenities to please your guests as well as yourself. No rule says you must be extravagant—but why not? •

LEFT: **Whiff of antiquity: This exceptional old marble basin counter was once installed with its rough edges against the wall, but here they're unpretentiously left in full view. The three-tier display makes the vintage hand-towel collection approachable and humorous: "Just mop off," they seem to say.** (Jeffrey Bilhuber)

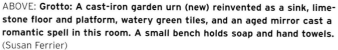

ABOVE: **Grotto:** A cast-iron garden urn (new) reinvented as a sink, lime-stone floor and platform, watery green tiles, and an aged mirror cast a romantic spell in this room. A small bench holds soap and hand towels. (Susan Ferrier)

RIGHT, TOP: **Charm:** A classic pedestal sink is key to the old-fashioned appeal of this powder room, which is in the French mode with a fresh pretty print fabric pasted to the walls, a gold-framed mirror, and a two-tier étagère. (David Kleinberg)

RIGHT: **Glamour:** Custom designed and built by a master craftsman, this elegant vanity has a tiny sink on one side and a cabinet for lotions and potions on the other, with a makeup table in between. A three-way standing mirror takes care of details; the mirrored wall reflects the lovely surroundings of this master powder room. (Paul Wiseman)

# The Choice Is Yours: **VANITIES**

Give your bath a
quick new look. What
a stylish way to start
the day.

# SHOWER TIME.
## Which Look Is Right?

Solo or double? Room for a bench? The color of rain, the ocean, or classic white? A walk-in shower can be customized in myriad ways. Depending on the space available, a shower can be nearly any shape and size you dream of, and placed in a corner, recessed in an alcove, or extended into the room. You have your choice of ceramic, stone, or glass tile in fabulous colors and of framed or frameless glass doors, which can be transparent or translucent. Or if you prefer, there are excellent readymade molded shower modules to which you can add whatever doors you like, or you can start with a stock base (called a pan or dish), tile the walls, and add your choice of doors—several sizes and shapes are available for both options.

The shower space is only half the story; the fittings are at least as important to your enjoyment and enhance the look as well. What will it be, a huge rain showerhead or a classic style? One that pulses? A spray bar with multiple jets on the wall? A handheld shower that rests in a bracket until you're ready to hose down? A mix of several of the above? Go shopping to see all the options.

**RIGHT: Reverse-painted glass tiles give this shower a deeply aquatic aura. The showerhead can be adjusted up or down on its mounting bar or removed and held by hand. Other amenities include a bench and inset niche for toiletries; the grab bar is required for safety.** (David Easton)

FAR RIGHT: **Forget the tiled floor and glass enclosure. Mother Nature doesn't require that kind of protection. At the beach, the lake, or in any country setting where there's sufficient space, an outdoor shower is the ultimate refresher. Do make sure the water drains safely away from the foundation of your house.** (Gil Schafer)

LEFT: **Clever idea: Have steel-and-glass casement window sash custom-fabricated for a shower enclosure. This one looks terrific with the granite floor and subtly hued tile wall (note the alternating bands of square and rectangular tile). Barely visible behind the door are small corner shelves, a hand shower, and a rain showerhead. The inward swinging door means no water drips on the floor when you exit the shower.** (Jeffrey Bilhuber)

# THE RULES OF . . .

## BATHROOM SAFETY

In a room where water, medications, and electrical appliances all find a home, it makes sense to take safety precautions. Be especially careful when residents or guests are elderly or too young to read.

- Install grab bars in the shower, by the tub, and next to the toilet. Look for these when you choose your towel bars and shower fittings.
- Put non-slip strips or decals in the tub or shower.
- Put non-skid mats under any rugs that don't come with a rubber backing.
- Make sure there is GFCI (ground fault circuit inter-rupter) outlet next to the basin; these protect against electrical shocks and are required by code.
- Store appliances such as hair dryers and radios away from wet areas and always unplug them after use.
- Keep all medications and cosmetics out of the reach of children (in a locked cupboard is recom-mended); keep the labels on the containers. Store cleaning chemicals in another room if at all possi-ble or place them where kids can't reach them.
- Place a nightlight in one of the electrical outlets.

# SO SEDUCTIVE.
## Which Tub Will You Choose?

When you're ready to soak, choose between two basic tub styles—freestanding or built-in. All tub types come in a number of sizes with various interior contours and whirlpool options can be found for each type. When you shop, don't be shy—climb in and test the fit. Freestanding tubs can be custom fabricated in all sorts of materials if you don't come across one you love; built-in tubs are usually enamel on cast iron or a cast resin. If your bathroom is on the second floor, be prepared for the contractor to grumble if you choose a stone or cast-iron tub!

A freestanding tub will have a sculptural presence, depending on the contours and material it may look very modern or charmingly classic; either way it will add a touch of elegance to your bath. There are two kinds of built-in tubs—those that are installed in a corner or alcove and fitted with a shower and shower curtain, and those that drop into a platform and are usually paired with a separate walk-in shower. The tub-shower is sometimes the only choice in a smaller bathroom; great tile on the walls will dress it up. There are also good looking tub-shower modules with integral walls. Platform tubs usually give a tailored look to a room. The tub can be set at any distance from the wall, the surrounding platform can be any size, and the top and

exterior sides can be finished with wood, tile, stone, or a combination. If the platform is more than a few inches wide, there is often a step next to it to make access easier and safer. When nicely finished these tubs can be quite elegant, and they have the great advantage of providing a place to put things (or for a companion to sit) while you bathe.

Choose fittings that complement the style of the tub and the look of the room. Even a simple tub-shower will be enhanced by a wonderful showerhead and classy faucet and controls. There are all sorts of stylish tub fillers for freestanding tubs, and sometimes they'll work for a platform tub too. Handheld showers are appropriate for all types, though perhaps not in a bath used by small children who can't resist aiming them outside the tub.

ABOVE: **This is a setting in Hawaii where the opulence of nature and the manmade seem to naturally intertwine and blur, as they do in this tub niche, where grand, rustic wood columns frame the entry and a bank of windows wraps the end and opens to lush vegetation. The travertine marble-faced platform around the tub can double as a banquette at the window or along the front.** (Douglas Durkin and Greg Elich)

LEFT: **This classic footed tub pairs well with the paneled wainscoting behind it. The filler includes a handheld shower; a basket across one end holds soaps and other accoutrements. Open-minded occupants chose to hang the Italian painting here so they could see it often, and drew the color scheme for the room from it.** (Paolo Moschino)

OPPOSITE: **All the surfaces in this very white, very calm master bath have a shimmery luster and the deep, sculptural tub completes the room's Byzantine feel, "like an Egyptian goddess should be rising from it," says the designer. Enhancing the effect are fittings with a finish somewhere between gold and silver.** (Sally Markham)

# The Choice Is Yours: **BATHTUBS**

They're self-indulgent and totally extravagant, but give so much pleasure. Don't think tub, think sculpture . . .

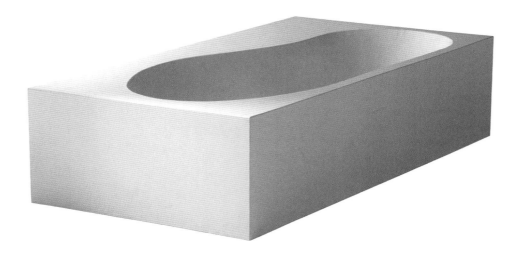
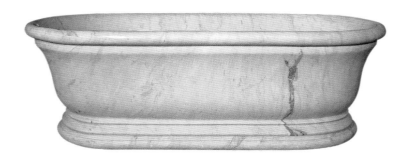
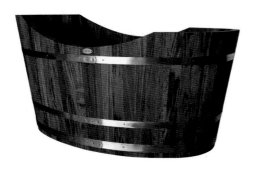

# LIGHTING FIXTURES:
## Use a Mix.

Practical and flattering is the goal of bathroom lighting and you can take your pick of stylish fixtures to create it. The flip of a switch should turn on enough general light to make the room comfortable and safe; your needs will vary with the size of the room but pendant lights, a chandelier, or multiple ceiling or wall fixtures can all work. You'll want ambient lighting that's soft, not glaring, so keep overhead and wall fixtures focused away from mirrors and shiny tiles, and choose shades that diffuse the light. Some fixtures incorporate heat lamps or exhaust fans; if these are on your list, look at the options first and think about how you'll pair them with the style of the other fixtures. If there's good daylight and the room is large, you may wish to use multiple fixtures that are individually switched so they can be used selectively, where needed, during the day.

Provide bright light at the mirror, placing fixtures on the side rather than above. If you choose small sconces for their decorative effect, you'll probably need the ambient fixtures to supplement them for grooming. Incandescent bulbs have the kindest glow but the newer compact fluorescent ones are less harsh than you might expect. Fixtures designed for bathroom use usually specify bulbs that give flattering light. Include reading light as needed and choose an overhead fixture for the shower, making sure it is designed for that installation.

OPPOSITE AND BELOW: **A large mirror over the tub bounces light from the window in the shower back into this bathroom and reflects the unexpected crystal chandelier. "I added sparkle wherever I could," explains the designer, who wanted this bath to be glamorous but not feminine. There are crystal teardrops on the silver-plated sconces beside the vanity mirrors, crystal knobs on the tailored cabinets, and lots of polished marble to catch the light too.** (Kari Cusack)

# ACCESSORIES:
## The Best Amenities.

As long as you're pampering yourself, don't stop when you've made the major decisions for your bathroom. You need mirrors (regular and magnifying), a place to hang towels (a warming rack would be so luxe), and cabinets, shelves, caddies, and racks for holding all manner of things. What about a bench or chaise? What about a rug? Would you like a hamper? Even a scrap basket has shape, color, and surface, which style will you choose? Many bathroom accessories are designed as part of the faucet and showerhead set, so, especially if you want good quality chrome pieces, look at the options when you're at the fixture store. Home stores and catalogs offer all manner of stylish designs for small cabinets, shower and tub racks, toiletry trays, soap dishes, candle holders, and baskets. Keep your eyes open for pieces from the dining room, living room, or kitchen that suit the look you wish to create. And don't forget the art.

ABOVE: **With a big double window at the middle of this vanity, tall narrow mirrors above the free-standing basins at the ends were a must. On the counter between, a rattan tray keeps things neat and tidy; the shadowbox with shells is a nice touch since this is a beach house. Little amenities were remembered here too: note the small hook below the sconce and the large one on the door reflected in the mirror.** (Susan Ferrier)

LEFT: **Large room, lovely prospect, dreamy tub, lots of amenities: For conversation, daydreaming out the window, or back-scrubbing, there are a big X bench and sweet slipper chair to pull up to the tub. For cold feet, there's a lush flokati rug. A neat hamper stands ready for soiled towels next to the large sink. The big mirror reflects the view and light; in front of it a small, railed shelf displays family photos (or cosmetics).** (Ruby Beets)

ABOVE: **Built-in open shelves answer the storage challenge in this very small bathroom; they're neat, precise, and charmingly integrated with the beadboard walls and the tub surround. There's a magazine rack incorporated in the basket over the tub, a towel bar on the wall above the spigot, and a small table nearby for things that must stay absolutely dry. A pair of framed botanicals draws the eye to the alcove and breaks up the expanse above the tub.** (Barbara Westbrook)

# PULL IT TOGETHER

You've decided. You know what you want your bathroom to be. Assemble your clipping and swatch files so you can begin to plan the specifics. Mix, match, and shuffle the pieces until you come up with a whole that is close to your dream look. However, unless you fall in the do-it-yourself category, don't worry if you don't have the perfect swatch, sample, or photo of each element—your goal is to create an annotated collage of ideas that you can share with the design pros who will bring your bathroom to life. If there's something eluding you, just note it as a question to be discussed with your designer.

### Ambience
Choose the key words that describe your dream bathroom—soothing, tranquil, a retreat, huge, intimate, modern, old-fashioned—whatever they may be.

### Layout
It's probably too early for a real floor plan, but do give some thought to the overall size and shape of your room. There's no point in planning a huge shower enclosure and a soaking tub in a 6-by-8 foot room.

### Color
Think of the overall palette, for instance blue and white, and also the color of specific elements like the floor, walls, cabinets, and fixtures. Consider what role pattern should play.

### Fixtures and controls
List the items: sink, toilet, and tub or shower for sure. Bidet? Two sinks? Choose the basic style, for instance, pedestal sink or vanity, claw-foot tub or one that drops into a platform enclosure? Get more specific if you can. Think about the shape and finish of the controls.

### Floor
What material will give you the look you're after? Can it be laid in a pattern and do you wish to use it that way?

### Walls
Do you favor paint, wallpaper, tile, wood, or some combination? Consider the long-term effects of dampness as well as the aesthetic possibilities.

### Storage
Do you favor a vanity? What do you wish to conceal in addition to toiletries and pharmaceuticals? What style of cabinetry appeals to you?

### Lighting fixtures
You'll need general light from overhead fixtures, and task light at the mirror. Do you read in the bath or shave in the shower? While you are considering light, think about an exhaust fan as well: some fixtures include both.

### Window treatments
Privacy is almost always a concern but style is up to you. Think about color and pattern as well. If access to the windows is awkward—say on the far side of a tub—take that into account; you might want blinds with electronic controls.

### Mirrors
Every bathroom needs at least one, over the sink; it can be framed, the door of a medicine cabinet, or part of the wall surface. Would additional mirrors enhance the ambience in your room?

### Accessories
Towel bars, tissue holders, soap dishes, and the like are practical items with decorative importance that you don't want to overlook. Artwork, small collectibles, even plants and flowers add personality.

### Furniture
Not every bath wants or can accommodate a chair, chaise, table, or freestanding cupboard; if these are in your dream room, choose the style.

OPPOSITE: **Moorish in inspiration and glamorous in effect, this bath features incredibly pure blue glass tiled walls that set off the crisp white of the cabinets, open vanity, and fixtures. Arched motifs distinguish the latticed cabinets and vanity apron. On the floor, black and white river stones replicate a Moorish interior courtyard; on the vanity, a freestanding basin with wall-mounted faucet lends romance. Ornate candle-style sconces with reflective backs flank the tiled-in mirror and a traditional lantern hangs overhead.** (Robin Bell)

# Making Your Plan

A vision, good communication, sourcing, decision-making, organization, time, and money: These are the seven essentials for the creation of your beautiful home. As you begin to make real interior design plans, it's useful to think of the process in these terms. Maybe you'll find the brevity of the list comforting, or perhaps you'll consider that each word encompasses a variety of things and be a bit daunted, but however you react, you can employ these as a framework for planning, put yourself into the picture, and decide what role you want to play. Neither the planning nor the work is conveniently linear, so read this section through to see how the pieces interact and fit together. The more aware you are of what's involved, the better prepared you'll be, the more smoothly the undertaking will go, and the happier the results will be. If you plan well, all the surprises will be good ones.

**A vision.** Parts One, Two, and Three of this book focus on finding the vision of the home that will make you happy. Each part approaches this from a different perspective, and together they encourage you to think through the way you live, the way your house works, and the aesthetic sensibility with which you wish to be surrounded. Before the vision can come to life it must be pretty specific; depending on the scope of the undertaking and your skills and tolerance for the other essentials on the list, you may or may not be the one to fully develop the vision or to facilitate it. That's fine; there are many people who are good at this and you'll probably be happy to work with them.

**Good communication.** There are lots of pieces to pull together and probably quite a few people involved. Being able to articulate the goals and parameters and specify the nature and terms of the work is critical. Listening is as important as speaking—you've got to understand the opinions and information offered by everyone else. And it starts at home; if you do not live alone, make sure your spouse, partner, or children are on the same page and develop a plan for apportioning responsibilities and resolving family differences privately.

**Sourcing.** Shopping—it's fun. It can also be frustrating and exhausting, and if you decide to work without a designer, you may not have access to the things you really want. The end of each chapter in Part Two of this book has tips for organizing your materials search. But there's more to sourcing than locating the perfect fabric or wall covering: you need talented, skilled, reputable tradespeople for most jobs. How many electricians and upholsterers are in your personal phone file?

**Decision-making.** Choosing a look you love and a way to bring it to your home is only the first step. There will be many

other choices to make, from which specific color or which piece of furniture to which painter to hire to how wide the molding should be to what to do when the tile order comes in wrong or the fabric you love most is discontinued. You'll definitely want to make—or at least approve—the big choices, but you may prefer to have a designer coordinate and be responsible for many of them.

**Organization.** You'll need a plan of attack and a schedule, and someone to coordinate the action and make sure that everything needed is ordered in a timely way and delivered when expected. There may be permits and contracts to manage, and there definitely will be a budget to oversee.

**Time.** Once your design plans are pulled together, you can develop a schedule (page 449). Obviously, it will depend on the complexity of the work, but the lead-time for items such as windows, cabinets, and furnishings to be created, prior commitments of any contractors or workrooms, seasonal weather conditions, and even a backlog at the local building inspector's office will affect the planned and actual progress of the undertaking. Developing the vision, sourcing, decision-making, and organizing all take time too; depending on how you proceed, that time may be yours and must be factored into the schedule.

**Money.** Only you know how much money you wish to allocate to your décor. When you are ready to get serious about the undertaking, make a real budget (see page 447) and be sure to set aside a contingency fund for unanticipated hiccups (things do show up once you open the walls). A contingency also allows you to make changes if someone has a brilliant idea once the work gets underway. Be sure you understand how and when things must be paid for.

# BRINGING IN PROFESSIONALS

Design professionals and the contractors who do the physical work all know things you probably don't and they have easy access to resources you may want. Whether, when, and which professionals to hire really depends on the scope of the work, your own talents, and the amount of time and attention you wish to devote to the undertaking. If you are happy and good at doing things yourself, you probably know it—if you really are good at this, you know your limits.

Whom might you need to help you create your new interior? An architect? Yes, if you plan new construction that will change the size or shape of your home. An interior designer? Yes, to create or refine your vision and bring it to life. A general contractor? Possibly; this depends on how much construction is involved and whether the architect or interior designer can supervise and coordinate it. Who else? Skilled tradespeople such as carpenters, electricians, plumbers, heating and air-conditioning mechanics, plasterers, painters, paper hangers, tile installers, upholsterers, drapery and pillow makers.

When you talk to an architect or interior design, ask how he or she would see a job of your sort being managed. Both may have the skills and contacts to manage construction or renovation; for a large job they or you are likely to need a general contractor to oversee, coordinate, and take responsibility for the construction. If you are redoing a kitchen or bath but not other parts of your home, you could work with a certified kitchen and bath designer, choosing one who works independently or one who is part of a business (including many large home stores) that provides and installs all the cabinets, appliances, fixtures, flooring, and other surfaces needed.

**AUXILIARY SPACE?**
Create a pantry.

Designate a closet, small ell, or even an adjacent room to supplement your kitchen. Pantries are at least partially concealed from the main work area, so utilitarian features can ride with ease; this is the ideal place to store staples and extra needs, set up room for pots and appliances. Depending on the space available and your needs, set up room for storage only to put in a sink and relegate the cleanup station or the coffee bar to it as well; if your culinary habits warrant it, you can even outfit a pantry with a second cooktop or more. If the primary purpose of a pantry is to store tableware, locate it near the dining room.

LEFT Who would think a place simple cupboard would hide such a surprise? It's like a walk-in closet, with an entire baking station tucked away with coverage for staples. Sand down, the items rack mounted on each side and pullout shelves fitted with convenient slide-within baskets make the most of the Italian marble counter.

ABOVE This little pantry would be the envy of many an apartment dweller just leaper for a bona residence it's an ordinate, fully equipped gray space adjacent to a large kitchen. On the left is a pass-through refrigerator tucked under 16th for a full view of the sale. To the left of the sink, drainage grooves have been incised in the Italian marble counter.

RIGHT Firm, function, and finish: Great looks were very much part of the plan in this butler's pantry. Flanking the sink cabinet are an undercounter refrigerator and ice maker; just visible on the left is a sink wine cooler, and on the right, sturdy china and glassware, are steel stainless-steel medical cabinets installed over counter drawers. The cabinets of the wall are satin-finish green; the backsplash over the stainless counter is bamboo suspended in aromatic.

RIGHT Tucked in the corner of a passageway, this pantry serves as coffee corner and light clean-up station (the large cabinet door on the right conceals a dishwasher). With beadboard wainscotting and ceiling, bright ceramic tile, herringbone floor tiles, it has a graceful old-fashioned charm; note the marble countertond-style backsplash supporting the sink from the lower woodwork.

# The designer's role

Interior designers are a wonderful cross between visionary creatives, psychologists, and pragmatic, skilled, resourceful worker bees. Their business is designing and creating interiors that are right for their clients and they are masters of minutia. They listen to the client to understand the goals, taste, preferences, time, and budget; look at the space; suggest ideas; develop a design; and calculate dimensions, find and order the materials needed, and commission made-to-order items. They usually coordinate and supervise the work too, and often manage the money. The more you know about your needs and preferences, the easier it will be for a designer to do his or her work and achieve your goals. That's why this book presents many ways to think about interior design, shows examples of hundreds of interiors, and encourages you to define and choose the things that will make your home be beautiful to you. If you do some preliminary gathering of ideas and examples as suggested in Part Two, you'll be able to visually share with a designer things that are difficult to describe in words.

Designers charge for their work in several ways. Some charge a flat fee (exclusive of expenses) for the entire job, some charge by the hour, some take a commission on all materials purchased. Often some combination of these methods is agreed upon. You can hire a designer to mastermind an entire job or to do some portion of it: create a design plan, rearrange and edit your existing furniture, or take you shopping or shop for you for some specific item or items. Most designers will happily have a preliminary meeting or conversation to learn about your project at no charge. If you decide to hire a designer, be very clear about the parameters of the work, the nature of the arrangement, and the responsibilities of both parties. It's to both of your advantage to be specific, and probably to have a contractual arrangement. Make sure you understand who assumes liability for what, just in case something goes amiss.

The Web site of the American Society of Interior Designers www.asid.org has more information on working with design pros and can help you locate a designer. The initials ASID after a designer's name indicate that he or she is a credentialed member of this organization, which requires specific education and training and has a code of ethics. Another good resource is the Interior Design Directory, www.i-d-d.com, which has a state-by-state designer directory and also a listing of design centers (buildings dedicated to manufacturers showrooms, open "to the trade" only) all around the United States. Some design centers provide a service that allows

consumers who are not working with a designer to shop for a limited number of items (contact the individual center to find out the details of this service) and many have designer referral programs. Many independent retail home furnishings stores are owned by interior designers or have them on staff; these are another good place to look for help, as are some of the large chain stores. If you wish to work with someone affiliated with a retail business, inquire whether your materials options are limited to merchandise the store sells.

## Resources for small jobs

Say your goal for the moment is modest in scale—for instance new draperies or upholstery, new tile in the bathroom, or built-in bookcases. You may not need an interior designer for isolated small projects and you could be quite happy working directly with a local workroom, tile vendor, or woodworker. These resources may or may not offer design services, so ask. They may ask you to provide a photo or sketch of what you're looking for, or they may charge for designing to your specifications. They can often source whatever materials are required, or will help you to do so.

## References and compatibility

If you're not already enamored of a specific designer or tradesperson, word of mouth is the best resource when you're looking for talent. Ask at local stores and workrooms. Ask an architect or general contractor, or a carpenter or painter. These people all will know who's active in the field locally and the kinds of work they do. They'll know too if a designer is considered pleasant or difficult to work with. Of course, if any of these referring parties work for the designer in question, you should know that and bear it in mind. Ask your friends too, they may recently have worked with a designer or know someone who has.

When you are thinking of hiring a specific designer, you can ask to see examples of his work—either to visit other homes he has designed or to see photos. If you do this, don't just look to see if you like the interior, but ask what the job involved: what were the goals and challenges? The client may have very different taste from yours; what you want to look at is the way the designer made that client happy. On the other hand, if the work looks dreadful to you, you are probably talking to someone whose sensibility is not in sync with yours. Ask if the designer works alone or has assistants; find out who will be your principal contact and be sure to meet her. And trust your instincts, you'll probably spend a lot time with whomever you hire; if you don't feel comfortable with him or her, admit it before the relationship is formal and costly.

# CREATING A BUDGET

If you've no idea what's involved and what to expect financially, do some preliminary shopping, talk to a designer or contractor and try to get a feeling for a basic budget; from that you'll know whether you should modify your dream right away or proceed as initially conceived. If you decide to work with a designer, be as straightforward about your budget as you can from the outset so he or she can work smartly and creatively to allocate your resources. You will be writing the checks, so be honest about the investment you are willing to make. Some things to consider: The time that you plan to live in the house, whether you are decorating for yourself or to sell in the near future, whether you will do the work in stages as more funds become available, and how often you tend to update your décor. If you plan to sell in the near future, you probably don't want to invest in eccentric or extremely personal structural or built-in details that others could find off-putting and costly to redo—say a bathroom completely covered in black marble. If you redecorate often, you could choose impact over quality for some furnishings, knowing they won't be in your life forever.

Is there a magic button that can calculate the cost for you? No. You know what the limit is, but the only way to see whether it is realistic for the look you want is to itemize the expenses you foresee and add them up. You need not have the specific prices for everything to make a preliminary

budget—list the items and assign a realistic amount to each based on the examples you see when shopping and labor costs quoted by workrooms or various tradespeople. If you are not working with an interior designer, individual tradespeople, workrooms, and other professionals can give you some ballpark estimates based on the quality of materials you're looking at and the square footage of the space—especially for kitchens and baths, upholstery and draperies, flooring, and painting.

A designer will know all the invisible costs that you might not anticipate—storage of your existing or newly purchased furniture, shipping, permits, disposal fees for demolition waste, travel expenses related to shopping, and also typical prices for the kinds of furnishings, appliances, surfaces, and finishes that are in keeping with the look and general tone of your home. And she'll give you options for how to maximize your funds, where to pinch pennies without sacrificing effect and where to be extravagant. Remember to include a contingency fund; 15 percent is a common amount, but ask your designer what makes sense for your situation. Make sure all the contractors carry insurance and ask your insurance agent if you need additional short-term coverage.

Add up your estimated costs. If there's a large discrepancy between the total and the amount you plan to spend, decide how to alter your design plan or choose to implement only some of it at this time.

## REVIEWING AND FINALIZING CHOICES

In an ideal world, you'll have samples of all the materials and specs for everything before you make final decisions on anything. But the world isn't ideal and chances are there will be unknowns at the beginning that may linger throughout the process. To some extent this can be advantageous; there may be things you really don't want to choose until you see something else in place or get a sense of the space if it is new or being extensively altered. However, the more options you can see at one time, the more confident you can be that you are choosing things that work together in whatever way you wish—some design plans (and personalities) welcome more serendipity than others.

At the end of each chapter in Part Two of this book are tips for gathering resources and design inspiration, and in Part Three there are tips for pulling together the look of each room; these give you a sense of how to consider the options. Your designer will know how and when to source and choose things for the specific work you are undertaking. While it makes sense to shop for like items at one time, say all the fabrics or all the tile for an entire house, of course you want to sort the samples by room, review everything needed for one room together, and then for the home as a whole to be sure there is pleasing continuity throughout. As much as possible, review samples on site so you get a real sense of the impact of scale and color in the space and light. And don't be shy about chalking furniture outlines on the floor to visualize their size and the flow around them.

The timeframe for your work may dictate when decisions must be made too. Be aware of lead-times for delivery of everything; you'll have to choose the size, color, finish, and similar details before you can order. It's easy to anticipate that custom-made cabinets, carpets, furniture, and draperies require some specific time for manufacture, but other items, for instance some light fixtures or even bathroom fixtures, may be stock designs but might not be created until an order is placed, or there may be a backlog in the supply, so it's smart to figure out early on if the things you are likely to want are always ready for shipping.

# WHAT HAPPENS WHEN

Here's an overview of the typical work sequence, starting with raw space (meaning new construction is closed in, or renovated space is gutted with new walls framed and windows in place). Your designer or contractor will know if and when the work requires inspection by the local building official. You can see that the carpenters, electrician, and plumber will make several visits to your home.

1. Wiring, plumbing, heating, and air conditioning are roughed in.

2. Walls are closed. Wallboard is taped and spackled.

3. Flooring is installed, but wood floors are not finished at this time.

4. Kitchen and bath cabinets and fixtures are installed; measurements are taken for countertops, which may be installed at any time before the room is painted.

5. Paneling, wainscoting, and trim moldings are applied.

6. Measurements may be taken for window treatments.

7. Heating and air conditioning are completed.

8. The space is painted; decorative stucco or Venetian plaster treatments are applied.

9. Wood floors are finished.

10. Wall coverings and wall-to-wall carpeting are installed.

11. Light fixtures, outlet covers, and switch plates are installed.

12. Appliances are installed; drop-in or countertop sinks are installed; plumbing controls are installed.

13. Everything should be tested to see that it works.

14. Window treatments are installed and furnishings delivered and arranged.

If you are redoing a home you live in full-time, consider the way the work will affect your life. Can you live with it, or will you move out? The larger the job, the less likely you want to be in the midst of it. If you are not moving out, be logical about the way the work is scheduled: don't gut all the bathrooms at once. Be considerate of the workers too; decide if you can designate a bathroom for their use or if you need a portable sanitary facility outdoors. If construction is part of the job, make plans to protect your landscape and determine where to place the debris container.

## MAKING A PROJECT TIMELINE

How much time is needed to create and implement your interior design plans? It depends on the scope of the work. Ask your designer how much time he anticipates the planning stage to require and discuss whether much of your time is likely to be needed while the plan is in development. Once you have a plan, make a list of the steps, or ask your designer to explain the process to you. If construction is part of the project, it may or may not affect the overall schedule because you may need that time for cabinets, furniture, or other made-to-order items anyway. Certainly building from the ground up will have an impact; rearranging interior walls or raising a roof may not. Prior commitments and other schedule conflicts among the various people involved can all affect the schedule.

How much lead-time is usual for custom-made items? Ten weeks to six months or more, depending on the item and supplier. It may not actually take that long for something to be made but you must allow the vendor time to schedule your work and for shipping. Only you know if this undertaking needs to be executed on a strict schedule or if there is flexibility for delivery of furnishings and selection of accessories. You may not mind if the sofa of your dreams won't be ready for a month after everything else is done, and you might prefer to shop for art or other accessories in a leisurely way. Or you may not tolerate those ideas at all.

## PULL IT TOGETHER

Creating an interior you love is certainly a complex undertaking, but you needn't be daunted by it. Write up your plan so you can distill it to its essential components. Make as many lists as you like. Do your research and your dreaming. Find good people to help you bring it to life. Trust your instincts—you have a beautiful home in you.

# CREDITS

# Interior Design

**Chapter 1: The Site**
Page 10: Fern Santini. 12–13: Architect: Michael Damore. 14, top right: Mimi Maddock McMakin, Kemble Interiors; bottom left: Sally Markham. 15: Betsy Brown. 16: Douglas Durkin and Greg Elich. 17: Myra Hoefer Design. 18–19: Architect: Bobby McAlpine. 20: Jill Morris. 21: Markham Roberts.

**Chapter 2: The Architecture**
Page 22: Karyl Pierce Paxton. 24–25: Robert Berman. 26–27: Erin Martin, Architect: Wayne Leong. 28: Ruthie Sommers. 29: Diamond Baratta. 30: Garrow Kedigan. 31: Kathryn Scott. 32, top left: Myra Hoefer Design. 32–33: Mona Hajj Interiors.

**Chapter 3: The Layout**
Page 34: Kathy Smith. 36–37: Michael S. Smith. 38: Susan Tully. 39: Architect: William F. Holland. 42–43: Robert Stilin. 44: Paul Siskin. 45: Katrin Cargill and Carol Glasser. 46: Bunny Williams, Inc. 48: bottom left: Alison Spear; top right: Kari Cusack. 49: Paula Perlini. 50, bottom left: Paul Wiseman; top right: Suzanne Kasler. 51: Fern Santini. 52: Sally Markham. 53: David Jimenez.

**Chapter 4: Ambience**
Page 56: Anne Miller. 58: Allesandra Branca. 59: Jeffrey Bilhuber. 60: Bunny Williams, Inc. 61: David Reed, Architect: Gil Schafer. 62: Ruby Beets Old & New. 63: Markham Roberts. 64, bottom left: Katrin Cargill and Carol Glasser. 64–65: Shannon Bowers, Shannon Bowers Designs. 66: Diamond Baratta. 67: Valerie Smith.

**Chapter 5: Color**
Page 68: Chad Eisner. 71: John Oetgen. 72: Douglas Durkin and Greg Elich. 73: Eldon Wong Design. 74: Robert Goodwin. 75, top: Meg Braff; bottom: Angie Hranowsky. 76: Libby Cameron. 78: Michael Whaley. 79: John Oetgen. 80: Kitchen Designer: Sandra Bird; Interior Designer: Rhonda Shipley. 81, top: Kathy Smith; bottom right: Christopher Maya. 82, left: Meg Braff. 82–83: Faye Cone. 84, bottom left: Ruthie Sommers; top right: Mary McDonald. 85: Kathy Smith. 86: Hilary Musser. 87, top: Jamie Gottschall; bottom left: Shannon Bowers, Shannon Bowers Designs; bottom right: Architect: Bobby McAlpine. 88–89: Franklin Salasky. 90: Alessandra Branca. 91: Phoebe Howard.

**Chapter 6: Lighting**
Page 92: Markham Roberts. 94–95: Tim Landy. 96: David Netto. 97: Charlotte Moss. 98: Andrew Flesher. 99, top left: Nancy Bozhardt; top right: Form Architecture and Interiors; bottom right: Anne Miller. 102: Michael Smith. 103: Susan Ferrier. 104: Susan Ferrier. 105: Bunny Williams, Inc. 106: Craig Schumaker and Philip Kirk. 107: Fern Santini. 108: Judith Barrett. 109, top right: Mary McDonald; bottom right: Anne Miller.

**Chapter 7: Fabric**
Page 110: Diamond Baratta. 112: Katrin Gargill and Carol Glasser. 113: Tom Scheerer. 114: T. Keller Donovan. 115: Karen Cohen and Ani Antreasyan. 116: Waldo Fernandez. 118–119: Alessandra Branca. 124, bottom left: Christopher Maya; top right: David Kleinberg. 125: Kathy Smith. 130: Angie Hranowsky. 131: Phoebe Howard.

**Chapter 8: Walls & Ceilings**
Page 132: Mary McDonald. 134 bottom left: Suzanne Kasler; top right: Myra Hoefer Design. 135: Jill Morris. 136–137: Robin Bell. 138: Albert Hadley, Inc. 139, left: Jeffrey Bilauber; top right: Markham Roberts; bottom right: Michael Whaley. 140, bottom left: Chantal Dussouchard; top right: Marshall Watson. 141: Michael Whaley. 142: John Oetgen. 144: Michael S. Smith. 145: Alessandra Branca. 146: Katrin Cargill and Carol Glasser. 147: Joan Schindler. 148: Marjorie Slovack and Martha Davis. 149: David Reed, Architect: Gil Schafer. 150: Kitchen Designer: Sandra Bird; Interior Designer: Rhonda Shipley. 151, left: Alessandra Branca; top right: Franklin Salasky; bottom right: Paul Siskin. 152: Jodi Macklin. 153: Amanda Kyser.

**Chapter 9: Floors**
Page 154: Marshall Watson. 156: Vicente Wolf. 157, left: Susan Tulley; top right: Barbara Westbrook; bottom right: Mick De Giulio. 158: Thomas Jayne, Architect: Peter Pennoyer. 159: David Reed, Architect: Gil Schafer. 160: Diamond Baratta. 161: left: Shannon Bowers, Shannon Bowers Designs; top right: Kim Freeman; bottom right: Nancy Boszhardt. 162, bottom left: Jonathan Rosen; top right: Marshall Watson. 163: Kay Douglass. 164: John Schindler. 165, left: T. Keller Donovan; top right: David Kleinberg; bottom right: Jacqueline Derrey Segura. 166: Emily O'Keefe. 167: Ken Fulk Design. 168: Valerie Smith. 169: Faye Cohen. 170: John Oetgen. 171: Douglas Durkin and Greg Elich. 172–173: Jeffrey Bilhuber. 174: Barclay Butera.

**Chapter 10: Window Treatments**
Page 176: David Kleinberg. 178: Kari Cusack. 179: Justine Cusing. 180: Michael Whaley. 181: Markham Roberts. 182: Marshall Watson. 183: William Hoogars. 184: David Kleinberg. 185: Phoebe Howard. 186: Merrill Stenbeck. 187: David Kleinberg. 188: Jason Bell. 189, left: Bunny Williams, Inc.; top right: Ann Miller; bottom right: Michael S. Smith. 190, top right: Fern Santini; bottom right: Kay Douglass. 191: John Peixinho. 192, bottom left: Albert Hadley, Inc.; top right: Celerie Kemble. 193: Charlotte Moss. 194: Amanda Kyser. 195: Michael Canter.

**Chapter 11: Foyers & Hallways**
Page 198: T. Keller Donovan. 200: Healing Barsanti. 201: Barbara Westbrook. 202: Jason Bell. 203: Ruthie Sommers. 204: Karen Cohen and Ani Antreasyan. 205, left: Robin Well; right: Ashley Whittaker. 206: Lee Bierly and Christopher Drake. 208: Betsy Brown. 209, left: Robert Godwin; top right: Neil Korpinen and Rich Erickson; bottom right: Garrow Kedigian. 211: Anne Miller.

## Chapter 12: Living Rooms

Page 212: Mary McDonald. 214: Nancy Boszhardt. 215: Susan Ferrier. 216, bottom left: Jonathan Rosen; top right: Marshall Walker. 217: Form Architecture and Interiors. 218–219: Barbara Westbrook. 220: T. Keller Donovan. 221: Paul Wiseman. 222: Ken Fulk Design. 223, left: Mitch Taylor and Suzanne Tucker; top right: David Mitchell; bottom right: Christopher Maya. 224: Richard H. Lewis. 225: Michael Smith. 228, top: Myra Hoefer Design; bottom: Suzanne Kasler. 229: Joe Nye. 230: Madeline Stuart. 232: Martha Angus. 233, left: John Peixinho; top right: Mona Hajj Interiors; bottom right: John Oetgen. 234: Robert Stilin. 235: David Jimenez. 236, top left: James Radin; bottom: Katrin Cargill and Carol Glasser. 237, top right: James Strickland and Suzanne Rester Watson; bottom right: Marshall Watson. 238: David Easton. 239: Diamond Baratta. 240: Kay Douglass. 241: Garrow Kedigian. 244–245: Meg Braff. 248: Eve Robinson. 249, left: Eve Robinson; top right: Betsy Brown; bottom right: Michael Canter. 250: Celerie Kemble. 253: Paula Perlini.

## Chapter 13: Dining Rooms

Page 254: Nancy Boszhardt. 256: Tim Scheerer. 257, top: Jodi Macklin; bottom right: Jacqueline Derrey Segura. 258–259: T. Keller Donovan. 260: Mary McDonald. 261: Susan Ferrier, Architecture: Bobby McAlpine. 262: Martyn Laurence-Bullard. 264: John Oetgen. 266, bottom left: Chad Eisner; top right: Alison Spear. 267: Vicente Wolf. 268: Christopher Maya. 269: Suzanne Kasler. 270: Kay Douglass. 271, left: Justine Cushing; top right: Diamond Baratta; bottom right: Myra Hoefer Design. 274: Abby Yozell. 277: Kathy Smith. 278: Myra Hoefer Design. 279: Markham Roberts. 280, bottom left: Jeff Andrews; top right: David Jimenez. 281: Myra Hoefer Design.

## Chapter 14: Kitchens

Page 282: John Oetgen. 284: Ina Garten, Architect: Richard H. Lewis. 285, top: Sally Markham, Architect: Joeb Moore; bottom right: Vicente Wolf. 286: Chad Eisner. 287: Nancy Boszhardt. 288: Hilary Musser. 289: Susan Ferrier; Architect: Bobby McAlpine. 290, top: Kathryn Scott; bottom: Waldo Fernandez. 291: Mallory Marshall. 292: Joan Schindler Interior Design. 293, top and bottom: Eldon Wong. 294: Alessandra Branca. 295, top: Kay Douglass; bottom right: Brenda Kelly Kramer. 296, bottom left: Robin Bell; top right: Healing Barsanti. 297: Susan Tully. 298: Carol Lalli. 299: Alexander Adducci. 300: Clare Donohue. 302: Jacqueline Derrey Segura. 303: Brenda Kelly Kramer. 304: Karen Cohen and Ani Antreasyan. 305: Jodi Macklin. 306: Eldon Wong Designs. 307, top left: Erin Martin; top right: Betsy Brown; bottom left: Carol Lalli; bottom right: Joan Schindler. 310: Mick de Giulio. 311, left: Joan Schindler; top right: Sally Markham; bottom right: Judith Barrett. 312–313: Hilary Musser. 314, bottom left: Michael S. Smith; top right: Shannon Bowers. 315: Ruthie Sommers. 316: Diamond Baratta. 317, top: Katrin Cargill and Carol Glasser; bottom right: Craig Schumacher and Philip Kirk. 318, bottom left: Beverly Ellsley; top right: Sandra Bird. 319, top: Todd Klein; bottom left: Mona Hajj Interiors. 320–321: Architect: Peter Fisher. 322. top left: Hilary Musser; bottom left: Joan Schindler; bottom right: Susan Tully. 323, top left: Phoebe Howard; bottom right: Carol Lalli. 324, bottom left: Jamie Gottschall; top right: T. Keller Donovan. 325: Betsy Brown. 326: Judith Barrett. 327: Amanda Kyser. 328: Kitchen Designer: Sandra Bird; Interior Designer: Rhonda Shipley. 329: Kitchen Designer: Sandra Bird; Interior Designer: Rhonda Shipley. 331: Paul Siskind. 332–333: Susan Ferrier. 334–335: Jeffrey Weisman and Andrew Weisman.

## Chapter 15: Libraries, Studies & Offices

Page 336: Phoebe Howard. 339: David Kleinberg. 340: Sally Markham. 341: Allegra and Ashley Hicks. 342, top left: Ruthie Sommers; top right: Jill Morris; bottom left: Betsy Brown. 343: Nancy Boszhardt. 344–345: Barbara Westbrook. 346: Jason Bell. 348: DD Allen. 350: Madeline Stuart. 351: Bunny Williams, Inc. 352: Christopher Maya. 353, left: Michael Whaley; top right: Paul Wiseman; bottom right: Alessandra Branca. 354, bottom right: Stephen Brady for Williams Sonoma Home; top: T. Keller Donovan. 355: David Easton. 358, bottom left: Douglas Durkin and Greg Elich; top right: Peter Forbes. 359: David Jimenez. 360: Craig Schumacher and Philip Kirk. 361, top: Chantal Dussouchaud; bottom right: Stephen Brady for Williams Sonoma Home. 363: Celerie Kemble.

## Chapter 16. Bedrooms

Page 364: Fern Santini. 366–367: Marshall Watson. 368, bottom left: Diamond Baratta; top right: Kay Douglass. 369: Erin Marin. 370: Healing Barsand. 371, top: Kari Cusack; bottom: Jodi Macklin. 372: Mona Hajj Interiors. 373: David Reed, Architect: Gil Schafer. 374: Vicente Wolf. 375: Phoebe Howard. 378: Charlotte Moss. 379, left: Ken Fulk Design; top right: Eldon Wong Design; bottom right: Keith Irvine. 380: Thomas Jayne. 382: Jeffrey Bilhuber. 383, left: Douglas Durkin and Greg Elich; top right: Karyl Pierce Paxton; bottom right: Bunny Williams, Inc. 384: Jacqueline Derrey Segura. 385, top: Form Architecture and Interiors; right: Barbara Westbrook. 386: Christopher Maya. 387, left: Franklin Salasky; top right: Michael Whaley; bottom right: Bunny Williams Inc. 388: David Mitchell. 389: Susan Ferrier, Architect: Bobby McAlpine. 390–391: Albert Hadley, Inc. 394: Markham Roberts. 395, left: Karyl Pierce Paxton; top right: David Easton; bottom right: Celerie Kemble. 396, bottom left: Marshall Watson; top right: Ruthie Sommers. 397: Eldon Wong Design. 398: T. Keller Donovan. 399: Valerie Smith. 400: David Jimenez. 401, left: Susan Tully; top right: Myra Hoefer Design; bottom right: Suzanne Kasler. 402, bottom left: Ruby Beets Old & New; top right: Sally Markham. 403: Sally Markham. 404: Myra Hoefer Design. 405, right: Tom Scheerer. 407: Robert Goodwin. 408–409: Elizabeth Ornstein. 410–411: Frank Roop.

## Chapter 17: Bathrooms

412: Paul Siskin. 415: Albert Hadley and Harry Heissmann. 416, bottom left: Betsy Brown; top right: Kathy Smith. 417: Paolo Moschino. 418: Kay Douglass. 419: Ken Fulk Design. 420: Waldo Fernandez. 421, top right: Diamond Baratta; bottom: Jill Morris. 422: Kerry Joyce. 423: Barbara Westbrook. 424: Anne Carson. 426: Nancy Corzine. 427: Phoebe Howard. 428: Jeffrey Bilhuber. 429, left: Susan Ferrier; top right: David Kleinberg; bottom right: Paul Wiseman. 432, bottom left: Jeffrey Bilhuber; right: David Easton. 433: Gil Schafer. 434, bottom left: Paolo Moschino; top right: Douglas Durkin and Greg Elich. 435: Sally Markham. 438–439: Kari Cusack. 440, bottom left: Ruby Beets Old & New; top right: Susan Ferrier. 441: Barbara Westbrook. 443: Robin Bell.

# Photography

**Chapter 1: The Site**
Page 10: Ngoc Minh Ngo. 12–13: François Dischinger. 14, top left and top right: Francesco Lagnese; bottom left: Pieter Estersohn. 15: Don Freeman. 16: Eric Piasecki. 17: Ray Kachatorian. 18–19: Don Freeman. 20: Chuck Baker. 21: Christopher Baker.

**Chapter 2: The Architecture**
Page 22: Kerri McCaffety. 24–25: Erik Kvalsvik. 26–27: Dominique Vorillon. 28–29: Don Freeman. 30: Pieter Estersohn. 31: Ellen McDermott. 32, top left: Tim Street-Porter. 32–33: Erik Kvalsik.

**Chapter 3: The Layout**
Page 34: John Gould Bessler. 36–37: Grey Crawford. 38: Laura Moss. 39: Karyn R. Millet. 42–43: Peter Murdock. 44: Pieter Estersohn. 45: Karyn R. Millet. 46: Don Freeman. 48, bottom left: Ken Hayden; top right: Karyn R. Millet. 49: Don Freeman. 50, bottom left: Tim Street-Porter; top right: Tria Giovan. 51: Ngoc Minh Ngo. 52: Pieter Estersohn. 53: José Picayo.

**Chapter 4: Ambience**
Page 56: Eric Piasecki. 58: John Gould Bessler. 59: Don Freeman. 60–62: Don Freeman. 63: Eric Pasecki. 64, bottom left: Karyn R. Millet. 64–65: Nathan Schroder. 66: Tria Giovan. 67: Miki Duisterhof.

**Chapter 5: Color**
Page 68: Karyn R. Millet. 71: Ngoc Mihn Ngo. 72: Eric Piasecki. 73: Michael Grimm. 74: Gridley & Graves. 75, top: Simon Upton; bottom: Timothy Kolk. 76: William Waldron. 78: Frances Janisch. 79: Ngoc Minh Ngo. 80: James Carrière. 81: John Gould Bessler. 82, left: Simon Upton. 82–83: Jeff McNamara. 84, bottom left: Don Freeman; top right: Dominique Vorillon. 85: John Gould Bessler. 86: Gridley & Graves. 87, top: Lizzie Himmel; bottom left: Nathan Schroder; bottom right: Don Freeman. 88–89: Pieter Estersohn. 90: John Gould Bessler. 91: Laura Moss.

**Chapter 6: Lighting**
Page 92: Eric Piasecki. 94–95: Kerri McCaffety. 96: Richard Felber. 97: Eric Piasecki. 98: Susan Gilmore. 99, top left: John Kernick; top right: Pieter Estersohn; bottom right: Eric Piasecki. 102: Lisa Romerein. 103: Don Freeman. 104: Eric Piasecki. 105: Don Freeman. 106: Nathan Schroder. 107: Ngoc Minh Ngo. 108: Eric Roth. 109, top right: Dominique Vorillon; bottom right: Eric Piasecki.

**Chapter 7: Fabric**
Page 110: Tria Giovan. 112: Karyn R. Millet. 113: Christopher Baker. 114: John Gould Bessler. 115: Roger Davies. 116: Tria Giovan. 118–119: John Gould Bessler. 124, bottom left: John Gould Bessler; top right: Eric Piasecki. 125: John Gould Bessler. 130: Timothy Kolk. 131: Laura Moss.

**Chapter 8: Walls & Ceilings**
Page 132: Dominique Vorillon. 134, bottom left: Tria Giovan; top right: Tim Street-Porter. 135: Chuck Baker. 136–137: Don Freeman. 138: Eric Piasecki. 139, left: Don Freeman; top right: Eric Piasecki; bottom right: Frances Janisch. 140, bottom left: Edmund Barr; top right: Eric Piasecki. 141: Frances Janisch. 142: Ngoc Minh Ngo. 144: Lisa Romerein. 145: Grey Crawford. 146: Karyn R. Millet. 147: Lucas Allen. 148: Jack Thompson. 149: Don Freeman. 150: James Carrière. 151, left: John Gould Bessler; top right and bottom right: Pieter Estersohn. 152: Anice Hoachlander/HDPhoto. 153: Ngoc Minh Ngo.

**Chapter 9: Floors**
Page 154: Eric Piasecki. 156: Vicente Wolf. 157, left: Laura Moss; top right: Pieter Estersohn; bottom right: Ellen McDermott. 158: Jonathan Wallen. 159: Don Freeman. 160: Tria Giovan. 161, left: Nathan Schroeder; top right: Dana Gallagher; bottom right: John Kernick. 162, bottom left: Eric Piasecki; top right: Nathan Schroeder. 163: Simon Upton. 164: Lucas Allen. 165, left: John Gould Bessler; top right: Pieter Estersohn; bottom right: Simon Upton. 166: Ellen McDermott. 167: Karyn R. Millet. 168: Miki Duisterhoff and Don Freeman. 169: Jeff McNamara. 170: Ngoc Minh Ngo. 171: Eric Piasecki. 172–173: Don Freeman. 174: Ken Hayden.

**Chapter 10: Window Treatments**
Page 176: Pieter Estersohn. 178: Karyn R. Millet. 179: Don Freeman. 180: Frances Janisch. 181: Eric Piasecki. 182: Nathan Schroeder. 183: Frédéric Vasseur. 184: Pieter Estersohn. 185: J. Savage Gibson. 186: Simon Upton. 187–188: Eric Piasecki. 189, left: Don Freeman; top right: Eric Piasecki; bottom right: Lisa Romerein. 190, top right: Ngoc Minh Ngo; bottom right: Simon Upton. 191: Don Freeman. 192, bottom left: Eric Piasecki; top right: Don Freeman. 193: Eric Piasecki. 194: Laura Moss. 195: Ngoc Minh Ngo.

**Chapter 11: Foyers & Hallways**
Page 198: John Gould Bessler. 200: John Gould Bessler. 201: Pieter Estersohn. 202: Eric Piasecki. 203: Don Freeman. 204: Roger Davies. 205, left: Don Freeman; right: Eric Piasecki. 206: Brantley Photography. 208: Don Freeman. 209, left: Gridley & Graves; top right: Tim Street-Porter; bottom right: Pieter Estersohn. 211: Eric Piasecki.

**Chapter 12: Living Rooms**
Page 212: Dominique Vorillon. 214: John Kernick. 215: Don Freeman. 216, left and top right: Eric Piasecki. 217–219: Peter Estersohn. 220: John Gould Bessler. 221: Tim Street-Porter. 222: Karyn R. Millet. 223, left: Dominique Vorillon; top right: Eric Piasecki; bottom right: John Gould Bessler. 224: Simon Upton. 225: Lisa Romerein. 228, top: Tim Street-Porter; bottom: Tria Giovan. 229: Jonn Coolidge. 230: Roger Davies. 232: Dominique Vorillon. 233, left: Don Freeman; top right: Erik Kvalsvik; bottom right: Ngoc Minh Ngo. 234: Peter Murdock. 235: José Picayo. 236, top left and bottom: Karyn R. Millet. 237, top right: J. Savage Gibson; bottom right: Wayne Cable. 238: John Gould Bessler. 239: Tria Giovan. 240: Simon Upton. 241: Pieter Estersohn. 244–245: Simon Upton. 248: Eric Piasecki. 249, left: Dominique Vorillon; top right: Don Freeman; bottom right: Laura Moss. 250: Don Freeman. 253: Don Freeman.

## Chapter 13: Dining Rooms

Page 254: John Kernick. 256: Christopher Baker. 257, top: Anice Hollander/HDPhoto; bottom right: Simon Upton. 258–259: John Gould Bessler. 260: Dominique Vorillon. 261: Don Freeman. 262: Tim Street-Porter. 264: Ngoc Minh Ngo. 266, bottom left: Karyn R. Millet; top right: Ken Hayden. 267: Vicente Wolf. 268: John Gould Bessler. 269: Tria Giovan. 270: Simon Upton. 271, left: Don Freeman; top right: Tria Giovan; bottom right: Ray Kachatorian. 274: Andreas von Einsiedel. 277: John Gould Bessler. 278: Ray Kachatorian. 279: Christopher Baker. 280, bottom left: Tim Street-Porter; top right: José Picayo. 281: Ray Kachatorian.

## Chapter 14: Kitchens

Page 282: Ngoc Minh Ngo. 284: Simon Upton. 285, top: Pieter Estersohn; bottom right: Vicente Wolf. 286: Karyn R. Millet. 287: John Kernick. 288: Gridley & Graves. 289: Don Freeman. 290, top: Ellen McDermott; bottom: Tria Giovan. 291: Laura Moss. 292: Frances Janisch. 293, top and bottom: Joshua McHugh. 294: John Gould Bessler. 295, top: Tria Giovan; bottom right: Laura Moss. 296, bottom left: Don Freeman; top right: John Gould Bessler. 297: Laura Moss. 298: John M. Hall. 299: Annie Schlechter. 300: Clare Donohue. 302: Simon Upton. 303: Laura Moss. 304: Roger Davies. 305: Anice Hoachlander/HDPhoto. 306: Michael Grimm. 307, top left: Dominique Vorillon; top right: Don Freeman; bottom left: Annie Schlechter; bottom right: Lucas Allen. 310: Ellen McDermott. 311, left: Lucas Allen; top right: Pieter Estersohn; bottom right: Eric Roth. 312–313: Gridley & Graves. 314, bottom left: Grey Crawford; top right: Nathan Schroder. 315: Don Freeman. 316: Tria Giovan. 317, top: Kathryn R. Millet; bottom right: Nathan Schroder. 318, bottom left: Laura Moss; top right: James Carrière. 319, top: Don Freeman; bottom left: Erik Kvalsvik; bottom right: Laura Moss. 320–321: Karyn R. Millet. 322. top left: Gridley & Graves; bottom left: Lucas Allen; bottom right: Laura Moss. 323, top left: J. Savage Gibson; bottom right: Annie Schlechter. 324, bottom left: Lizzie Himmel; top right: John Gould Bessler. 325: Don Freeman. 326: Eric Roth. 327: Ngoc Minh Ngo. 328–329: James Carrière. 331: Pieter Estersohn. 332–333: Eric Piasecki. 334–335: Grey Crawford.

## Chapter 15: Libraries, Studies & Offices

Page 336: J. Savage Gibson. 339–340: Pieter Estersohn. 341: Simon Upton. 342, top left: Jeremy Samuelson; top right: Chuck Baker; bottom left: Don Freeman. 343: John Kernick. 344–345: Pieter Estersohn. 346: Eric Piasecki. 348: Peter Margonelli. 350: Roger Davies. 351: Don Freeman. 352: Eric Piasecki. 353, left: Frances Janisch; top right: Tim Street-Porter; bottom right: John Gould Bessler. 354, bottom right: Ellen McDermott; top: Tria Giovan. 355: John Gould Bessler. 358, bottom left: Eric Piasecki; top right: William Waldron. 359: José Picayo. 360: Nathan Schroder. 361, top: Emanuel Baer; bottom right: Ellen McDermott. 363: Don Freeman.

## Chapter 16. Bedrooms

Page 364: Ngoc Minh Ngo. 366–367: Eric Piasecki. 368, bottom left: Tria Giovan; top right: Simon Upton. 369: Dominique Vorillon. 370: John Gould Bessler. 371, top: Karyn R. Millet; bottom: Anice Hoachlander/HDPhoto. 372: Erik Kvalsvik. 373: Don Freeman. 374: Vicente Wolf. 375: J. Savage Gibson. 378: Eric Piasecki. 379, left: Karyn R. Millet; top right: Michael Grenier; bottom right: Simon Upton. 380: Christopher Baker. 382: Dan Freeman. 383, left: Eric Piasecki; top right: Kerri McCaffetty; bottom right: Don Freeman. 384: Simon Upton. 385, top and right: Pieter Estersohn. 386: John Gould Bessler. 387, left: Pieter Estersohn; top right: Frances Janisch; bottom right: Don Freeman. 388: Eric Piasecki. 389: Don Freeman. 390–391: Eric Piasecki. 394: Eric Piasecki. 395, left: Kerri McCaffetty; top right: John Gould Bessler; bottom right: Don Freeman. 396, bottom left: Nathan Schroder; top right: Don Freeman. 397: Michael Gruen. 398: John Gould Bessler. 399: Don Freeman. 400: José Picayo. 401, left: Laura Moss; top right: Tim Street-Porter; bottom right: Tria Giovan. 402, bottom left: Don Freeman; top right: Pieter Estersohn. 403: Pieter Estersohn. 404: Tim Street-Porter. 405, right: Christopher Baker. 407: Gridley & Graves. 408–409: Tara Striano. 410-411: Eric Roth.

## Chapter 17: Bathrooms

412: Pieter Estersohn. 415: Don Freeman. 416, bottom left: Don Freeman; top right: John Gould Bessler. 417: Simon Upton. 418: Tria Giovan. 419: Karyn R. Millet. 420: Tria Giovan. 421, top right: Antoine Bootz; bottom: Chuck Baker. 422: Tim Street-Porter. 423: Pieter Estersohn. 424: Ricky Zehavi. 426: Ken Hayden. 427: J. Savage Gibson. 428: Don Freeman. 429, left: Don Freeman; top right: Pieter Estersohn; bottom right: Tim Street-Porter. 432, bottom left: Don Freeman; right: John Gould Bessler. 433: Don Freeman. 434, bottom left: Simon Upton; top right: Eric Piasecki. 435: Pieter Estersohn. 438–439: Karyn R. Millet. 440, bottom left: Don Freeman; top right: Eric Piasecki. 441: Pieter Estersohn. 443: Don Freeman.

# Index

tone-on-tone, 81
tying in with window treatments, 180, 181, 188, 189
vibrant, colorful, 78, 79
Planning, 444–449. *See also specific elements of design; specific rooms*
budget and, 445, 447–448
for closets, 47
decision-making during, 444–445. *See also* Questions to ask
envisioning plan, 30, 444
for furniture placement, 50
good communication during, 444
for lighting, 106, 109
making plan, 444–449
making project timeline, 449
organizing for, 445
professional help with, 445–447
pulling it together, 449
reviewing and finalizing choices, 448
sourcing and, 444
time and schedule development, 445, 449
Porches
front-porch swing, 278
gabled, 22, 23
office space in, 343
screened, for sleeping, 14
transitioning indoors/outdoors, 14, 15, 20, 21
Powder rooms, 428–429
Professionals
bringing in, 445
compatibility with, 447
designer's role, 446–447
references for, 447
for small jobs, 447
types of, 445
Project timeline, 449
Proportion
assessing, 28
defined, 28
examples illustrating, 28–29, 42–43, 383
furniture placement and, 48
of open-living plan, 334
pattern and, 78
scale and, 28, 384
of sofas and chairs, 225

**Q**
Questions to ask
about ambience, 58, 66
about architecture, 23–24
about bathrooms, 413, 414
about color, 72
about dining rooms, 255, 256–258
about floors, 155

about foyers, 199, 210
about kitchens, 283, 284
about layout, 35, 36, 38
about libraries, studies, offices, 337, 338
about living rooms, 213, 214, 216, 252
about outdoor living spaces, 279–280
about painting, 134
about rugs and carpets, 168
about site, 11, 15–17
about transitioning indoors/outdoors, 15–17
about wallpaper, 140
about window treatments, 177, 178
about woodwork, 146

**R**
Railroading, defined, 114
Range hoods, 108, 109, 282, 283, 285, 320, 321, 324, 329, 330, 331
Reading areas. *See also* Libraries, studies, and offices
in bedroom, 366, 375, 390
easy chair or sofa for, 224–225
foyers as, 200
lighting for, 94, 99, 103, 109, 252, 324, 366, 375, 396, 406, 438
storing reading materials in, 248–249
Refrigerators, 306, 311, 320, 322, 348, 383, 385
Regional looks, 64–65, 140, 162, 168, 216
Repeat, defined, 114
Resilient flooring, 155, 166–167
Rheinstein, Suzanne, 128–129
Rios, Mark, 19
Room-by-room analysis, 197. *See also specific rooms*
Rubber flooring, 155, 166
Rugs and carpets, 168–173
adding style with, 168
considerations for using, 168, 171
defined, 172
designer's top ten tips on, 171
for dining rooms, 256, 276
as focal point, 168, 171
for living rooms, 252
painted floor mimicking, 161
questions to ask about, 168
runners on stairs, 171
sample file for, 172

**S**
Sample files
for ambiance, 57, 67
for colors, 90
for flooring or floor coverings, 172

setting up clipping file, 67
for walls and ceilings, 152
for window treatments, 195
Sanders, Scott, 84–85, 231
Scale, defined, 28
Seating groups, 53
Secretaries, 352–353, 358, 359, 416, 417
Selke, Annie, 122–123
Setting, of house. *See* Site
Shade, defined, 70
Shades. *See* Window treatments
Showers
dramatic, free-standing, 414, 415
fittings and faucets, 414–415
outdoor, 432, 433
planning for, 432
reverse-painted glass tiles and bench, 432–433
safety rules, 433
size and clearance rules, 421
steel-and-glass encased, 432
Shutters, 185, 190–191, 192
Sideboards, 256, 257, 274, 276
Sightlines, 334
Sinks and faucets
bathrooms, 414, 421, 426–427, 428, 429, 442
kitchens, 318–319, 330
skirting below, 112
Site, 11–21
assessing, 11
as basic design aspect, 10
celebrating or accommodating, 15
describing setting, 11
design considerations, 10
landscape, design and. *See* Landscaping
location, environment and, 12–13
questions to ask about, 11, 15–17
Skylights
in bathroom, 414, 415
in kitchen, 108, 109
in office, 342
Slipcovers
on dining room chairs, 261, 270–271
fabric examples, 110, 111, 115
on kitchen chairs, 302
Small spaces
bathroom examples, 422, 423, 441
bedroom examples, 368, 396, 397, 399
dining room examples, 254, 255, 266–267, 274
kitchen examples, 284, 285, 286, 290
mirrors ehancing perception of, 266, 267, 408, 423

optimizing studio apartments, 408–411
tips for small dining rooms, 266–267
Sofas
cover, 225
cushion filling, 224
cushion style, 224–225
frame construction, 224
padding, 224
pillows for. *See* Pillows
safety considerations, 225
sectional, examples, 226–227
shopping for, 224–225
springs, 224
Sourcing, 444
Stairways
design elements around, 32, 38, 152, 153, 161, 200, 202, 204
runners on, 161, 171
seating on landing, 189
using nooks/crannies around, 350
Stokes, Stephanie, 106–107, 425
Storage. *See also* Cabinets; Closets; Kitchen cabinets
in bathrooms, 414, 423, 440, 441, 442
in bedrooms, 366, 400–401, 406
of books, 350. *See also* Bookcases/shelves
in libraries, studies, and offices, 350, 362
in ottomans, 409
in studio apartments, 409
Stoves/ranges, 289, 320, 324, 328, 329, 330, 331
Structural changes, 30
Studio apartments, optimizing, 408–411
Subtle (Instant Room fabrics by Wayne Nathan and Carol Egan), 126–127
Sunlight
affecting interior colors, 20, 82
kitchen basking in, 108, 109, 329
kitchen paint colors celebrating, 300–301
lighting emulating, 103, 107
window treatments filtering, 177, 185, 190, 362
Swatches. *See also* Instant Room fabrics
defined, 114
file folder/box for, 90, 130
functions of, 114
Swedish style
blue paint colors, 301, 348
colored look of, 64, 83, 156
country style, 162, 163, 236, 237

# Paint Color Index

(by name, manufacturer, designer)

Front cover collage designed by Eddie Ross, photograph by Antonis Achilleos.
Back cover photograph by Erik Kvalsvik, interior design by Mona Hajj Interiors.

Page 2: photograph by Timothy Kolk, interior design by Angie Hranowsky. Page 4, top left: photograph by Erik Kvalsvik, interior design by Mona Hajj Interiors; top middle: photograph by Karyn R. Millet, interior design by Katrin Gargill and Carol Glasser; middle: photograph by Ray Katchatorian, interior design by Myra Hoefer Design; bottom left: photograph by Simon Upton, interior design by Jacqueline Derrey Segura; bottom middle: photograph by Dana Gallagher, interior design by Kim Freeman. Page 7, left: photograph by Ray Katchatorian, interior design by Myra Hoefer Design; right: photograph by Karyn R. Millet, interior design by Molly Isaksen.

Additional photography credits appear on page 452.

**HEARST BOOKS**
Publisher: Jacqueline Deval
Editorial Director: Marisa Bulzone
Project Editor: Carol Spier
Art Director: Celia Fuller
Book design by Tanya Ross-Hughes/Hotfoot Studio
Floor plan illustrations by Glenn Wolff

10  9  8  7  6  5  4  3  2  1

Published by Hearst Books
A Division of Sterling Publishing Co., Inc.
387 Park Avenue South, New York, NY 10016

House Beautiful and Hearst Books are trademarks of Hearst Communications, Inc.

www.housebeautiful.com

Distributed in Canada by Sterling Publishing
C/o Canadian Manda Group, 165 Dufferin Street
Toronto, Ontario, Canada M6K 3H6

Distributed in Australia by Capricorn Link (Australia) Pty. Ltd.
P.O. Box 704, Windsor, NSW 2756 Australia

Manufactured in China

ISBN 978-1-58816-770-5

# EVERYONE HAS A BEAUTIFUL HOME IN THEM.